The Dark Sahara

About the Author

From the *Times Literary Supplement*: 'Jeremy Keenan, like the Tuareg, is his own man: brave, authoritative and a master of his environment by dint of scholarship and experience.'

Jeremy Keenan is a Professor of Social Anthropology and an internationally recognised authority on the Sahara and its peoples. He first visited the Tuareg of southern Algeria in 1964. Between then and 1972 he spent almost three years with them, learning their language and travelling literally thousands of miles on foot and camel through much of the Central Sahara. Few Europeans know the great desert better. The studies he undertook then comprised his PhD thesis (1972) and were published in his seminal work: *The Tuareg. People of Ahaggar* (Allen Lane Penguin 1977).

Subsequent work, first on apartheid, poverty, conflict and underdevelopment in southern Africa, and then on the problems of the economic, social and political transition of Eastern Europe and the former Soviet Union, alongside the development of the European Union, kept him away from North Africa until the mid-1990s, by which time Algeria's 'civil war' was at its height. However, following the 'election' of Bouteflika as Algeria's President in 1999, Keenan was able to return to the Sahara. For the last decade, his research has focused almost exclusively on developments, notably the 'war on terror', in the Saharan and Sahelian regions of Algeria, Niger and Mali, but with extensive travels in both Libya and Mauritania and with an eye on Chad, Western Sahara, Morocco and Tunisia, while being attached, in a somewhat nomadic style, to the universities of Cambridge, East Anglia, Exeter, Bristol and SOAS.

Jeremy Keenan's writings on the Sahara are extensive and authoritative. *Sahara Man: Travelling with the Tuareg* (John Murray) was published in 2001, with a paperback edition in 2003 and a US edition in 2004. *The Tuareg: People of Ahaggar* (Sickle Moon) was republished in 2002. These were followed by *The Lesser Gods of the Sahara: Social Change and Contested Terrain amongst the Tuareg of Algeria* (Cass 2004 & Routledge 2005) and *The Sahara: Past, Present & Future* (Routledge 2007). Further research and writing on the Sahara and its peoples is found in 18 book chapters, over 40 peer-reviewed journal articles and 15 professional reports, as well as numerous radio and TV broadcasts and other media reports. He has made 5 full-length TV documentary films on the Sahara. *Travelling with Tuareg* (2006) and *The Lesser Gods* (2006) were shot in Algeria while *A Forgotten Civilisation* (2007) and *Waters Under the Earth* (2007) focus on Libya's 'lost' civilisation of the Garamantes and Libya's rich cultural heritage respectively.

He advises several 'international consultancies' on Saharan political and security matters, as well as a number of NGOs, including the IWGIA, UNHCR and other UN agencies, media organisations, mining and oil companies. He also briefs a number of governments, including the US State Department and the UK's Foreign and Commonwealth Office.

The Dark Sahara

America's War on Terror in Africa

JEREMY KEENAN

PLUTO PRESS
www.plutobooks.com

First published 2009 by Pluto Press
345 Archway Road, London N6 5AA and
175 Fifth Avenue, New York, NY 10010

www.plutobooks.com

Distributed in the United States of America exclusively by
Palgrave Macmillan, a division of St. Martin's Press LLC,
175 Fifth Avenue, New York, NY 10010

British Library Cataloguing in Publication Data
A catalogue record for this book is available from the British Library

ISBN   978 0 7453 2453 1   Hardback
ISBN   978 0 7453 2452 4   Paperback

Library of Congress Cataloging in Publication Data applied for

This book is printed on paper suitable for recycling and made from
fully managed and sustained forest sources. Logging, pulping and
manufacturing processes are expected to conform to the environmental
standards of the country of origin. The paper may contain up to
70 per cent post-consumer waste.

10   9   8   7   6   5   4   3   2   1

Designed and produced for Pluto Press by
Chase Publishing Services Ltd, Sidmouth, England
Typeset from disk by Stanford DTP Services, Northampton, England
Printed and bound in the European Union by
CPI Antony Rowe, Chippenham and Eastbourne

CONTENTS

In memory of

Mokhtar

*without whom this book neither would
not nor could not have been written*

ACKNOWLEDGEMENTS

Aleksandr Solzhenitsyn, who died shortly before this book was completed, said that while an ordinary man was obliged 'not to participate in lies', artists had greater responsibilities. 'It is within the power of writers and artists', he said, 'to do much more: to defeat the lie!' In what is a sad reflection on the state of the world in which we live, it has increasingly become the task of anthropologists to 'defeat the lie'.

At a time when our universities are taking on an increasingly mercenary hue and social scientists coming under growing pressure to politicise their research and so ease the passage of 'the lie', it is a regrettable indictment of academe, but perhaps not surprising, that my acknowledgements are so brief. I would like to have thanked, as I have done frequently in the past, a number of funding agencies and research councils, but I am not able to do so. The prolonged fieldwork and research on which this work and its sequel (*The Dying Sahara*) are based have received no such funding. Nor would it be anything but hypocritical of me to express any gratitude to the universities to which I have been attached during the period of this work, notably Bristol and Exeter, other than to thank a small number of colleagues (they know who they are) and those students whom I have taught, both undergraduate and postgraduate, for the stimulation, friendship and support they have given me.

This lack of institutional financial support has inevitably made both the research and the writing of these two books extremely difficult. I am therefore grateful to my publisher, Roger van Zwanenberg, for his constant encouragement and forbearance when deadlines inevitably came and went, and to my copy-editor at Pluto, Charles Peyton, for his much appreciated endeavours. I am also grateful to a number of academic journal editors for affording me the space in which to write and for giving me their support on those occasions when this work became especially difficult. In particular, I should single out Jan Burgess and Ray Bush at *Review of African Political Economy* and Gustaaf Houtman, who, through his own brand of editorial genius, has almost single-handedly turned *Anthropology Today* into a 'must-read'. I would also like to give special thanks to Fançois Gèze and his colleagues and associates at *Algeria Watch International*, who have accomplished extraordinary work in monitoring and reporting human rights abuses in Algeria.

I owe a great intellectual and personal debt to Claude Meillassoux. He embodied an immense humanity. Travelling with him in Africa was a privileged experience that enabled me to share his unique approach to and understanding of the anthropological domain. But, in the same way as there were no free lunches for Mrs Thatcher, there are no free journeys for anthropologists. Our privileged insight into the anthropological domain is one that is afforded us by the 'other', and like all 'gifts' (for that is what it nearly always is) it requires reciprocity, in the form, so I believe and when requested, of our engagement.

Anthropological engagement, however, brings responsibilities and raises multiple ethical questions. Knowing what is 'right' and 'wrong' is one thing, but putting what is 'right' into practice is often neither easy nor clear-cut, and rarely without costs. Amid the romanticism that shrouds our subject, we should not underestimate the latter. Mokhtar, without whom this book neither would not nor could not have been written, died suddenly and unexpectedly while in its formative stages. In his all-too-short life, he gave inspiration, meaning and insight to life in the Sahara. In his own inimitable way, he stood up and spoke 'truth to power'. And for that he died; some would say of a broken heart. This book is written in his memory. In 2007, Tuareg in Niger took up arms against perceived injustice. *The Dying Sahara* describes and explains why their women, children and old men suffered grotesque crimes at the hands of Niger's US-trained armed forces. That is not the anthropology of exotica, but the anthropology of 'bearing witness'.

I first visited and lived among the Tuareg of the Sahara in 1964. Over the succeeding years they gave me much, enabling me to serve my traditional apprenticeship and then establish myself as a professional anthropologist. Over the last ten years they have again given me more than can be described in mere words: that hospitality which is so noticeably rare in our own culture, deep friendship and, of course, understanding. I cannot thank them all here by name for their own safety, but they too know who they are. I cannot say that this book and its sequel, *The Dying Sahara*, were written 'for them', because that is not wholly true. Rather, they were written 'with them', with my role sometimes being little more than as scribe – a recorder 'bearing witness', so that others might understand the circumstances under which they now live. Most of all, however, they were written for us, so that we can better understand both the nature and the consequences of the lies and deceptions that have been perpetrated in the name of 'Western civilisation' through the instrument of the Bush administration's 'global war on terror' – not just in the Sahara–Sahel, but elsewhere in Africa and across the world.

These two books (*The Dark Sahara* and *The Dying Sahara*) are the fifth and sixth books I have written on the Sahara and its peoples. In all of them I have paid tribute to the brave and long-suffering people of Algeria, including the hundreds of thousands who are obliged or have chosen to live in exile because the repressive conditions in their own country are so intolerable. They have a special place in my heart, and I use these pages once again to pay them my respects.

Finally, I would like to thank my family, to whom I apologise for what must seem like an eternal preoccupation with the Sahara, and those many friends, among whom I include those journalists, travellers, broadcasters, colleagues and researchers in the UK, Germany, Malta, North Africa, elsewhere in Europe, and not least the US, who have given me invaluable help at one time or another, especially in collecting and/or verifying difficult-to-obtain information, translating documents, and reading and commenting upon earlier drafts. I regret leaving you nameless, but those of you in Algeria and the Sahel especially know why it has to be like that. Thank you all. Your many contributions have helped to 'defeat the lie'.

ABBREVIATIONS

AFP – Agence France-Presse
AFRICOM – US Africa Command
AIS – Armée Islamique du Salut
AQIM – Al-Qaeda of the Islamic Maghreb
ATAWT – Association des Agences de Tourisme Wilaya de Tamanrasset
AWACS – Airborne Warning and Control System
BBC – British Broadcasting Corporation
BKA – Bundeskriminalamt
CIA – Central Intelligence Agency
CPMI – Centre Principal Militaire d'Investigation
DCE – Direction du Contre-Espionnage
DDSE – Direction du Documentation et de la Sécurité Extérieure
DGSE – Direction Générale de la Sécurité Extérieure
DRS – Direction des Renseignements et de la Sécurité
EIA - Energy Information Administration
FAN – Forces Armées Nigeriennes
FBI – Federal Bureau of Investigation
FFS – Front des Forces Socialistes
FIS – Front Islamique de Salut
FLN – Front de Libération Nationale
FNIS – Force National d'Intervention et de la Sécurité (Niger)
GIA – Groupes Islamiques Armées
GIS – Groupe d'Interventions Spéciaux
GSPC – Groups Salafiste pour le Prédication et le Combat
GWOT – Global War on Terror
HCE – Haut Comité d'Etat
HCS – Haut Conseil de Sécurité
HUMINT – Human Intelligence
ICC – International Criminal Court

ICG – International Crisis Group
IMET – International Military Education and Training Program
IMF – International Monetary Fund
JCIT – Jerusalem Conference on International Terrorism
JSOC – Joint Special Operations Command
LNG – Liquefied Natural Gas
MAOL – Mouvement Algérien des Officiers Libres
MBM – Mokhtar ben Mokhtar
MDJT – Mouvement pour la Democratie et la Justice au Chad
MEI – Mouvement pour l'Etat Islamique
MIA – Mouvement Islamique Armé
MNJ – Mouvement des Nigériens pour la Justice
NATO – North Atlantic Treaty Organisation
NEPD – National Energy Policy Development (Group)
NSA – National Security Agency
OEF – Operation Enduring Freedom
OPEC – Organization of the Petroleum Exporting Countries
PMC(s) – Private Military Companies
PNAC – Project for the New American Century
PSI – Pan-Sahel Initiative
RDJTF – Rapid Deployment Joint Task Force
RFI – Radio France Internationale
ROAPE – Review of African Political Economy
SACEUR – Supreme Allied Commander Europe
SAP – Structural Adjustment Programme
SM – Sécurité Militaire
SOA – School of the Americas
TSCTI – Trans-Saharan Counter-Terrorism Initiative
UNATA – Union Nationale des Associations des Agences de Tourisme Alternatif
UNDP – United Nations Development Programme
USEUCOM – United States European Command
USSOCOM – United States Special Operations Command
VOA – Voice of America
WMD – weapons of mass destruction
WTO – World Tourism Organisation

GLOSSARY

(Tk. = Tamahak; Ar. = Arabic; Fr. = French)

ag (Tk.) – son of

ben (Ar.) – son of

borgne (Fr.) – one eyed

Bundeskriminalamt (Ger.) – Federal Criminal Police Office of Germany (BKA).

daira (Ar.) – an administrative division of a *wilaya* (analagous to municipality; see *wilaya*)

Dawa wa Jihad (Ar.) – The name sometimes used in Arabic for Algeria's *Groupe Salafiste pour la Prédication et le Combat* (GSPC) (from *dawa*, the 'call to Islam'; *jihad*, struggle or 'holy war')

douaniers (Fr.) – customs

emir (Ar.) – leader

erg (Ar.) – sand sea

ishomar (Tk.) – berberised version of the French word *chômeur* (an unemployed person or redundant worker). The word categorises the young men who left Niger and Mali during the drought of the 1970s, and more recently in search of work in Libya. Many joined Gaddafi's Islamic Legion. With the collapse in the oil price and Gaddafi's humiliating military withdrawal from Chad in the late 1980s, many of the them returned home and became the main fighters in the Tuareg rebellions in the 1990s.

Islamic – pertaining to the religion of Islam. An Islamic state is one in which the religion of Islam is implemented fully into state and society (see Islamist).

xvi THE DARK SAHARA

Islamist/-ism – As distinct from Islam, refers more to a political ideology culled, often very selectively, from the history of Islam and sometimes equated with Islamic fundamentalism. Islamists are generally associated with political movements and ideologies advocating an Islamic state.

jihad (Ar.) – struggle, 'holy war'

laouar (Ar.) – one-eyed

kel (Tk.) – people of

mairie (Fr.) – mayoralty, office of mayor, town council, town hall

maquis (Fr.) – underground movement

mujahideen (Ar.) – religious freedom fighter

mukhabarat (Ar.) – intelligence force; often used with connotation of repression in the context of the state security system.

oued (Tk.) – valley

parrain (Fr.) – godfather, patron

piste – (Fr) track

pouvoir (Fr.) – power; used in Algeria to denote the political–military elite which effectively holds the power behind the formal arrangements of government.

Salafist/-ism – an early Sunni Islamic movement. Salafists in Algeria and North Africa are generally regarded as Islamic 'fundamentalists', in that Salafism is sometimes regarded as a simplified version of Islam in which adherents focus on a few commands and practices (see GSPC). Often used interchangeably with Wahhabiism.

shott (Ar.) – impermanent lake

Tablighi Jamaat (Ar.) – a Muslim missionary and revival movement claiming to be non-political

trabendo (Tk. From Fr.) – smuggling

trabendiste (Tk. from Fr.) – smuggler

troc (Fr.) – barter exchange/trade

wali (Ar.) – governor of a *wilaya*

wilaya (pl. *wilayat*) (Ar.) – an administrative division of Algeria, usually translated as 'province'

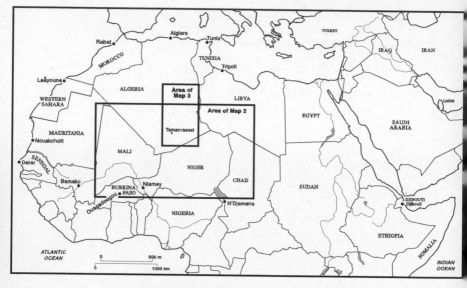

Map 1   Northern Africa (Catherine Lawrence)

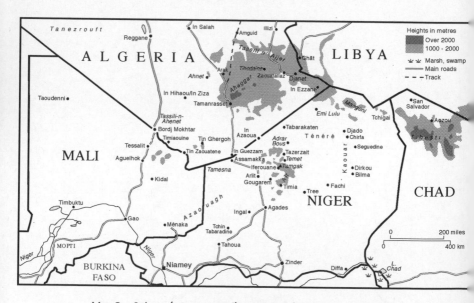

Map 2   Sahara (west-central) and Sahel (Catherine Lawrence)

xviii

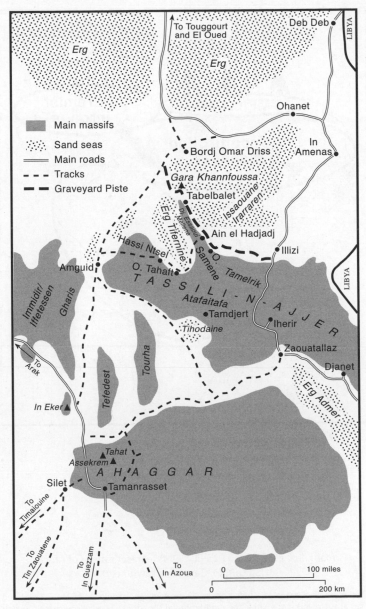

Map 3 Southern Algeria: the 'Graveyard Piste' (Catherine Lawrence)

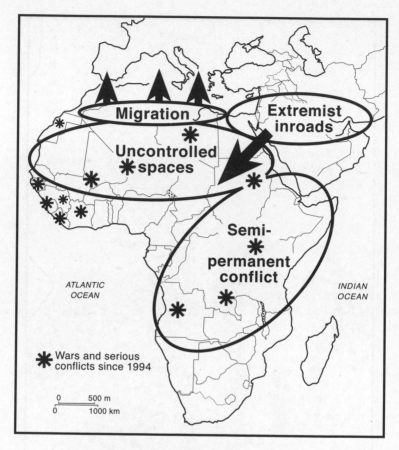

Map 4a   War and serious conflicts since 1994

Maps 4a,b,c: Pentagon (US EUCOM) representations of Africa
(US EUCOM/Catherine Lawrence)*

*The originals of maps 4a, 4b and 4c, in vivid colour, were compiled by US EUCOM and
used at their workshops within the programme of the Africa Clearing House, a discussion
forum on security issues in Africa. The maps were used to demonstrate the urgency of the
Pentagon's Pan-Sahel Initiative (PSI). Map 4c was used to justify the expansion of the PSI
into the Trans-Saharan Counter-Terrorism Initiative (TSCTI).

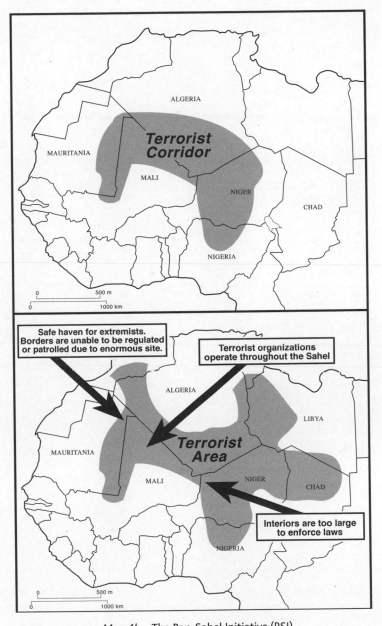

Map 4b The Pan-Sahel Initiative (PSI)

Map 4c The Expanded Terrorist area – Pan-Sahel Initiative: Intrinsic Forces

INTRODUCTION

In early 2003, a few weeks before the US invaded Iraq, 32 European tourists, in seven separate parties, disappeared seemingly into thin air in the depths of Algeria's Saharan desert. The so-called 'Graveyard Piste' ('La Piste des Tombeaux'), the region where they disappeared, became the Sahara's Bermuda Triangle.

The first chapter describes how these disappearances were transformed, over the course of several weeks, from a sinister desert mystery into the belief that the tourists had been taken hostage by Islamic extremists belonging to Algeria's 'terrorist' organisation, the Groupe Salafiste pour le Prédication et le Combat (GSPC), now known as 'Al-Qaeda of the Islamic Maghreb' (AQIM).

After three months of captivity in the open desert, 17 of the hostages were released when the Algerian security forces launched a helicopter and ground assault on their hideout. The 15 remaining hostages, who had been held captive in another desert mountain hideout some 300km away, were then taken on a momentous journey, estimated at some 3,000km, into the remote desert regions of northern Mali, with one of them, Michaela Spitzer, dying from heat-stroke on the way. After a further month of negotiations, the alleged payment of a 5 million euro ransom and a total of six months of captivity in the searing heat of the Central Sahara, these remaining 14 were finally released.

The leader of the kidnappers was Abderrazak Lamari. Sometimes known as Amari Saifi, or a dozen other aliases, he was usually referred to by his *nom de guerre*, 'El Para', a name derived from his time as a parachutist in the Algerian army. The Bush administration quickly branded him as Osama bin Laden's 'man in the Sahara'. Chapter 2 describes how El Para and his 60 or so terrorists, after four months in Mali, were driven out of their desert retreats somewhere to the north of Timbuktu and chased

1

by a combination of US, Malian, Nigerien and Algerian forces across the southern Saharan tracts of north-east Mali, the Aïr Mountains and Ténéré desert of northern Niger, and on into the Tibesti Mountains of northern Chad. There, in the first week of March 2004, forces of the Chad regular army, supported by US aerial reconnaissance, surrounded them. Forty-three of El Para's men were reportedly killed in the ensuing battle. El Para himself and a handful of followers managed to escape the carnage, only to fall into the hands of Chadian rebels.

Even before the hostages had been released, the Bush administration had identified the Sahara as a new front in its global war on terror (GWOT). With El Para holed up in Chad, Washington was not short of hyperbole in portraying this new terrorist threat as having spread right across the wastelands of the Sahel, as the southern 'shore' of the Sahara is known in Arabic, from Mauritania in the west, through the little known desert lands of Mali, southern Algeria and Niger, to the Tibesti mountains of Chad, with beyond them the Sudan, Somalia and, across the waters, the 'Talibanised' lands of Afghanistan and the debacle that was Iraq.

The White House, the US Office of Counterterrorism and the Pentagon moved quickly. On 10 January 2004, President Bush's Pan Sahel Initiative (PSI), designed to fight terrorism in these vast, ungoverned wastelands of Africa, rolled into action with the disembarkation in Nouakchott, Mauritania's sand-blown Atlantic coastal capital, of an 'anti-terror team' of 500 US troops. This was no mean affair. US Deputy Undersecretary of State Pamela Bridgewater, in Nouakchott to oversee what locals called the 'American invasion', announced to the accompanying press corps that 400 US Rangers would be deployed into the Chad–Niger border regions the following week. US troops, so Ms Bridgewater told the world, would do the work in Mauritania and Mali, while Los Angeles-based defence contractors Pacific Architects and Engineers would pick up the work in Niger and Chad.

The generals of America's European Command (US EUCOM), based in Stuttgart but charged with responsibility for most of Africa, were fully energised. While General James (Jim) Jones, Supreme

Allied Commander, Europe (SACEUR) and the Commander of US EUCOM, talked enthusiastically about constructing a 'family of bases' across Africa, his deputy commander, with responsibility for Africa, the gung-ho Air Force General Charles Wald, described the Sahara as a 'swamp of terror', a 'terrorist infestation' which 'we need to drain'. Back at the White House, press officers described the Sahara as 'a magnet for terrorists', while, almost within minutes of El Para's flight across the Sahel becoming public knowledge, western intelligence and diplomatic sources were claiming to be finding the fingerprints of this new terrorist threat everywhere. It took only a few days after the Madrid train bombings for that atrocity to be linked to al-Qaeda groups lurking deep in the Sahara, with western intelligence and security services soon warning that al-Qaeda bases hidden deep in the world's largest desert could launch terrorist attacks on Europe. America's military commanders did much to alert Europe to the threat of terrorist activity from North Africa. They pointed explicitly to the bombing of a synagogue in Tunisia in 2002; suicide bombings in Casablanca that had killed 33 innocent civilians and wounded more than 100 in May 2003; the arrest of al-Qaeda suspects in Morocco; and the abduction of the 32 tourists in Algeria. They warned of the region, Europe's back-door, becoming another Afghanistan; of terrorists from Afghanistan and Pakistan swarming across the vast ungoverned and desolate regions of the Sahara desert; that the GSPC had already emerged in Europe as an al-Qaeda recruiting organisation; and that in North Africa it sought nothing less than the overthrow of the Algerian and Mauritanian governments.

The threats of terrorism that lurked in the Sahara's vast empty spaces, and of which the Bush administration and its military commanders were warning the world, especially Europe, were literally terrifying. However, they were stories and warnings that were not recognised by the local people who lived in the Sahara, notably the nomadic Tuareg tribesmen in whose traditional domain most of the El Para incidents had been played out. Indeed, long before the hostages were released, a few people who knew the Sahara well, including myself, were beginning to question whether their abduction was all that it had appeared. Local people, especially the Tuareg, sensed something sinister. As the drama unfolded, they became increasingly suspicious of the role played by the Algerian government, its security establishment – the *mukhabarat* – and especially the 'dirty tricks' department of its secret military intelligence and counterterrorism service, the Direction des Renseignements et de la Sécurité (DRS), formerly the Sécurité Militaire (SM).

My own suspicions were such that, before the first group of hostages had been released, I had told some of their families, as well as official representatives of their governments, that although we were witnessing an act of 'terrorism', it was possibly one of 'state terrorism' being orchestrated by the military and intelligence services. But whose military and intelligence services? This was the question that dogged me from soon after the 32 tourists were taken hostage, and the one that I have pursued, almost without break, during the months, now years, since their release. As my research progressed, it became apparent that the Sahara had been the stage for one of the world's most elaborate and diabolical intelligence deceptions.

If this book, as I suggest in Chapter 3, begins to sound a bit like a 'whodunit', that is what it is, but with the mystery not so much being the 'who' as the 'why' and 'how'. The 'who' is the US and Algeria – or, to be more precise, elements within their respective regimes. The questions of 'why' and 'how' raise complex and far-reaching issues about the nature of both the Bush administration and the Algerian regime, and about why they have ventured into such heinous territory. In the case of the Bush administration, the answer to these questions goes beyond mere reference to the GWOT. My analysis of Washington's Saharan front in the GWOT unmasks much that underlies the real nature, direction and dynamics of America's 'new imperialism': its energy crisis; the views and dreams of the neo-conservatives within its government; the real forces and ideologies of neo-liberalism; the rise of the 'religious right'; turf wars within both the military and the intelligence services; fears of Chinese expansionism and more intense competition for global resources, especially in Africa; and, perhaps most dangerous of all, what some people have seen as the dislocation and dismemberment of the Western world's most corrupt government, and a military that is 'out of control'. As I reveal in the case of the Sahara, America's GWOT has involved the fabrication of a fiction of terrorism that in turn has created the ideological conditions for the US's militarisation of Africa and the securing of US strategic national resources – notably, but not exclusively, oil. On the wider, global scene it added in no small measure to the Bush administration's 'information war': the quagmire of lies and propaganda that served to justify the US invasion and occupation of Iraq.

This book presents the evidence of this deception, thus enabling us to make sense of what has been happening in North Africa and in the Sahelian Sahara over the last half-dozen or so years. It also explains what drove both the US and Algeria to conspire in this duplicity and what they sought to achieve from it. In the sequel, *The Dying Sahara: US Imperialism and Terror in Africa*, I illustrate and explain the 'blowback'– the resistance to this US 'invasion' – as well as the implications that the US militarisation of Africa has had, and will continue to have, for the peoples of both the Sahara–Sahel and the rest of Africa.

Chapters 4, 5 and 6 set out the initial suspicion, and then the gradual accrual of evidence, that convinced both me and those few others with whom I was investigating these events that neither the kidnapping of the 32 European tourists nor El Para's activities in the Sahel were all that they seemed. Chapter 4 examines the evidence that led us, as well as some of the hostages, to believe that the Algerian army's secret intelligence services were involved in the kidnapping. Chapter 5 pieces together what we now know of the GSPC's alleged expansion across the Sahel. Chapter 6 raises questions about El Para's identity, and about his ties to both America's and Algeria's secret military intelligence services – notably Algeria's.

These three chapters take us to the same conclusion as that of Salima Mellah and of François Gèze, director of Editions Le Découverte and Algeria Watch, Algeria's respected human rights organisation, who said:

> We have undertaken an in depth enquiry into the affair of the European hostages in the Sahara. A close study of the facts shows that there is no other explanation for this operation than the directing of the hostage-taking by the DRS, the Algerian army's secret service.[1]

If elements in the US and Algerian regimes had indeed colluded in fabricating this deception in order to justify launching a Sahara–Sahelian front in the GWOT, as the evidence suggests, then the $64,000 question is: Which one of them initiated it? On face value, it might appear as if the US was 'suckered' into the region by Algeria's secret military intelligence services. Indeed, there is much circumstantial evidence to suggest that that may have been the case. However, the more closely we look at how much both countries have benefited from these events, and how closely their secret intelligence services have been working together, especially since 9/11, the more it seems that the US, at the very least, was happy to be 'suckered' into the region in this way.

However, to understand the nature and closeness of this collusion fully, and to throw a clearer light on the question of which party might have taken the initiative in this affair, we need to step back in time a little so that we can get a better understanding of what has brought the US and Algeria into such a potentially cataclysmic alliance. This involves departing from the narrative for three chapters, in order to provide the reader with an understanding of the forces and dynamics that have driven the two countries towards each other. Chapter 7 examines the main driver behind the Bush administration's policy towards this part of Africa. It explains the importance of America's energy crisis in determining US foreign policy and the specific shaping of America's new imperialism, along with other recent drivers of US foreign policy in Africa. These include the importance to the US of the continent's other natural resources apart from oil, and other aspects of what Noam Chomsky has called America's 'grand design'. Other key factors behind US policy towards Africa are touched on in subsequent chapters and in *The Dying Sahara*, including the relationship between the invasion of Iraq and the launch of a new front in the GWOT across the Sahara–

Sahel; military and intelligence turf wars; concern for China's expansionism and increasing investment in Africa; pressure from the religious right; and the Bush administration's obsession with both the arrogation of 'war powers' to itself, to the exclusion of Congress, the Constitution and civil rights and liberties, and the associated militarisation of 'almost everything' – from the administration of bird flu jabs in the American mid-west to education programmes in the Sahel. Indeed, if Africa, and more especially its empty desert spaces, at times appear peripheral to the main thrusts of American foreign and domestic policies during the Bush–Cheney era, these subsequent chapters and *The Dying Sahara* highlight the role that the GWOT in Africa, notably in the Sahara–Sahel, has played in enabling the Bush administration to globalise the war on terror and to authorise, among other things, the largest CIA covert action programme since the Cold War.

Chapters 8 and 9 focus solely on Algeria. They are designed to help readers who are unfamiliar with the country's recent history to appreciate how it has come to its present critical condition. Chapter 8 provides a summary analysis of the traumatic years of the late 1980s that led up to the elections of 1991/92, which would have brought to power the world's first democratically elected Islamist government. Chapter 9 provides an equally succinct account of the course of events and forces at play in Algeria's violent civil war – or 'Dirty War', as it is commonly known – which followed the army's annulment of the elections in January 1992, in what was effectively nothing more than a military coup. This coup – which received more than the proverbial wink and nod from France, Algeria's former colonial ruler, the US, other western powers and, most significantly, neighbouring Arab states, and which led to Algeria tearing itself apart in an almost unimaginable spiral of violence and human suffering – has not only singularly failed to address the country's most glaring and fundamental problems, but, in the words of one Algerian journalist, El-Kadi Ihsane, 'has turned Algerians into bootlickers who have chosen to make a pact with the most reactionary and dangerous American administration in the last hundred years'.[2] El-Kadi Ihsane, is, of course, referring to the Algerian government and not his fellow citizens, the great majority of whom he describes as detesting the Bush administration.

The key question throughout this book is: Why? What drove the US administration to implicate itself in, perhaps even to orchestrate, this heinous act and its duplicitous aftermath? The 'banana theory' of terrorism, as I have dubbed it, and which provides the title of Chapter 10, explains how the Bush administration has 'theorised' ('imagined' would be a better word) how terrorists were dislodged by American forces from Afghanistan only to spread to the Horn of Africa, and then 'swarm' (to use the US military term for it) across the Sahel, through what is now a banana-shaped curve across US military maps of Africa, then to link up with terrorist movements in North Africa's Maghreb, notably Algeria's GSPC – from where they stand poised, lurking in the unknown spaces of the great desert, to threaten the heart of Europe. The theory is grand, persuasive, terrifying, and untrue. As Chapter 12 explains, it was based on no credible intelligence.

This lack of US intelligence lies at the heart of the extraordinary US–Algerian relationship that, since 9/11, has linked two of the world's most accomplished proponents of state terrorism together. Algeria, suffering from an effective arms boycott and from international pariah status as a result of its Dirty War during the 1990s, needed US military technology and wanted to regain its international status. The Bush administration was able to provide both. The US, in turn, needed 'terror' in the Sahel. It needed to validate its 'banana theory' of terrorism, which provided the ideological conditions and justification for the militarisation of the rest of Africa, and for the securing of its resources – notably oil.

Chapter 10 also documents for the first time a particularly sinister event that took place in a remote and little-known corner of the Sahara some four months before El Para came on the scene, and five months before the US invaded Iraq. The event enables us to place subsequent incidents and developments, notably the abduction of the 32 European tourist hostages, in their proper and wider context, which until now has been shrouded in the elaborate web spun from the disinformation and lawlessness that have become the hallmarks of both the current US and Algerian administrations.

Chapter 11 illustrates, through an analysis of the Algerian media in the run-up to El Para's hostage-taking, how the media disinformation was prepared prior to the opening of the Saharan–Sahelian front in the war on terror. One is left wondering if anything much has changed since Ronald Reagan launched his own war against international terrorism in 1981. A 1982 Masters thesis on that moment in history concluded:

> ... a successful propaganda operation ... the entire notion of 'international terrorism' ... rests on a faulty, dishonest, and ultimately corrupt information base ... The issue of international terrorism has little to do with fact, or with any objective legal definition of international terrorism. The issue, as promoted ... and used by the Regan administration, is an ideological and instrumental issue. It is the ideology, rather than the reality, that dominates US foreign policy today.[3]

The concluding chapter describes how the 'US invasion', as locals described it, has led to 'blowback', or what I prefer to call resistance. Terrorism in the Sahara–Sahel, fabricated to justify the launch of the GWOT in Africa, has now become a self-fulfilling prophecy. Multiple Tuareg rebellions have transformed the Sahara–Sahel region from what the Bush administration and military imagined as a 'terror zone' into a very real war zone. The chapter also introduces other issues raised in *The Dying Sahara*, notably how this most shameful of US foreign policies has been responsible for a horrific loss of both life and livelihoods in the Sahara–Sahel region. *The Dying Sahara* also explains and illustrates how the militarisation of Africa, which has been justified by this duplicitous policy, has not brought to Africa the 'peace, security and development' promised by the American president and his military commanders, but conflict, insecurity and suffering.

THE DOSSIER

Djanet, Algerian Sahara, 10 March 2003

The anger was palpable. Black blinds were drawn in all but one front window of the cramped auditorium to shield the audience from the glare of the Saharan sun. As he spoke, he sensed the eyes in the packed rows of predominantly blue-, black- and white-turbaned heads and veiled faces focusing on him. He was one of only three Europeans there. The other two were from the United Nations Development Programme (UNDP) and the World Tourism Organisation (WTO). He spoke in French, for longer than he had planned, and slowly, because it was not his native tongue and also to enable the many self-appointed interpreters among the audience to murmur almost simultaneous translations into both Arabic and Tamahak, the language of the Tuareg who live in this remote corner of the Algerian Sahara. By the time he had finished he was sure that his audience had a clear understanding of the history and contents of what was to become known colloquially as 'the dossier'. What he could not explain at that time was why the Algerian authorities had singularly refused to act upon it. That explanation would only come much later.

He had been invited to the conference by representatives of the local people themselves; notably the president of the Union Nationale des Associations des Agences de Tourisme Alternatif (UNATA) and members of the Association des Agences de Tourisme Wilaya de Tamanrasset (ATAWT), two local organisations in the forefront of the battle to protect the Sahara's fragile environment both from mass and unregulated tourism, and from the rampant looting of the region's prehistoric artefacts: stone axes, arrow-heads, grinding stones, stone jewellery and figurines, ostrich shell beads, pottery; on occasion, even paintings and engravings hacked from rock-faces were being spirited out of the country by the truckload to be sold on the world's illicit markets for stolen antiquities. It was not just the peoples' cultural heritage that was being destroyed, but their future livelihoods, for tourism – based on the region's fantastic scenery, prehistoric rock art and associated archaeology – was the region's major industry, and the one which gave the indigenous Tuareg peoples a modicum of control over the way in which what remained of their traditional way of life was being integrated into the modern and increasingly globalised economy.

The compilation of the dossier had begun in 2001, shortly after the Algerian Sahara had reopened to tourism after almost ten years in which violent political strife between Islamic militants and the government's security forces had claimed an estimated 150,000 to 200,000 lives. As tourists trickled back into the Sahara, the looting recommenced – in Algeria, Libya, Northern Niger; in fact almost everywhere where the Sahara's rich prehistory lay exposed and accessible to plunder. Government agencies paid lip-service to the conservation of cultural heritage, but seemed both uninterested and unwilling to intervene. In some Saharan countries looters knew that a small bribe, combined with bureaucratic ignorance of the value of the artefacts, could go a long way. The looters, mostly Europeans, entered the Sahara with their own, often false-bottomed, vehicles, sophisticated navigational and communications systems, and other high-tech accoutrements. The Sahara was ripe for their exploitation.

The Tuareg knew all this. Those that understood the implications – and they were rapidly growing in number – were incensed by it, but could do little without concrete evidence. The internet became their means of gathering such evidence. Soon after its arrival in Tamanrasset, the administrative capital of Algeria's extreme south, in 2001, they began searching the websites of European tourism agencies advertising tours to the Sahara. Using code names, they elicited a stream of information from the chat rooms of Swiss, French, German, Italian and English Saharan travel websites. As they found data – names, addresses, telephone numbers, Saharan travel itineraries, photographs and sale prices of stolen artefacts – they transferred them to archaeologists in Cambridge for safekeeping until such time as they would be required as evidence in a court of law. The first big 'stash' they found was that of a German, Helmut Artzmüller, and his Munich-based Rolling Rover operation. It contained everything from past and future itineraries to web-pages of looted artefacts and accompanying prices, and the bright, smiling, confident faces of his team of collaborators. One operator had undertaken as many as 80 raids on the Sahara.

The dossier grew to the point where it was ready for a court of law. But where would the arrests be made? Advice from all fronts was unequivocal: the criminals would have to be caught, red-handed, in the country they were pillaging. In the spring of 2002, the dossier was handed over to the Algerian government. By the winter of 2002, the Algerian authorities had done nothing: Rolling Rover, according to its own itineraries, was still moving freely around the country. In December 2002 the Tamanrasset agency, Tarahist, sent copies of the dossier, with an urgent plea to act against Rolling Rover and other known German looters, to the Ministers of Culture and Tourism in Algiers, and to the regional directors of Tourism, the Ahaggar National Park and the Customs, in Tamanrasset. The Algerian authorities, however, still took no action.[1] Local Tuareg were both perplexed and cross at their government's failure to act, and therefore decided to use the Djanet conference to bring the dossier's contents to public attention.

Within days of the dossier's revelation, Algeria's newspapers had given headlines and extensive coverage to the scandal. It seemed unlikely that the Algerian Sahara would ever again be such a carefree place for German travellers.

MISSING

Two parties of travellers returning from the Algerian Sahara were booked onto the Tunis-to-Genoa night ferry of 9 March 2003. One comprised four Swiss who had been touring the Algerian Sahara in a Toyota Hiace camper van; the other a young Dutchman and three Germans who had been travelling in the same part of the Sahara on motorbikes. None of them made it to the ferry. Twenty days earlier, three other Germans had crossed into Algeria and checked into a hotel in El Oued for the night. They stored their vehicle and trailer at the hotel, and the following morning set off southwards on motorbikes. They were seen four days later at the wells of Hassi Tabelbalet, heading in the direction of Illizi, the desert town just to the north of the Tassili-n-Ajjer Mountains, where the four Swiss had camped the previous night before heading eastwards towards Aïn el Hadjadj, a well 65km to the south-east of Hassi Tabelbalet. They were booked onto the Tunis ferry a few days after the other eight, but they too didn't make it.

As Algeria's newspapers began their denouncement of Helmut Artzmüller and the looting of the country's national heritage, eleven European tourists – all German-speakers – were being reported by their families as missing. The immediate reaction of the Algerian authorities was to do little other than note and circulate the details. They – like many of the travel agencies in Algeria's southern Sahara, who were beginning to receive anxious phone calls from the tourists' friends and families – were not altogether surprised: the Sahara, after all, is a vast place in which many travellers do silly things. It was conceivable that they might simply have crossed into a neighbouring country without passing through a frontier post, and be heading home by a different route. The possibilities of such routes and of what might have befallen them were myriad.

But, as the days went by, concern began to grow. For three separate groups of relatively experienced travellers to disappear in roughly the same place and at about the same time was beginning to look sinister. Then, on 28 March, six more Germans, who had been travelling together in three vehicles in the same region, also failed to turn up for the Tunis ferry. On the next day, 29 March, another group comprising three Germans and a Swede, travelling in two vehicles, failed to arrive in Tamanrasset as planned. Twenty-one people had now disappeared. A week later, on 5 April, the number rose to 29, as a group of eight Austrians, travelling in four vehicles, also failed to make their return booking on the Tunis ferry. This group had last been seen at a service station at Deb Deb, close to the Tunisian–Libyan border, on 21 March, and was known to be travelling via Amguid into the Ahaggar region of Algeria's vast south. On 11 April the number rose to 31, as two more Austrians also failed to make the ferry.

Between 21 February and 11 April 2003, seven groups of tourists, numbering 31 persons (15 Germans, 10 Austrians, 4 Swiss, 1 Dutchman and 1 Swede), had literally disappeared without trace in the Algerian Sahara. Later, the number was amended to 32, with the inclusion of a German archaeologist who had been travelling alone in the region under mysterious circumstances. The 'missing' had three things in common. Although they were not all German nationals, they were all German-speakers. Secondly, they were all travelling 'off-piste' and without guides. Thirdly, they had all disappeared within the broad triangle of desert between the oasis towns of Ouargla, Tamanrasset and Djanet. A more careful reconstruction and analysis of their last known movements and contacts indicated that most of them had disappeared in a more narrow region, somewhere to the south of Bordj Omar Driss, around the Erg Tifernine,[1] on or close to a route previously known as the 'Timbuktu route' but now dubbed by Saharan travellers, a little sinisterly, as the La Route des Tombeaux – the Graveyard Piste.[2]

1

THE SAHARA'S BERMUDA TRIANGLE

Does the Sahara have its own 'Bermuda Triangle'? It was a question that both the world's press and many of the Sahara's inhabitants began to ask. People might occasionally disappear without trace, especially in remote areas, but surely not 32 of them – and especially when they were in at least seven separate groups. Although the idea of a Saharan Bermuda Triangle was fanciful, the facts were stark: between 21 February and 11 April 2003, 32 people had disappeared into thin air.

People only start being registered as 'missing' when they don't turn up. There may therefore be quite a time lag between actually getting lost, being abducted, or whatever else might cause one to disappear, and other people becoming aware of it. In this case, it was not until the second week of March, around the time of the Djanet conference and the public divulgence of the dossier on German looters, that tourism agencies in Illizi, Tamanrasset and Djanet began to receive the first anxious phone calls from friends and relatives in Europe. I had both been at the conference and heard the phone calls from friends and relatives at first-hand. My immediate thought was that enraged locals, or perhaps even the Algerian authorities themselves, had taken the law into their own hands. It was a chilling possibility which lingered for several weeks, until it became clear that the first disappearances had actually preceded the groundswell of anti-German sentiment that emanated from the Djanet conference.

If the disappearances had nothing to do with looting, then what had happened to those missing? By the second week of April the Algerian government had mobilised 1,200 troops, later to be increased to some 5,000. Ground patrols with local guides spread across the region, targeting especially the area around Aïn el Hadjadj, while satellite surveillance, two helicopters (later reported to be ten) and one reconnaissance plane, all running four sorties a day, searched from above.[1] Still there was nothing: no bodies, no vehicles (and there were ten all-terrain vehicles and more than half a dozen motor bikes missing), no clothes, no tracks. Simply nothing.

For several weeks, the question of what had happened to the tourists was almost the sole topic of conversation in the Sahara, while the world's media, especially in the countries from which the missing people came, became increasingly preoccupied with the mystery. Speculation was rife, ranging from the plausible to the ridiculous. In the early stages of the drama, the Algerian media were keen to suggest that the tourists had simply had an accident; they had got lost, perhaps as a result of sandstorms or, more likely, because their GPS systems were malfunctioning. Indeed, in the wake of a few prominent articles, most of the country's population tended to believe that the Americans had scrambled GPS systems to confuse the Iraqis prior to the start of their invasion of that country. The Algerians made much of the fact that the tourists were all travelling without guides – were 'off piste'– and that some of them, as Algeria's President Abdelaziz Bouteflika at one time suggested, had even entered the country illegally. Other 'official spokesmen', keen to absolve Algeria from any blame and further tarnishing of its image, suggested that the tourists had simply strayed into neighbouring countries such as Libya, Niger or Mali. Even if they had, this didn't explain why they had not communicated. One such spokesman even suggested that the tourists had staged their own disappearance, although for what end was not altogether clear. Following in this vein, one Algerian newspaper, no doubt still thinking of what had been revealed at the Djanet conference, suggested that they were 'looters' who had staged their disappearance to cover their misdeeds. Perhaps the most bizarre suggestion came from a European source which claimed that the tourists had been abducted by a group of Rommel's World War II followers who had been holed up in the Tibesti Mountains for the last 50-odd years and were now in search of healthy, young (German) breeding stock!

A slightly less fanciful theory, but one which found some resonance in the region, was that the disappearances had been engineered by Tunisian, or perhaps even Moroccan, tourism interests who saw the pick-up in Algeria's Saharan tourism since 2000 as a threat to their own tourism industries, neither of which could match Algeria's expansive and magnificent Saharan destinations.[2]

Kidnapped: by Smugglers or Islamists?

However, as the days went by, fears grew that the tourists had been kidnapped. But by whom? No one had claimed responsibility. Speculation swung between two schools of thought. One was that the tourists had fallen into the hands of smugglers, or *trabendistes*[3] as they are known, the other that they had been abducted by Islamist militants. But these were not mutually exclusive categories: those familiar with the conflict that had racked Algeria during the 1990s were only too well aware that the Armed Islamic Groups (Groupes Islamiques Armées – GIA) were also heavily involved in *trabendo*, as too were elements of the country's military. It was a complicated mix, even before the Sahara was added into it.

The Sahara is best imagined as a sea, across which trade, in one form or another, has flowed since time immemorial. The only differences between today and earlier times are the modes of transportation, the nature of the goods transported, and their greater commoditisation. The camel (and before that the horse) has largely given way to all-terrain (four-wheel-drive) vehicles, while the main smuggling lines are now in cigarettes, drugs, and the trafficking of arms and illegal migrants. Fuel, vehicles (stolen) and various electronic goods, such as satellite phones and GPS systems, also have their own markets and operational networks. Perhaps the main difference between present-day smuggling and earlier forms of trade is that, whereas the latter's routes were determined largely by the location of water points (wells, oases,

and so on), which determined the caravan routes across the
Sahara, modern-day smugglers are obliged to steer clear of such
locations, as they are the nodal points of the security forces – the
military, *gendarmerie*, police and *douaniers* (customs). Smuggling
across the Sahara today thus has to be fast and flexible, with
success being heavily dependent on having the right sort of all-
terrain vehicles and on the ability to keep one step ahead of the
security forces in finding new routes.

It is this simple matter of geography that enables us to
understand the suggestion that the tourists had fallen into the
hands of smugglers. Suffice to say that the Sahara, with its sand
seas, mountainous scarps, minefields and military zones, has
a limited number of north–south passages, even for all-terrain
vehicles and the most brazen drivers. When the French started to
penetrate the Sahara in the late nineteenth century, they were faced
with the dilemma of whether to push across the Sahara to the
east or west of the Ahaggar-Tassili mountain complex of southern
Algeria, or to head directly through the massif. Today, smugglers
face the same dilemma. The ideal route is through the massif, but
this is complicated by the fact that the precipitous scarps of the
northern Tassili allow very few crossing points. Those that exist
– namely the main road across the Tassili between Zaouatallaz
(Bordj el Haoues, Ft. Gardel) and Illizi (and its side tracks through
Afara, Imihrou, and so on), and the two gorges of Amguid and
Arak, are well-guarded by the security forces. Clandestine traffic is
therefore pushed eastwards, across the extreme south-east corner
of Algeria and into Libya; or increasingly further west of Ahaggar
through the Ahnet region, across Asedjrad; or even further west
into the exposed plains of the Tanezrouft. The holy grail for
trabandistes is to find new, unguarded passages that can take
them across the near-impenetrable barrier of the northern Tassili
ranges into south-central Algeria, from where they can strike out
into North Africa's lucrative market of 80 million people and the
even bigger markets of Europe beyond. One such passage worms
its way through the Tassili to the north of Erg Tihodaine, past the
mountain range of Atafaitafa and out into the area of the Piste
des Tombeaux around the southern end of Erg Tifernine and the

Oued Samene – precisely where many of the lost tourists had last been heard of.

This corner of the Sahara, although recommended as 'safe' by the popular German guidebook they were using, is known by locals to be the haunt of smugglers, and therefore an area best avoided. Smugglers take great care not to be seen, for fear of having their presence reported. Thus, when it became clear that many of the lost tourists were travelling without guides and had last been seen or heard of in this area, it was only reasonable to suspect that they had stumbled across smugglers – who, to avoid their presence being reported, might have killed them and hidden their remains. This was the most widely accepted theory among local people in the first few days of the disappearances.

Another line of argument, also suggesting that the tourists had fallen into the hands of smugglers, was advanced at various stages in the drama by a number of 'Saharan experts', including both the Algerian authorities and the French journalist Richard Labévière, who was regarded in many circles as being especially well-informed on Algeria's terrorism and other such intrigues. It is a thesis to which I shall return later. In essence, it postulated that the trans-Sahara smuggling business, especially narco-trafficking,[4] had been becoming progressively boxed in since about 1999, when the Algerian security forces began to go on the offensive. This increasing pressure on the smugglers coincided with the reopening of the Algerian Sahara to tourism. From a mere handful of tourists in 1999, the number visiting the region at the time of the disappearances had risen to around 8,000 a year.[5] The thesis put forward by Labévière and others was that the major smugglers – notably Mokhtar ben Mokhtar, who was known as 'le parrain Marlboro'[6] and who was the major trafficker in the few years prior to the disappearances – had decided that kidnapping European tourists for ransom might be a more profitable form of business than narco-trafficking. Although this argument has a number of flaws, which I shall consider later, it had considerable plausibility at the time.

The notion that the tourists had been abducted by Islamic extremists also had many variants. One view, which enjoyed considerable currency for a brief time in the early stages of the drama, was that Islamist extremists had deliberately sought out and abducted German tourists in an attempt to exchange them for four Algerian 'terrorists' recently gaoled by a Frankfurt court. The four had been accused and charged with planning to bomb a bustling market alongside Strasbourg Cathedral on New Year's Eve, 2000. This theory was soon discounted when it was realised that no demands had been received by the German authorities. Nor did the dates fit: the Frankfurt verdict was given on 10 March, some days after the first hostages had been taken.[7]

After a few weeks most news reports were tending to settle on the idea that the tourists had been kidnapped by the GSPC (Groupe Salafiste pour la Prédication de le Combat) – Algeria's most active terrorist group at that time, and widely held by the authorities to be linked to al-Qaeda – in order to obtain a ransom to help fund their violent campaign to establish an Islamic fundamentalist state in Algeria.

Others postulated that the tourists had been kidnapped by a group associated with al-Qaeda simply to demonstrate that al-Qaeda had global reach, and had the means to strike anywhere at any time. Several reports suggested a more political motivation, such as anger at America's build-up to war against Iraq, or the increasing rapprochement between Algeria and the US in the wake of the al-Qaeda attacks of 11 September. Back on the domestic front, there were many who believed that the disappearances were related to internal political struggles, possibly as attempts to embarrass and weaken President Bouteflika in the run-up to the country's general and presidential elections, even though these were still more than a year away.

There was a glimmer of hope on 5 April when German television, citing local police sources, reported that an abandoned vehicle, possibly belonging to one of the tourists, had been found hidden by branches close to a system of underground tunnels 50km east of Illizi, close to the Libyan border. This quickly turned out to be a false alert, with neither the vehicle nor the tunnel complex having anything to do with the missing tourists.

On the following day members of Germany's Federal Criminal Investigation Bureau – the Bundeskriminalamt or BKA, as it is more widely known – flew to Algiers to join a BKA officer who was already there. With Algerian troops and aircraft reported to be scouring the region, and with kidnap fears rising, Germany placed its special service forces, the GSG9, on standby. But, as the drama moved into the second week of April, there were still no clues as to what had happened to the tourists – in spite of the widespread search activity, the proliferation of theories as to what might have befallen the tourists, and experts insisting that it was impossible for so many people to disappear without trace.

On 11 April the tension heightened further, as two more Austrians were reported lost. The total of 'disappeared' had now reached 31. Then, on 12 April, came two important announcements. The first came from Austria's Foreign Affairs Minister, Benita Ferrero-Waldner, who, on returning from Algiers, reported that she had received information from the Algerian government that the ten Austrians were alive on 8 April. She gave no further details, although it was later leaked by the Algerians that they had found a message scratched on a rock in the Illizi region dated 8 April, saying, in German: 'We are alive'.[8] The second announcement was from the Algerian authorities who, according to *Der Spiegel*, had told Berlin 'that they were now convinced that the disappearances were the work of an Islamic terrorist group'.[9] Even more significant were the subsequent reports in the Algerian press that the only known terrorist group operating in the Ouargla–Tamanrasset–Djanet triangle was that led by Mokhtar ben Mokhtar, who was reputed to be linked to Hassan Hattab's GSPC – which was itself now being portrayed by the authorities as part of the al-Qaeda organisation.

Mokhtar ben Mokhtar, Hassan Hattab and the GSPC

Most fingers, at least for the moment, pointed to Mokhtar ben Mokhtar. The question of who is, or was, Mokhtar ben Mokhtar, is not answered easily. He has been – and still is, six years later – a major player in the Sahara's political scene, while already having become part of its mythology. To introduce him at this stage in the story is necessary but difficult, for a key feature of myths is that they are subject to both varying interpretations and change over time. In Mokhtar's case, there are plenty of people in the Sahara who even question whether he is alive, or even whether he ever existed – which is not surprising since his death has been reported in the Algerian media on at least six occasions! As this story unwinds, the reader will come to understand why he is often known as the 'phantom' of the Sahara, and how useful such phantasmatic qualities can be to the pullers of political strings. But let me begin at the beginning, bearing in mind that the 'facts' of Mokhtar's life are open to constant revision and question.

At the time of the hostage-taking, Mokhtar was still a young man – approaching 31 years of age. He is a member of the Arab Chaamba tribe, reportedly born in 1972 in the small town of Metlilli, a day's walk to the south of the Mozabite capital of Ghardaia in the northern part of the Algerian Sahara. Like most families of the Mzab region, Mokhtar's family was involved in commerce – a profession which, in post-Independence Algeria, has become almost a euphemism for smuggling (*trabendo*), or what most of the Sahara's population would be more inclined to see as *le troc*: the recognised system of quasi-barter exchange that enabled the flow of many commodities across the desert's national and regional frontiers. Mokhtar seems to have grown up into this business, while also performing his national service, like most young men, in the Algerian army. Mokhtar – or MBM, as he is frequently know in the media – has many aliases and nicknames. The best-known of the latter are 'Belmokhtar', a derivative of his full name, Le Borgne, and 'El Laouer' or 'Belaouer', the French and Arabic terms, respectively, for someone who is blind in one eye. This nickname was apparently acquired from a wound he received while allegedly fighting as a *mujahideen* against the Russians in Afghanistan. While many of Algeria's Islamist militants were known to have fought in Afghanistan, a question-mark must be placed over Mokhtar ben Mokhtar's time there, for the simple reason that, if the Algerian army's records are correct, he would have been only seven at the time of Russia's invasion of

Afghanistan, and only seventeen by the time of their departure. That does not mean that he might not have gone there as a very young man, or, more likely, after the Russians had left. Whether myth or fact, Mokhtar ben Mokhtar's service as a *mujahideen* and the loss of an eye in their cause is now firmly part of his established image – although I have heard Tuareg cruelly question whether his damaged eye might not merely be trachoma, a disease suffered by many Saharan children of his generation.

As with his blindness and exploits in Afghanistan, both the deeds and dates of his elevation to 'super-outlaw' status are equally enigmatic. Two formative incidents in his life as an outlaw are thought to have been the killing of his brother in a shoot-out with a customs patrol and his own killing of a German tourist who resisted the theft of his vehicle. According to those of my informants who have met Mokhtar, he claims to have been driven by a determination to avenge his brother's death, which in turn may explain his aversion to gratuitous killing and his claim that his 'war' is with the Algerian state, not its peoples. However, his killing of a German tourist, reported to have been in 1995, made him a wanted man.[10] Mokhtar's control over the Algerian Sahara and the northern Sahel regions of Niger, Mali and Mauritania seems to have developed in the second half of the 1990s, and probably reached its peak in 1998, by which time he had established a near-stranglehold over much of Algeria's extreme south. Most of the main trans-Saharan routes were at his mercy, with transport only moving in army-protected convoys, as he played cat-and-mouse with the security forces – notably the gendarmerie and the national oil company (Sonatrach), who were his main targets in provisioning him with all-terrain vehicles. During 1998 he reportedly downed a military aircraft that was attacking him, and also made off with precisely 365 four-wheel-drive vehicles – one for each day of the year![11] In 1999 the Algerian forces went onto the offensive and gradually penned him back into the southern frontier zones and the Azaouagh Valley area of north-west Niger and north-east Mali. There is little doubt that he was then running much of the huge trans-Saharan smuggling businesses.

I first came across Mokhtar ben Mokhtar on my return to Ahaggar in 1999.[12] During the course of the next two years, I had several meetings with a major oil company, at which we discussed the possibility of my arranging a meeting with him to negotiate some sort of protection deal on their behalf. But, as the Algerian security forces reclaimed the initiative, so the idea fell away. Nevertheless, although our meeting did not materialise, I had spent much time learning all that I could of his movements and operations, while making undercover plans to meet with him in the Azaouagh region of northern Niger or Mali. As the hostage drama unfolded, I, along with others in the Sahara who had come to know something of his modus operandi, was convinced that it bore none of his hallmarks.

However, if Mokhtar was implicated, the obvious question was why he should have got himself involved in the perilous business of hostage-taking? The many press articles, nearly all of which claimed to be relying on sources within or close to Algeria's security services, took one of two positions. One was that the *emirs* (leaders) of Algeria's armed Islamic groups – the GIA and Hassan Hattab's more recently formed Groupe Salafiste pour la Prédication et le Combat (GSPC), to the last of which Mokhtar was considered to be associated – were driven more by the financial imperatives of their informal economies than by any religious ideology. In Mokhtar's case, this simply meant taking advantage of the emerging market presented by the redevelopment of Saharan tourism, which, as he had no doubt observed from the recent hostage-taking on oil platforms in the waters off the Niger Delta and Equatorial Guinea, might generate millions of dollars in ransom money. Some also considered that this new business tactic was a means of countering the presumed fall in margins in his cigarette-smuggling businesses, resulting from the Algerian security forces' greater success since the end of the 1990s against both the armed Islamic groups and smugglers.[13] The second point of view gave primacy to ideological rather than commercial motives, suggesting that the GSPC's practice of kidnapping for ransom was designed to fund its establishment of an Islamic fundamentalist state in Algeria.

By the end of April, there was still no concrete news on what had happened to the missing tourists. The most frustrating aspect of the entire business was that the Algerians were operating a thoroughly confusing news output. Seemingly impregnable walls of silence at governmental levels were punctuated by an almost continuous series of facile, confusing and usually quite contradictory 'officially sourced' statements in the media. A report issued one day was likely to be contradicted by a spokesman for another government department or agency the next. Not even experienced Algeria-watchers, who knew that the country's authorities exercised considerable control over their national media, could fathom the messages they were trying to convey. Denials by ministers that negotiations were going on with 'any possible kidnappers' were almost immediately followed by statements that talks with the abductors had 'broken down'. Similarly, details of ransom demands in both the Algerian and foreign media tended to be denied about as quickly as they were published.[14]

As the drama dragged on into May, it was becoming increasingly clear that the Algerian authorities knew more than they were revealing. Indeed, as early as 19 April, an Austrian television reporter in Algiers, Franz Norman, had broadcast that the hostages were being held in two groups in locations that were known to the Algerians. He also warned that a quick solution was unlikely, as the Algerians were concerned about the hostages' safety. Although his report was immediately denied by a spokesman for Algeria's gendarmerie, it suggested that some sort of negotiation process was probably in hand, and that an armed assault was being ruled out, at least for the time being. Further credence was given to this view by a report in the 11 May issue of the German magazine *Focus*, which stated that President Bouteflika had not only rejected Germany's offer to send in more terrorism specialists, but that he had also refused to allow the German government to negotiate directly with the hostage-takers.

On Monday 12 May, the German foreign affairs minister, Joschka Fischer, accompanied by officers of Germany's Federal Intelligence Agency, held talks in Algiers with Algeria's President Bouteflika. Fischer declined to give details of the talks, other than to say that he hoped the tourists would return home quickly, 'safe and sound', and that his government did not want a 'solution by force'. This was the first time that the German foreign minister had referred explicitly to 'hostage-takers'.

The First Release of Hostages

Twenty-four hours later, 17 of the hostages (ten Austrians, six Germans and one Swede) had been freed. A spokesman for the Algerian army stated that the 17 foreigners, who had been kidnapped by the GSPC, an Islamic group linked to Osama bin Laden's al-Qaeda network, had been freed unharmed after an army assault lasting 45 minutes on a GSPC hideout, during which all precautions had been taken to ensure the safety of the hostages. Both the hostages and their respective governments declined to give details because of their concern for the safety of the 15 tourists who were still missing. The hideout was later identified as being in the Gharis region of the Immidir Mountains, not far to the west of Amguid and only some 200km as the crow flies from where they were first abducted. Initial reports gave the impression that all the hostage-takers had been killed, although the army stated that nine (later reduced to seven) had been killed, with the rest being hunted down by army trackers.

With the freed hostages remaining silent, little more became known about the circumstances of their capture, other than the Algerian army's confirmation that they had been taken by Hassan Hattab's GSPC, whose *emir* in the south of Algeria was Mokhtar ben Mokhtar. Not surprisingly, the media was almost immediately full of conflicting reports, denials, and further speculation about the nature of the alleged negotiations and ransom demands, and about the role of Mokhtar ben Mokhtar – with some reports even questioning whether the hostages had in fact been freed by an armed assault, as described by the Algerian army. However, with the focus of concern and attention turning almost immediately to the fate of the remaining 15 hostages, now believed to be held in the Tamelrik region some 300km east of Gharis, questions regarding the release of the first group tended to be put to one side. I, too, shall return to them later.

On the morning of 19 May, exactly one week after the freeing of the first group of hostages, I was up well before dawn in order to catch the early morning flight from Tamanrasset to Djanet, and from there to Algiers. In Djanet, where the old Boeing 737 disgorged most of its human cargo before taking on a handful of new passengers, I switched to a left-side window seat, knowing that our flight path would take us just a little to the east of the Tamelrik massif. As I peered down through the haze of the near-mid-summer heat onto the black, sun-baked plateau of Tamelrik, with its labyrinth of gorges squashed into dolls-house proportions, I imagined the 15 remaining hostages staring up at us. I wondered if they had heard the news of the assault on Gharis, and that their own release was anticipated at any time.

We touched down in Algiers shortly before midday, forty minutes before my scheduled meeting with a government minister. As I came into the empty baggage hall, the minister's secretary, whom I knew, was walking towards me, all smiles and waving arms. 'You've heard the news?' he asked rhetorically, bursting with excitement, and without even enquiring after my well-being. 'The second group of hostages', he hastened to add, 'has just been liberated by the army'. It flashed through my mind that this must have been taking place when I was flying over them. 'Come quickly, we can listen on the car radio.' The secretary's driver waited to pick up my bag while the pair of us rushed out to the official car parked by the terminal entrance. 'That's Lamari speaking', he said, presuming that I would not recognise the voice of the head of Algeria's army, as we listened intently to the details of the drama being broadcast on the national radio service. The driver joined us a few minutes later and we sped off to the Ministry, with the two officials highly excited at the news that the 15 remaining hostages had been freed safely after another army action. 'Now we really have something to export to the world', said the secretary, turning to me in the back seat and punching the driver's arm so frenetically in his enthusiasm that he was forced to continue his race through the traffic with only one hand on the wheel. 'Our army can teach everyone how to free hostages', he said. There was no let-up in excitement at the Ministry, where my meeting with the minister was reduced to the pair of us leaning over a small radio placed in the middle of an otherwise empty glass-topped coffee table as he proudly accepted my effusive congratulations at his army's successful intervention.

After my meeting I was driven to my hotel, where I caught a couple of hours' sleep before going on to fulfil a longstanding appointment at a reception at the Embassy of one of the countries involved in the hostage crisis. I anticipated a festive atmosphere now that the three months of anxiety and tension were over; but before I had even finished proffering my congratulatory remarks to the ambassador, he interjected in an unmistakable tone of anger: 'There is no good news. Everything has been denied: no assault and no freeing of the hostages. Lamari himself has given a complete denial.' I was utterly flummoxed: I had not only heard the radio reports in the company of a government minister, but he had even confirmed them to me. The ambassador could not, or was not prepared to, say anything more, leaving his embarrassed guests to shuffle around the reception for the minimally acceptable amount of time before making their departures. I too left, thinking that I could have made more sense of the Mad Hatter's tea party.

Transferring the Hostages to Mali

At the time of the ambassador's reception, both Radio France Internationale (RFI) and NTV, the German television network, had already broadcast the news that the hostages had been evacuated safely and were on a flight to Algiers. Indeed, by the evening most European networks, relying on military and diplomatic sources in Algiers, had confirmed the hostages' safe release.[15] Nor was this unexpected, as press reports had been commenting for several days on the build-up of military activity in the region and the anticipated release of the second group. Local papers had reported the presence in Illizi of both General Smaïn Lamari, head of the secret military intelligence's counter-intelligence unit,[16] and members of the German security forces, while members of Algeria's Groupes d'Interventions Spéciaux (GIS) and General Mohamed Lamari, military chief of staff, were known to have moved into the region on the Sunday. Something had clearly gone disastrously wrong. But what?

What followed the 'false release' of 19 May was even more mysterious than the first three months of the hostage crisis, as Algeria sent out a stream of confusing and often quite contradictory signals. Some of the initial reports suggested that an assault was still imminent, others stated that negotiations were still on-going, and still more reported that bad weather in the form of sandstorms had put a temporary hold on things. At the end of May, a report that the hostages had been split into several groups to make their rescue more difficult was immediately contradicted by the Algerian President, who said they were all being held in the same place. Speculation also began to build up that Libya might be playing a role in resolving the crisis. Although it was denied that Bouteflika's visit to Tripoli on 18 May had anything to do with the hostage situation, no such denials followed a further visit to Tripoli to meet with Colonel Gaddafi four days later (22 May). Several high-ranking Libyan officials were also reported to be in Algiers at the beginning of that week. There were also confusing signals over Germany's role in the proceedings. While Bouteflika intimated that he had allowed the involvement of German special forces, reports emanating from the security forces stated that, while German navy jets and spy drones were being used in air searches, no German forces were being used on the ground, for reasons of national sovereignty. Similarly, a report that the captors and their hostages had left Tamelrik (in spite of its being surrounded by Algerian troops) and had been seen by local nomads moving north towards Bordj Omar Driss, and then possibly towards Libya, was immediately denied by the security forces, who confirmed that the hostages were still being held in Tamelrik.

By early July, Algeria had succeeded in shifting the focus of attention eastwards, to Libya. Several reports now gave the impression that the International Gaddafi Foundation, managed by his son Saif al-Islam Gaddafi, held the key to the hostages' release. In 2000, Gaddafi claimed to have negotiated the release of six tourists kidnapped by the Islamist Abou Sayyaf terrorist group on the Philippines' island of Jolo. Cynics argued that Gaddafi was simply turning his historic relations with terrorist organisations to some benefit, and that by doing so he was still supporting terrorism. Instead of paying the groups out of his own pocket, as one western commentator remarked, 'the Libyan leader now just bargains with other countries for the right price to pay in exchange for their kidnapped citizens'.

Whatever the veracity of that argument, we now know that Libya was almost certainly not involved. In fact, at the time the Algerian media reported the hostages being moved close to the Libya frontier, they were, as we were soon to find out, already far to the south-west. An interesting side issue of the Libyan ruse is that the Algerian security services confirmed that German spy planes (drones), which had earlier been operating out of Illizi, were no longer 'in the sky'. The possibility that the Algerians put out the Libyan story as a reason for keeping the German drones grounded so that they could not see what was going on in the region is one to which I shall return later.

On 9 July, almost immediately after the Libyan reports, the Algerian media confirmed that the captors and their hostages were still in Tamelrik, where they were effectively trapped by Algerian troops, and that negotiations with the captors were difficult as they had no means of communication. On 12 July the Algerians said they had lost track of the captors, who had moved the hostages under cover of a sandstorm, which was as unlikely as it was untrue. Four days later, their communications problems were miraculously overcome when it was reported that a passing nomad had delivered a note to the Algerian military in Illizi saying that the hostage-takers were 'ready to negotiate'. The Algerian security forces immediately issued a statement to the media saying that the crisis could be over in a few days, and that they were therefore ordering a partial withdrawal of troops from the Oued Samene and Tamelrik areas. The European media paid little attention to this new 'breakthrough' as on the next day, 18 July, German radio reported that the hostages and their captors were in Mali, well over 1,000km as the crow flies to the south-west.

The Final Hostage Release

The final stage of the drama was played out in Mali, where negotiations between the hostage-takers, the German and Mali authorities, a number of intermediaries and, of course, the Algerians, dragged on for some weeks. It was not until 18 August, precisely one month after German radio had reported their arrival in the country, that the hostages were finally released. With their release, it was learned that their journey from Tamelrik to Mali, undertaken in the intense heat of summer, had lasted for six weeks and taken them – by their own estimates – over 3,000km. Sadly, only 14 of them returned home. One of them, Michaela Spitzer, had died of heatstroke shortly after leaving Tamelrik.

Although it was denied by the German authorities, it is generally recognised that the German government paid a ransom of 5 million euros in the form of 'reparations' to the Malian government, which then allegedly found its way to the hostage-takers.

While the hostages were being moved from Tamelrik to Mali, a new name entered the equation. On 10 July the Algerian newspaper, El Watan, known to have close ties with the military, reported that another GSPC emir – not Mokhtar ben Mokhtar – may have been responsible for the abduction of the tourists.[17] The name of this new emir was Abderrazak Lamari, sometimes known as Amari Saifi or a dozen or so other aliases, but more generally referred to as El Para, after his stint as a parachutist in the Algerian army. This was not the first time El Para's name had been associated with 'terrorism'; it had come up in a number of articles in the Algerian press in the last couple of months of 2002, before acquiring notoriety at the beginning of January when he was held responsible for an attack on an Algerian army convoy at Teniet El-Abed in the Aures mountains of north-eastern Algeria, in which 43 soldiers had been killed and 19 wounded.[18] Not surprisingly, his name was among those mentioned in the press in the weeks immediately after the disappearances, but it was not until the *El Watan* report in July that he became regarded as the chief suspect.

On Friday 22 August, four days after the release of the hostages in Mali, journalists in Algiers received a faxed statement in which El Para claimed responsibility for the kidnapping of the 32 tourists. According to the Reuters desk in Algiers, it was not possible to authenticate the document independently; nor was any government official immediately available for comment.[19]

2

RECONSTRUCTING TORA BORA

A New Front in the Global War on Terror

Even before the hostages were released, the Bush administration was branding the Sahara as a new or 'second' front in the global war on terror (GWOT).[1] Indeed, little more than six months later, by March 2004, this new terrorist threat was being portrayed by Washington as having spread right across the Sahel.[2]

According to the European hostages who were taken to Mali, 62 'terrorists' accompanied them into that country.[3] What happened in the region for the remainder of the year is not entirely clear, in spite of some of the hostages, now back in Europe, receiving satellite phone calls from their former captors. From these calls, as well as corroboration from local people in the region, it is clear that the hostage-takers believed that a deal had been made with the Malian authorities allowing them to remain freely in Mali as long as they did not cause trouble or bother local people.[4]

The telephone conversations indicated that the hostage-takers were apologetic for what they had inflicted on the tourists, and that they were happy and seemingly content with their new lives in Mali. However, there seemed little likelihood that they would be left in peace for long. At a conference on terrorism in Bamako two months after the hostages' release, Algeria's ambassador to Mali, Mohamed Antar Daoud, warned that the terrorists who kidnapped the Europeans were still in Mali. 'They have euros', he said. 'What's to stop them recruiting Malians and trafficking in arms?'[5] In spite of this veiled threat, the kidnappers appear to have remained in Mali, keeping a very low profile, at least until December. During the intervening time there was little news of them, apart from the occasional press story speculating on the ambassador's questioning of their expenditure of the ransom money on arms and recruitment.

Back across the border, in Algeria, the atmosphere in the wake of the hostage crisis remained tense, especially in the regional capital of Tamanrasset, where the government was actively harassing a number of local people – especially prominent members of civil society, who had not only begun to voice concern about increasing corruption and poor governance, but were also letting their beliefs be known that the Algerian authorities had been involved in the hostage-taking. Apart from harassing these people, the government's strategy for repressing this discontent was to emphasise and exaggerate the 'terrorist threat' to the region. Within a month of the hostages' release, rumours were spreading around Ahaggar and the Tassili-n-Ajjer[6] that 'bandits' from Niger were operating in Algeria's extreme south. I was filming throughout most of this region during September and October, on permits that had been issued some months earlier by the central government in Algiers. Throughout the filming, we were perpetually harassed by local officials, notably the Tamanrasset *wali*,[7] who at one time insisted that we could only film from the main road. Phone calls to ministers in Algiers got around this restriction, although at no time were we free from the presence of a military escort that stuck to us like limpets as we filmed across several thousand kilometres of southern Algeria. Shortly after our departure from the region, the Algerian authorities reported that 'bandits', allegedly identified by their accents as being from Niger, had staged a hold-up near Amguid.[8] The name that began circulating around Ahaggar was that of Aboubacar Alembo, a Niger Tuareg[9] who had come to prominence in 2002 after conducting a number of highway robberies in Niger, before taking hostages and killing two policemen. After eluding the army and hijacking more vehicles, he and his gang escaped to Algeria.[10] There the group split: some reportedly fled to Libya, others sought refuge around Djanet, and the remainder, along with Alembo, made their way to Tamanrasset, where they were apparently arrested. However, according to the Algerian authorities, no such arrests were made![11] Alembo received even greater prominence later in the year, being held responsible for a particularly brutal hold-up of French tourists near Chirfa, on the eastern side of Niger's Ténéré desert.[12] Although none of the tourists were killed, the women were violated and the men beaten up. The incident was enough to damage seriously Niger's fledgling tourism industry. It was also enough for certain members of Niger's government to decide that the young renegade should be 'brought in'. I shall return presently to the bizarre circumstances of Alembo's attempted 'elimination' and his involvement with Algeria's security services, as they have significant implications for our understanding of many subsequent events in the region.

For the moment, though, let me stay with El Para's 60 or so GSPC terrorists holed up in northern Mali. After more than three months of relative calm, things began to stir. On 13 December, Agence France Press (AFP), citing Malian military sources, reported that the kidnappers had returned to Algeria the previous week to avoid being trapped by a military offensive from Algeria. Algerian military aircraft were reported to have overflown the region a few weeks earlier in search of them.[13] The AFP report made no mention of the type of aircraft, but we can assume that it was probably helicopters, especially as they appear to have landed and picked up two local people whom they mistook for terrorists.[14] It is not clear whether this raid captured or perhaps even collected some of the kidnappers.[15] However, from subsequent reports and events, it would appear that few if any of them actually left Mali at that time.

A few weeks later, on 12 January 2004, a party of German tourists ran into a group of heavily armed Algerian Islamists 60km north-east of Timbuktu. The Germans stayed the night with the Islamists and were allowed to photograph them. The Islamists said that they had been involved in the original hostage-taking. This was confirmed by the former hostages, who identified some of their captors in the photographs.[16] In the same week, two stages of the Dakar Rally were cancelled, ostensibly because French intelligence services had learned that 100 Islamist militants, apparently led by El Para, were going to kidnap rally competitors.[17]

By this time – the beginning of 2004 – the Algerians and the US, for reasons that I shall explain presently, were working with the other governments in the region – namely those of Mauritania, Mali, Niger and Chad – in a new initiative to counter terrorism in this part of Africa. The undertaking, known as the Pan-Sahel Initiative (PSI), had first come to public attention just over a year earlier, in November 2002,[18] when two officials from the US Office of Counterterrorism had visited Chad, Mali, Mauritania and Niger to discuss a scheme designed to fight terrorism, control illicit trade and enhance regional security.[19] Not surprisingly, such a low-level visit did not make the headlines. However, as we shall see in the following chapters, the date of that visit was particularly significant. Little more was heard of the scheme until the PSI rolled into action more than a year later, with the disembarkation of a US 'anti-terror team' in Nouakchott, Mauritania's capital, on 10 January 2004. According to the press statement given by US Deputy Undersecretary of State Pamela Bridgewater on her visit to Nouakchott the following day, the team comprised 500 US troops and the deployment of 400 US Rangers into the Chad–Niger border region the following week.[20] According to Undersecretary Bridgewater's initial announcements, US troops would do the work in Mauritania and Mali, while Los Angeles-based defence contractors Pacific Architects and Engineers would pick up the work in Chad and Niger.[21] In fact, what Undersecretary Bridgewater failed to say was that the PSI had got underway at least two months earlier, when the small number of US Special Forces already based at Gao and Tessalit in northern Mali had begun preparing counter-terrorism activities with the Algerian and Mali militaries.

Expanding the GWOT Across the Sahel

The first major move against El Para's terrorists took place in the latter part of January, when Algerian forces led by General Benali, the commandant of Algeria's VIth military region – namely Tamanrasset – were reported to have undertaken their first joint-action offensive with their new American allies. French sources confirmed the presence in both southern Algeria and northern Mali of American military experts, as well as the fact that the Algerian military, using night-vision equipment provided by the US and images from US spy satellites that had been permanently positioned over the Sahel for several months, had launched a vice-like sweep in coordination with the Malian army through the Algerian–Malian border region.[22]

Precisely what took place during this reported military sweep is not clear. Testimony to its effectiveness may be found in the fact that the kidnappers made no further telephone calls to their former hostages after 6 January. Their last call was uncharacteristically downbeat, giving the impression that they perhaps knew they were cornered and about to be attacked.

A profusion of media reports, all seemingly originating from Algerian military intelligence sources, gave the impression that there may have been a number of military engagements around this time. However, a careful reading of these reports suggests that they may have been different accounts of one single engagement in the Tamanrasset region (wilaya) in which at least four Islamic extremists were killed and a large quantity of arms captured.[23] Algeria's military intelligence services gave the impression that the four terrorists killed belonged to the GSPC group that had kidnapped the European tourists the previous year, that the arms had been bought with their ransom money, and that the arms were on their way to GSPC cells in northern Algeria.[24] If these media reports were correct, then it would suggest that these four were the first of the kidnappers to be killed since their arrival in Mali. However, as we shall see, this incident may also have been fabricated or reported disingenuously and out of context.

A few days later, however, a European intelligence source claimed to have received information from their Algerian counterparts that 30 of the former hostage-takers had just been killed in an Algerian army offensive in the Malian sector. This intelligence was received in Europe on 6 February. It complies with a report in the Algerian Press on 5 February[25] saying that the Algerian military, with the close support of the Americans, was about to launch a second and much bigger offensive. Both sources confirmed that the terrorists had been located and tracked with the assistance of US spy satellites.[26] But the source did not say whether the attack had taken place on Algerian or Malian territory. Irrespective of where the attack had taken place, the Americans would have been impressed by the enthusiasm of their new-found allies in their global war on terror. It also provided Algeria's president, Abdelaziz Bouteflika, who was running for re-election on 8 April, with a timely and high-profile success against terrorism.

By early 2004 a number of media reports, coming mostly from Algerian sources, began to give the impression that the combined Algerian–Malian–US military operations had succeeded in dislodging El Para's GSPC terrorists from their bases in northern Mali. These military engagements, along with the numerous media reports of the GSPC's purchase of arms and recruitment of personnel in Mauritania, Mali and Niger, alerted the Sahel to the imminent likelihood of its becoming an active battleground in the war on terror.

We do not know the precise circumstances under which the GSPC terrorists initially spread out or were driven from their alleged redoubts in northern Mali. It was not clear how many of the original 62 GSPC terrorists, and possibly their new recruits, had been either killed in the reported military sweep through the Algerian–Malian border regions or flushed out of Mali. A few incidents involving attacks on vehicles and tourists, first in the Tamesna region and then, in late January, in southern Aïr, suggested that they had travelled eastwards from Mali into northern Niger, possibly even travelling as far south as below the In Gall-Tchin Tabaradene-Tahoua corridor, before heading north-east into the Aïr mountains. These mountains, one of the great massifs of the Sahara and a bastion of the Kel Aïr Tuareg, extend for some 450km from just north of the regional capital of Agades in the south to the Algerian frontier in the north. The hold-up of a group of tourists near Timia in south-central Aïr on 24–25 January, in which one four-wheel-drive vehicle and luggage was stolen,[27] was thought by some to be the handiwork of El Para's men, although others, because of the language and accents of the attackers, thought they were local bandits from the In Gall region, possibly recruited to the GSPC.

Any uncertainty as to whether the GSPC were really on the rampage in the Sahel was put to rest on 23 February 2004, when several European tourists[28] were held up by some 50 of El Para's men at Temet in north-eastern Aïr, around 250 kilometres by road north of Timia. One of them confirmed his identity to the tourists as El Para, and insisted that they took his photograph. Some of the Europeans taken hostage the previous year subsequently confirmed the photograph as being of El Para. The incident, which received much media coverage both locally and in Europe, was followed by a series of media reports describing how El Para and his band of GSPC terrorists were pursued through the mountains of Aïr and across the Ténéré desert of northern Niger 'by US Special Operational Forces in cooperation with North African Militaries' and US air surveillance.[29] Raffi Khatchadourian, writing in the style of Iraq's 'embedded' journalists, describes the pursuit quite graphically:

> With the multinational force closing in, and American reconnaissance planes observing from above, Saifi's [El Para's] convoy raced across Niger toward the Chadian border. As the vehicles pushed forward, weapons rattled in their mountings and the roar of engines cut through the desert silence. Stray rocks and loose sand battered the vehicles' exteriors. Windshields clouded over with sediment...[30]

When asked by Khatchadourian if US troops assisted in the hunt for El Para across the Sahel, Col. Vic Nelson, the director of West Africa policy at the Pentagon, replied, 'We didn't have any forces on the ground.'[31] However, according to Khatchadourian, a Niger defence official 'confirmed that US Special Operations forces, working with their Algerian counterparts, had tracked Saifi (El Para) in the desert, during his race from Mali through Niger to Chad, and that Americans were present during at least one fight'.[32]

El Para's men were finally chased by the pursuing forces into the Tibesti Mountains of northern Chad. There, thanks to US air surveillance, they were ambushed by regular forces of the

Chad army on 8 March. Forty-three of the group were reportedly killed in a battle that lasted for three days. However, El Para and a handful of followers escaped the carnage only to fall into the hands of the rebel Mouvement pour La Democratie et la Justice au Chad (MDJT).

Within the matter of precisely one year, from the kidnapping of the 32 European tourists in March 2003 to El Para's flight into Tibesti in March 2004, the Sahara–Sahel had become a new and significant front in the global war on terror. Prior to March 2003, there had almost certainly been no act of terror, in the conventional meaning of the term,[33] anywhere in this vast region of Africa. And yet, by the end of 2004, senior US military personnel were describing the Sahara as a 'swamp of terror', a 'terrorist infestation', which, in the words of US Air Force General Charles F. Wald, deputy commander of US-EUCOM,[34] 'we need to drain'.[35]

Within no time at all of El Para's flight across the Sahel, western intelligence and diplomatic sources were claiming to be finding the fingerprints of this new terror threat almost everywhere. Indeed, it was only a matter of days after the Madrid train bombings of 11 March 2004 that that atrocity was linked to al-Qaeda groups lurking deep in the Sahara. Under the same headline – 'Swamp of Terror in the Sahara' in the US's *Air Force Magazine* – Charles Powell, now describing the Sahara as 'a magnet for terrorists', wrote:

> Were the deadly Madrid train bombings plotted by Muslim terrorists in the Sahara? The answer, quite probably, is yes. The Moroccan daily *Al-Ahdath Al-Maghribia* has reported that those March 11 attacks were conceived and launched from the 'terrorism triangle,' a desolate zone encompassing parts of Morocco, Mauritania, Algeria, and Mali.
>
> According to the newspaper, Moroccan intelligence agencies tracked the movements of the terror bombers to what was described as an 'al Qaeda rear base' in the Sahara.[36]

It required little more imagination for the media–intelligence services to warn that al-Qaeda bases, hidden deep in the Sahara, could launch terror attacks on Europe itself. Indeed, US-EUCOM's top commanders – notably General Jones, Nato's supreme commander, and General Charles F. Wald, deputy commander of US European Command in Stuttgart – did much to alert Europe to the threat of terrorist activity in North and West Africa. Referring explicitly to the bombing of a synagogue in Tunisia, the arrest of al-Qaeda suspects in Morocco, and the Algerian hostage-taking, they warned of the region – Europe's backdoor – becoming another Afghanistan. They warned of terrorists from Afghanistan and Pakistan 'swarming'[37] across the vast, ungoverned and desolate regions of the Sahara desert – through Chad, Niger, Mali and Mauritania. The GSPC, they attested, had now emerged in Europe – only a stone's throw away across the narrow Straits of Gibraltar – as an al-Qaeda recruiting organisation, while in North Africa it sought nothing less than the overthrow of the Algerian and Mauritanian governments.

By the summer of 2004, the only thing missing from this new 'terror scenario'[38] was the actual discovery of an al-Qaeda base in the Sahara. This, however, was soon remedied by an Algiers-based correspondent of *Jeune Afrique* claiming that El Para had been in touch with al-Qaeda's military leader, Mohamed Atef (alias Abou Hafs el-Misri) before he was reputedly killed by the American bombing of Kabul in November 2001, and that Atef's last wish had been to turn the mountains of the central Sahara into 'a sort of Saharan Tora Bora'.[39] Right on cue, an obscure French Sunday newspaper, *Le Journal du Dimanche*, quoting the vague, unattributed but ever-dependable 'source proche d'un service de contre-espionnage européen' ('a source close to a European counter-espionage service'), claimed that Libyan security forces had intercepted members of El Para's GSPC terrorists 'ready to strike', and that the GSPC had established an operations base in the desert mountains of Tibesti.[40] Tora Bora had been recreated in the heart of the Sahara.

3

'WHODUNIT'

The Suspicions of the Tuareg

Long before the hostages were released, a few Saharan 'experts' were beginning to question whether their abduction was all that it appeared. Local people, especially the indigenous Tuareg of Algeria's extreme south, in whose lands the kidnappings had occurred, were even more suspicious. They, like almost everyone else, were mystified for the first few weeks of the drama by what might have befallen the tourists. However, as they listened to the frequently far-fetched, contradictory and geographically incorrect statements by Algerian government spokespersons, and their incrimination of first Mokhtar ben Mokhtar and then the GSPC and El Para, they became suspicious of the Algerian government itself, especially its security establishment – the mukhabarat – and the 'dirty tricks' department of its secret military and state intelligence services, notably the Direction des Renseignements et de la Sécurité (DRS).

From almost the outset of the drama, local Tuareg sensed something sinister. They knew better than anyone that this part of the Sahara was one of the safest places on earth for foreign tourists. They had even gone to the trouble in the previous year of making representations to a number of European foreign ministries advising them on the safety of foreign travel in the region. They pointed out that there had been no serious incidents involving foreign tourists, barring accidents and illness, in Algeria's extreme south in recent memory, and that the regions of Ahaggar and Tassili-n-Ajjer, so they claimed – and quite truthfully – were the safest places for tourists in the entire Sahara, perhaps even the world. Even during the troubles of the 1990s,[1] Algeria's extreme south had been spared the violence that enveloped most of the rest of the country. Indeed, the Saharan oasis towns, especially those in the extreme south such as Tamanrasset, became refuges for many thousands of Algerians who wanted to shelter themselves and their families from the violence that ravaged the northern, more populated regions of the country. The Sahara, especially the extreme south, was a refuge of safety and comparative tranquillity.[2]

There was one fact in particular that convinced the Tuareg that elements within Algeria's own security forces were involved in the kidnapping, and it was to do with Mokhtar ben Mokhtar. They knew that Mokhtar would not mess up his own patch. His smuggling business, worth far more than the ransom money allegedly paid, was heavily dependent on not disturbing the livelihoods of the peoples of the central Sahara – the Tuareg of Ahaggar and the Tassili-n-Ajjer,[3] whose territories he traversed and on whose good will he relied for ensuring arms, fuel and other such caches. The Kel Ahaggar and Kel Ajjer themselves were not much involved in trafficking or smuggling, at least in the years prior to the onset of the war on terror, nor did they hold particularly strong views on it. They knew smuggling was illegal, and therefore not something to be condoned, but trade of one sort or another had gone on across the Sahara since time immemorial. Indeed, the Tuareg had controlled many of the trans-Saharan caravan routes in pre-colonial times, and while only a few of them now participated in such smuggling, most of them knew someone who had been engaged at one time or another in a little *troc*. With regard to the new trans-Saharan smuggling and trafficking businesses that have become big business in the last decade or so, the ethic among the Tuareg has been broadly one of 'live and let live'. This has meant that the activities of the traffickers should not in any way upset local people, and especially their main livelihood – tourism – on which many of them depended for much of their cash income. The big operators, such as Mokhtar ben Mokhtar, knew that any incident involving a tourist – hijacking, robbery, assault, kidnapping, death – would damage the tourism industry and thus incur the wrath of the

Tuareg, who in turn were more than capable of mobilising against them and putting a stop to their trafficking. It was thus in the interest of traffickers of all kinds to ensure that the regions and people of Ahaggar and Tassili were well protected, and the tourists who travelled in them not harmed.

Unaware of this critical and delicate relationship, Algerian and French journalists instead filled column inches with the suggestion being put to them by the Algerian authorities that the *emirs* running the trans-Saharan smuggling networks, such as Mokhtar ben Mokhtar, had decided, in the wake of the Algerian army's recent purported successes against the smugglers, to abandon the diminishing returns from smuggling and take a leaf out of the book of those who had successfully kidnapped and ransomed oilmen from platforms in Africa's Gulf of Guinea. Their new business, so it was being suggested, would be the expanding Saharan tourism market.

This suggestion bordered on the absurd for at least three reasons. Firstly, the 5 million euro ransom allegedly paid by the German government for the release of the hostages paled into insignificance alongside the revenues earned from cigarette smuggling, not to mention hard drugs, arms and people-trafficking. I will come back to the trafficking business later, but for the moment let me simply say that the size of this market at the time of the hostage-taking might have approached 1 billion euros a year. Single convoys, travelling north from Mali or Niger into Algeria for the North African–European markets, regularly carried as much as 2 million euros of cigarettes, at European street prices, on each trip, with convoys worth some 12 million euros being not unheard of. Secondly, such kidnappings could only be pulled off once, or perhaps twice, before tourism to the Sahara completely ceased. Thirdly, for Mokhtar ben Mokhtar, or any other such *emir*, to 'diversify' into such kidnapping activities would force the army to come after him, with the inevitable destruction of both him and his substantial business base.

Thus, the more the Algerian authorities pointed their collective finger at Mokhtar ben Mokhtar, the more the local Tuareg knew they were creating a smokescreen. But a smokescreen to cover what?

Local Knowledge and Research Methodology

That is the question on which I have been working, more or less continuously, since the hostages were released. Following the publication of Mustafa Barth's article in 2003,[4] which raised the question of Algeria and the US's complicity in this affair, I have written 70 or more articles and briefings and contributed to numerous radio and television broadcasts detailing the way in which America's GWOT has unfolded across the Sahara and Sahel. These, of course, raise questions about my own knowledge of the region and its peoples, and the overall methodology by which my research has been undertaken.

My knowledge of the area goes back many years, to when I was very much younger and travelled extensively on foot, by camel and vehicle through most of these parts of the Central Sahara, getting to know them like the proverbial back of my hand. I also spent much time with the local Tuareg, and wrote a doctoral thesis on the history of their society, and its transformation during both the colonial and post-colonial periods.[5] The thesis, polished with some further research, was published and became something of a standard reference on the Tuareg of Ahaggar.[6] During the last ten years, I have again had the good fortune to spend much time in the central Sahara, rarely being away from Algeria's south and neighbouring regions for more than a few months at a time, and sometimes visiting the region as many as five or six times a year. In the months before, during and immediately following the hostage crisis, I had – by chance – visited or travelled through most of the places that were central to the drama: Arak and the well at Tin Ghergoh, where key events[7] took place in the lead-up to the 2003 hostage-taking; the regions around Amguid and Gharis, where the first group of hostages was held and subsequently liberated; the western and southern margins of Tamelrik, where the second group of hostages was held; much of the terrain extending out into the Tannezrouft from a line drawn roughly between the Ahnet-Assejrad region, In Hihaou (In Ziza) and the Mali frontier; Tamesna and south to below the Tahoua-Tchin Tarabaradene-In Gall-Agades corridor; much of Aïr, including both Timia and Temet; Adrar Bous and the route allegedly taken by El Para's men across the Ténéré desert in February–March 2004, including the Emi Lulu and northern Djado regions, and crossing the Algerian and Libyan borders in the In Ezzane-San Salvador region; the Kaouar oases that fringe the eastern Ténéré; and the extreme north-eastern parts of Niger, bordering on Libya and Chad, including the Djado and Mangeni plateau regions which El Para would have had to circumvent by one route or another on his way into Chad.

With chance often playing a more significant role than the best laid plans, it happened that I was in the region when the hostages were being captured in March 2003. I was able to listen to the telephone calls being made by some of their anxious friends and relatives in Austria, Germany and Switzerland, and to observe and even talk with members of the Algerian security forces, who, at that time, showed remarkably little concern over the apparent disappearances. Again, by chance, I was in Ahaggar when the first group of hostages was liberated, on 13 May 2003, and also a week later when the Algerian army claimed, and then later denied, that it had liberated the second group. I was in the region again two weeks after their release in Mali, in August 2003, and travelled extensively throughout the region during the rather uncertain period between then and the onset of the reported military push against the GSPC in Mali at the end of the year. In 2004 I was able to check on the alleged activities of both Mokhtar ben Mokhtar and GSPC opposition groups in Mauritania, but found little or no evidence of their presence, which suggested that their activities in the country had been exaggerated by the Mauritanian–US–Algerian intelligence and media services. I was back again in more central Saharan regions during the period of El Para's subsequent return to Algeria.[8] More recently I have been able to reconnoitre trafficking and related activities along some of the key border regions, as well as several of the key regions in the Sahel in which 'banditry' (putative terrorism, as Washington calls it) has again become a problem. In particular, I was closely associated with elements of the Tuareg rebellion in Mali in 2006, and the subsequent Tuareg rebellions in Niger and Mali that began in 2007, while also having the opportunity to travel extensively in the Libyan Sahara.

Although my research into the hostage-taking and what lay behind it began from the moment of their disappearance, I had actually been undertaking more or less continuous social-anthropological research in the region since 1999. I had returned to the central Sahara in 1999, as soon as the Algerian government had reopened its Saharan regions to foreign tourists.

In January 1992, Algeria's army annulled the results of a general election that would have brought to power the world's first ever democratically elected Islamist government. This effective coup d'etat led to a vicious conflict between Islamists and the security forces, which resulted in the deaths of an estimated 150,000 to 200,000 people, mostly innocent victims. Throughout this period, from 1992 to 1999, the Algerian Sahara was closed to foreign tourism. During much of this time, most of northern Niger and northern Mali were also closed to the outside world, because of the Tuareg rebellions in those countries. To complete the global isolation of much of the central Sahara during these years, Libya was also closed to foreigners throughout much of this period as a result of UN and US sanctions.

As Algeria's violent conflict diminished and its Saharan regions reopened to the outside world, I was able to return and recommence my social-anthropological research into the state of nomadism, the nature of governance in southern Algeria, and a number of other issues relating to the Tuareg, whose homelands had been effectively cut off from the outside world for the best part of a decade.

The Tuareg with whom I worked – my informants – were in many cases very old friends, or, to be more precise, the sons (and sometimes daughters) of old friends with whom I had lived and travelled more than thirty years earlier, in the years immediately following Algerian independence. For them this period, from 1999 to the time of the hostage-taking in early 2003, was like a reawakening from nearly a decade of dormancy. They had had many years to think about their own livelihoods and futures, and what they might do when the country returned to some sort of normality. They had seen the beginnings of mass tourism in the late 1980s and the environmental damage that it had done. They were now determined that the renewal of tourism should be directed specifically towards the conservation of the region's environment and cultural heritage.

I was able to help them in this endeavour by forming a travel company in the UK, which provided them with select clients who shared their aim. I thus took on two roles. On the one hand, I worked with them in my capacity as a social anthropologist – that, in a sense, was my 'internal' role, and it was in that role that my work became increasingly that of scribe and witness to the events that are documented here. In my other, 'external' role, I was a supplier of tourism clients!

As my anthropological and archaeological work became increasingly focused on the problems of cultural heritage conservation, and how the Tuareg were trying to engage the government in the establishment of a more environmentally sustainable tourism industry in the region, so both of my roles became increasingly bound up with their own endeavours. We therefore collaborated closely, with the bulk of the field research being done by the Tuareg themselves. We were assisted increasingly by Tuareg working on similar issues in the neighbouring regions of Niger, Mali and Libya, as well as a small number of other external researchers who had access to various aspects of national and regional governments and officialdom across much of this extensive area. Thus, when the first hostages were taken captive in early 2003, local people especially were even more attuned than usual to what was happening in their region, since an established network of local 'fieldworkers', comprising both nomads and town-dwellers, was already in place. Moreover, my experience of running a tourism company in the Sahara at that time gave me unique access to and understanding of the relationship between Algeria's legal and security systems and the many difficulties associated with tourism in Algeria, especially its Saharan regions.

In addition to what traditional social anthropologists might refer to as a good grounding and network of informants in the field, I also had close contacts with key parties involved in the hostage drama as it was unfolding, such as close relatives of hostages and their support groups – and later, after their release, some of the hostages themselves; representatives of their governments and their governments' intelligence services; members of the Algerian government and many of the local people, especially the local tourism agencies and nomads, who had been involved in aspects of the search; and many other local people who had witnessed specific events, or who have been involved in or affected directly by the overall unfolding of the GWOT across the Sahara.

But let me go back to the earliest days of the disappearances when I, like many others who knew the Algerian Sahara, became increasingly suspicious of the information being offered by the Algerian authorities, and of the possibility of their involvement in the events. My suspicions that things were not what they appeared were heightened further when I was able to learn from the group of hostages released in Gharis on 13 May about the details of their liberation by the Algerian army, the nature of their debriefing by the Algerian authorities, and the experience of both their capture and their time in captivity. Indeed, by the time the second group of hostages was released in Mali, I was almost certain, as were many local peoples of the Sahara, that the whole affair was very different from what the Algerians and their American allies had been telling the world. Indeed, even before the first group of hostages had been released, I had told some of their families, as well as official representatives of their governments, that although we were witnessing an act of 'terrorism', it was possibly one of 'state terrorism' being orchestrated by the military and intelligence services and played out as 'theatre'.

But whose military and intelligence services? At the time, I could not be sure. But the more I began to question and analyse the kidnapping, along with the hostages' experiences in captivity, their subsequent debriefings, and the information disseminated by the Algerian and US authorities, as well as a number of other events that had taken place in the region in the months before and after the hostage-taking, the one hypothesis that began to offer an explanation for both the hostage-taking and El Para's subsequent escapades in the Sahel was that both had been fabricated by elements within the Algerian and US military intelligence services.

I continued my research and investigations during the months, now years, after the release of the hostages and El Para's subsequent activities in the Sahel. Now, at the time of finally completing this book, I have had the benefit of several more years in which to research the Bush administration's GWOT in the Sahara and Sahel, and elsewhere in the world. Not surprisingly, my network of informants during this time has expanded further to include key contacts in the US State Department, the US Department of Defense, the FBI, and European intelligence services. The evidence laid out in this book (and its sequel, *The Dying Sahara: US Imperialism and Terror in Africa*) has thus been acquired cumulatively through an ongoing process of reassessment which is now into its sixth year since the 32 tourists disappeared. For example, some 50 pages of files on the hostage-takers, compiled by Algeria's own security and intelligence forces in April 2004, only came into my possession in 2006, three years after the hostages had been released. More such evidence will undoubtedly come to light, although its veracity will almost certainly become harder to assess as actual memories of events become blurred with the passage of time.

A Diabolical Intelligence Deception

As this research continued, at times painstakingly slowly, it began to appear that the Sahara had been the stage for one of the world's most elaborate ruses.

If this is beginning to sound a bit like a 'whodunit', that is what it is – but with the mystery not being so much the 'who', as the 'why' and 'how'. The 'who', as will become evident, is the US and Algeria, or, to be more precise, elements within their respective regimes. The questions of 'why' and 'how' raise complex and far-reaching questions about the nature of the

Bush administration and why it has ventured into such heinous territory. Mere reference to the GWOT explains very little, in that America's post-9/11 GWOT masks much that underlies the real nature, direction and dynamics of America's 'new imperialism': its energy crisis; the views and dreams of the neo-conservatives within its government; the driving ideologies of neo-liberalism; fear of Chinese expansionism; the rise of the 'religious right'; turf wars within both the military and the intelligence services; and, perhaps most dangerous of all, what some people have seen as the dislocation and dismemberment of the Western world's most corrupt government and a military that is 'out of control'. In the case of the Sahara, as I shall show, the GWOT involved the fabrication of a fiction of terrorism that has created the ideological conditions for the US militarisation of Africa and the securing by the US of strategic national resources – notably, but not exclusively, oil. On the wider, global scene it added in no small measure to the quagmire of lies and propaganda that have served to justify the US invasion and occupation of Iraq.

The 'why' question is: What it is that has brought these two seemingly unlikely bedfellows – America and Algeria – together in such a duplicitous conspiracy? The 'how' questions focus on how this deception could have been mounted and sustained over such a vast geographical area, for what has now been almost six years. Three points should be made in answer to the latter question. The first is that, if one is going to fabricate an incident, it helps enormously if the place chosen for its enactment is 'out of sight' and 'beyond verification'. The Sahara, with its vast empty spaces, is the perfect location.

The second point relates to my use of the term 'intelligence-media services'. The success of this deception has been reliant on the compliance of a gullible and uncritical media – both local and international. In the case of the Algerian press, the main public source of information in this affair, this is not surprising. Anyone who knows the Algerian media appreciates that its apparent relative freedom masks the fact that many of its journalists and editors, especially those handling military-security matters, are in the control of the country's military intelligence and security services, and thus act as conduits for whatever scenarios those services might wish to purvey. The international media, with its greater 'real' freedom, is especially culpable. The sloppiness of its working practices, notably its cut-and-paste culture and failure to do its own research,[9] has meant a piecemeal and quite uncritical acceptance of US–Algerian official briefings and press statements which, for most of this period, have been little more than 'spin'.

Furthermore, a combination of neo-con thinking, government-compliant press interests, a blind acceptance of the Bush–Blair line on terrorism, and the fact that terrorism – especially for the specialist intelligence and security services and their publications – has become not only big but good business, has ensured the rejection of articles that have offered a more critical analysis of alleged terrorism both in the Sahelian Sahara and elsewhere. Indeed, in the context of 'business', we should not lose sight of the fact that, for neo-liberalism – as Deepak Lal, Professor of International Development Studies at UCLA and former advisor to both the World Bank and IMF, has affirmed – 'the "War on Terror" can be seen as merely an extension of [the defence of the capitalist market]'.[10]

The broad trajectory and objective of this media-intelligence hype and disinformation over the last six years becomes even clearer when we re-examine the account of Saharan events that it presents within the dual contexts of the established pattern of 'dirty tricks' undertaken by both the US and its main regional ally, Algeria, and the interests of the main beneficiaries of this deception – namely, US imperialism, the beleaguered Bush administration, and elements within both the Algerian military and local Sahelian governments.

I include within the 'intelligence–media services' many of the quasi-academic, impressively titled institutes that have proliferated in recent years, especially within the US, as well as, sadly, a few of the genuine pillars of the academic world,[11] which have played integral roles in the Bush administration's use of Orwellian 'reality control'. During their illegal support of the Contras in Nicaragua in the 1980s, the neo-conservatives who surrounded President

Reagan based their propaganda on the concept of 'perception manipulation' – a crude but effective mixture of exaggeration and distortion. Twenty years later, the neo-cons have simply perfected the same crude technique: if the facts don't fit the storyline, just deny the facts; or, as has been more the case in the Sahara, create the facts to fit the storyline.

The third point concerns the knowledge and perceptions of the local peoples of the Sahelian Sahara. They do not recognise the picture that the intelligence–media services have painted of their region over this period. They know that most, if not all, of the alleged terrorist incidents attributed to it have been either exaggerated or fabricated by some sort of combination of US–Algerian–local government interests. In the short run, this does not pose much of a threat to the efficacy of the deception, as the local populations are relatively sparse in number and politically marginalized, with little or no effective means of representation through which to express their views. The few who have raised concerns, notably in Algeria, have been subject to state harassment, and possibly even assassination. However, as I have argued repeatedly over the last five years, and as we are now seeing in the Tuareg rebellions that developed in Niger and Mali in 2007, the perceptions and actions of these peoples are becoming increasingly – perhaps critically – important.

4
GROUNDS FOR SUSPICION IN THE ALGERIAN SAHARA

Kidnapped on the 'Graveyard Piste'

Only 17 per cent of the Sahara, or thereabouts, is actually covered by sand. The rest is a mixture of gravel plains, rocky plateaux, and an extraordinary array of mountains, rising to over 3,300m in the Tibesti, almost 3,000m in Ahaggar, and just over 2,000m in Aïr, which offer the tourist almost every shape and form of volcanic contortion, scarp and gorge imaginable. Most tourists coming to the Algerian Sahara with their own vehicles take the ferry to Tunis and then the main road to Algeria's north-eastern oasis town of El Oued. From there they travel south, past the oilfields of Hassi Messaoud and along a sand-blown asphalt road that somehow manages to wind its way for more than 200 miles between the massive dunes of the Great Eastern Erg, before reaching Bordj Omar Driss (formerly Ft Flatters), the last point of replenishment for many desert travellers heading into Algeria's deep south. Here, the traveller has a choice, as the town, on the northern edge of another sand sea, the Issaouane Irarraren, is just to the south of one of the Sahara's crossroads. The traveller can either follow the asphalt road eastwards, around the northern edge of Issaouane Irarraren to the oil and gas fields of Ohanet and In Amenas, close to the border with Libya, and then turn south to the *wilaya* capital of Illizi and across the Tassili-n-Ajjer to Djanet, or he can head south-west and follow the desert track to the Amguid gorge – one of two vehicular accesses from the north into the great massif of Ahaggar.[1]

But there is another route that leads south from Bordj Omar Driss. About 30 or 40 miles south-west of the town, the track forks: the right branch continues to Amguid, while the left veers towards the south-east, taking the traveller onto the now infamous Route des Tombeaux – the Graveyard Piste.[2] It was at this fork that a group of eight Austrians, travelling in four four-wheel-drive vehicles, turned left on 22 March 2003. Unbeknown to them, 17 other travellers had disappeared in the vicinity of the Graveyard Piste in the preceding couple of weeks. However, unlike those who had already disappeared, the Austrians were not planning to follow the Graveyard Piste. The Graveyard Piste crosses over the neck of dunes that link the Issaouane Irarraren to the Issaouane Tifernine, one of the Sahara's more discrete sand seas, passes the 2,000ft-high Gara Khannfoussa, an outlying peak of the Tassili ranges to the south and a well-known landmark, and then runs south-east to Hassi Tabelbalet and Ain El Hadjadj, two wells some 65 miles apart in a long corridor that is bounded on the east by the sand dunes of the Issaouane Irarraren and to the west by a series of ranges running north–south – notably the Djebel Essaoui Mellene – that separate the Issaouane Irarraren from the Issaouane Tifernine. South of Ain El Hadjadj the track gradually swings in a more easterly direction, passing the exit of the Oued Samene, where many of the travellers were kidnapped and later held captive, and on to the town of Illizi. The Austrians were planning to take the Graveyard Piste only as far as Gara Khannfoussa, which they wanted to climb. They then planned to head due south along the Essaoui Mellene valley, which runs along Tifernine's eastern margin, thus taking them in a big loop around the bottom of Tifernine and back to the main Amguid track, via Hassi Ntsel.

Just before they reached Gara Khannfoussa, the Austrians ran into an Algerian army post of around 30 soldiers. The Austrians were stopped and asked about their destination, but allowed to continue after explaining that they were going direct to Gara Khannfoussa, before turning south down the Essaoui Mellene valley and then back to the Amguid piste. One of the Austrians, Ingo Bleckmann, who spoke French, asked the military, as he had done at all previous checkpoints along their route, if there were any problems in the area, especially 'bandits'. Although the Algerian army was by now well aware that at least eleven tourists had disappeared in the region of the Graveyard Piste, Bleckmann was told that there were no problems.

The Austrians accordingly drove on to Gara Khannfoussa and climbed to its summit. When they returned to their vehicles they were met by a smaller group of men in army camouflage uniforms, who had driven out from the military post in four beige ('type 80') Toyotas. The unit commander asked Gerhard Wintersteller, the Austrians' tour guide, more about their destination. When Wintersteller repeated that they were heading south, the commander told them that that was impossible, as it was a military zone. After what the Austrians described as a 'typical argument between travellers and officials', the commander asked Wintersteller to show him on the map precisely where they wanted to go. Wintersteller pointed out their route down the eastern margin of Tifernine, round its southern tip and then westwards to the Amguid track. The commander told them that he was not allowed to let them continue, but would on the condition that, if they were stopped by another military patrol, they were to say that they were searching for four motorcyclists. After providing the commander with their personal and vehicle details, the Austrians set off from Gara Khannfoussa in the early afternoon of 22 March on their planned route down the eastern margin of Tifernine.

On the previous day, 21 March, a group of five Germans and Harald Ickler, a Swede now living in Bavaria, who had been heading north from Ahaggar in three vehicles,[3] were seized and taken capture at about 4pm in the Oued Tahaft, roughly 25 miles due east of the southernmost point of Tifernine. The vehicles were taken into a nearby valley, where they were stripped of their registration plates and roof racks.

The next day, only a few minutes after the Austrians had left Gara Khannfoussa, the kidnappers holding the Germans leapt into action. They quickly replaced both the roof rack and number plates on the Land Rover[4] and sped off in it northwards. At about the same time as they were leaving the Tahaft area, Gerhard Wintersteller's party of Austrians were coming off the last dunes to the south of Gara Khannfoussa. The two groups were about 100 miles apart and heading directly towards each other along the Essaoui Mellene valley. They could have been expected to meet well before sunset. But they didn't. As the Austrians were coming off the dunes, one of their vehicles, an Opel Frontera, pitched in soft sand and broke its roof rack. With a sandstorm whipping up and several hours repair work ahead of them, they decided to spend the night in the dunes. In the morning, with the Frontera repaired, they recommenced their journey down the Essaoui Mellene valley, only to be confronted by a German Land Rover driving towards them at high speed. To their surprise, it was filled not with German tourists, but with eight heavily armed bandits.

'What has taken you so long?' the bandits asked in French. From this and other remarks and questions, it was clear that the kidnappers had been waiting for the Austrians. They knew not only the Austrians' precise route, but their expected time of arrival. A close friend of the Austrians, who published an account of their capture a month after their liberation, stated that they were convinced that the army commander was in direct contact with the kidnappers and had passed on this crucial information to them. How else could they have known? Indeed, from several interviews with these two groups of hostages back in Austria and Germany after their release, it is absolutely clear that the kidnappers were expecting the eight Austrians.[5] What the army commander could not have foreseen was that the Frontera's luggage rack would break, and that they would be running behind schedule.

There was nothing untoward about the army having a checkpoint on the Khannfoussa track. Not only was that passage a known conduit for smugglers, but also, at that particular time the Algerian authorities already knew that at least eleven tourists had disappeared in the Graveyard Piste region. The job of the soldiers, as their initial remarks to the Austrians seemed to signify, should therefore have been to stop them entering the area. Why then did the commander allow them to pass? Perhaps he did not consider the disappearance of so many people to be very serious. Or perhaps the tourists tugged so pitiably on his heart-strings that he couldn't deprive them of their detour around the back of Tifernine. Or perhaps, as the circumstantial evidence strongly suggests, he was in cahoots with the kidnappers; if not, the kidnappers' comments, actions and timing were, to say the least, extraordinary.

Later, on reflection, these tourists considered that the army commander's instruction to them – to tell any other military patrol they came across that they were searching for four motorcyclists – was an indication that he knew that 'loyal' troops were on their way into the region. That would also explain why the kidnappers, presumably warned by the army commander, made such a rapid departure from the region, heading out of the area with all their hostages (now 14) on the same evening as their capture of the Austrians.[6]

This incident also helps resolve the question of why the Austrians were travelling in an 'unsafe' area and, in a strictly technical sense, illegally. Although Gerhard Wintersteller, the tour party leader, was an experienced Sahara traveller, neither he nor members of his group knew at that time about the other disappearances. Nor, it seems, did they know about the smuggling traffic through that area. There were two particular reasons for this. One was that this corner of the Sahara, especially Tifernine and the Graveyard Piste, had become very fashionable among German Sahara travellers. The other was that the popular German-language guidebook on the area used by many of these tourists not only stated that the area was safe, but advised travellers not to pay attention to Algerian travel regulations. Algeria's regulations stated that the use of category C routes, such as the Graveyard Piste (Der Gräber-Piste), 'est à priori interdit à cause des dangers persistants. Il faut une autorisation spéciale de la wilaya concernée dans laquelle sont exigé des mesures de sécurité supplémentaire aux mesures définit dans la catégrie B.' Moreover, 'Il est interdit de quitter les routes et les pistes…'[7] In the light of these regulations, much media coverage was given to the supposed 'illegality' of the hostages' travel arrangements. While this was prompted by the Algerian authorities to exonerate them from culpability, it had the effect of dampening public sympathy for the hostages in their own countries. However, in the light of what we now know took place at Gara Khannfoussa, it would seem that Wintersteller's group could hardly be accused of being in the area 'illegally'.

The Khannfoussa incident remained firmly lodged in the minds of the Austrian group – especially that of Ingo Bleckmann who, as a French speaker, had the most conversational contact with both the soldiers at the checkpoint and their captors during their 51 days of captivity. The more he thought about the incident, the more convinced he became that the army commander or one of his men must have radioed or telephoned their details to the kidnappers. It was therefore almost the first thing that he mentioned to Generals Abdennour Aït-Mesbah (alias Sadek)[8] and Smaïn Lamari,[9] head of Algeria's counterterrorism service, the DRS, who debriefed the hostages at Amguid immediately after their liberation on 13 May.[10] Smaïn's reaction was extraordinary. Instead of taking details and asking further questions, as might be expected, he verbally attacked Bleckmann for besmirching the army's reputation, suggesting that he, as a foreigner, could not distinguish the different uniforms and vehicle colours of the various branches of the security forces, and that the people at Khannfoussa might even have been impostors! For such an experienced intelligence officer to react in this way suggests that he may have been more than a little anxious about what Ingo Bleckmann was telling him.

Bleckmann and his compatriots were not the only hostages to wonder whether Algerian army agents had tipped off their captors beforehand. Harald Ickler recounts in his book on his capture[11] that, on his way north through Ahaggar, his group ran into the same Algerian film team on several occasions shortly before their capture, and that later, after his release, on looking at a French website, he thought he recognised the boss of the film crew as a member of Algeria's secret military service.[12]

The Hostage Liberation

The suspicions of both these men, and of other members of the group, were raised further by the events surrounding their liberation, which now appears to have been stage-managed by the Algerian army's secret intelligence services. The account of the liberation comes from four main sources: the Algerian army; the hostages themselves; the Algerian media, which has close ties with the Algerian military and government; and the foreign media, which, in this instance, means specifically Radio France International (RFI). According to the first brief communiqué on Algerian radio, the Algerian military stated that all 17 hostages held near Amguid (in the Gharis mountains) had been liberated following an assault by the Algerian army on the morning of 13 May. Subsequent reports in the Algerian media, quoting official military sources, stated at first that all the terrorists – confirmed as being members of Hassan Khattab's GSPC – had been killed. This claim was modified over the next few days, with numerous 'official' reports in the Algerian media – notably the newspaper *El Watan* – which is close to the military, putting the number of terrorists killed at nine, then four and finally seven.[13]

There are major discrepancies between the accounts of the attack given by the Algerian authorities and the hostages. The attack was described by the Algerians as a 'dawn raid'.[14] Eighteen 'terrorists' were involved in the action, of whom seven, according to the final reports, had been killed. Those not killed or captured were reportedly tracked down by the surrounding troops.

The hostages' version is rather different. The attack began at 11am, with three army helicopters firing one or two rockets into a gully on the opposite side of the valley from where the hostages were sheltering. The assault lasted for three-quarters of an hour. Ingo Bleckmann, who had an excellent view of proceedings and whom I have interviewed several times about the details of the attack,[15] is adamant that he saw three or four of his captors run into the gully into which the rocket(s) were fired. He saw no bodies himself, but is absolutely certain that 'no one could have survived the explosion'. When the two groups of hostages were finally able to compare notes, Marc Heidegger and Harald Ickler, who were both in the group held in Tamelrik and later taken to Mali, confirmed to Ingo Bleckmann that all the 'terrorists', except four who were killed in the Gharis attack, were picked up by El Para and accompanied the hostages to Mali.

At the debriefing of the liberated hostages at Amguid, they were told by General Abdennour Aït-Mesbah (Sadek) that the army had shot dead four of their abductors, presumably trying to escape, in one of the hostages' own vehicles. The hostages were shown the vehicle, riddled with bullet holes and parked in the Amguid barracks. The vehicle was later returned to Germany, where forensic analysis revealed no traces of blood.[16] Moreover, Harald Ickler confirmed in a radio interview in 2007 that the four terrorists who had allegedly been shot in this vehicle had in fact rejoined their colleagues in the Mouydir/Iffetessen Mountains and travelled with them to Mali![17]

From the information given by the two groups, notably Ingo Bleckmann, Marc Heidegger and Harald Ickler, there are many other things that we now know for certain. First, some 30 terrorists had originally held the Gharis hostages. During the week or so before their release, the hostages were forced to walk several hours each night in order to reach the site that now appears to have been pre-selected for their liberation.[18] Each day, however, the number of their captors diminished. 'It was as if', in Bleckmann's words, 'a couple of them flaked off and disappeared each night. By the time we reached the "liberation site" only about 15 remained.'[19] This number roughly equates to the army's 18. Second, the *emir* (El Para) drove from Tamelrik in one of the hostages' vehicles[20] – which had remained hidden in spite of 5,000 troops sweeping the area – and picked up a number of his men who had been at the Gharis assault, driving them back to join the group in Tamelrik. This action alone almost certainly proves that the Algerian army did not have both sites surrounded with some 5,000 troops, as it repeatedly claimed. Alternatively, and as I believe, it indicates that El Para was given special passage at night by the DRS. Third, we also know from the second group of hostages that El Para picked up the remainder of the Gharis terrorists a week or so after their departure from Tamelrik on 16 May, while on their way to Mali. Thus, all the 'terrorists', save the four killed in the Gharis assault, were taken by El Para to Mali.

'No Assault, No Islamists, No Victims, No Ransom!'

In short, the statements issued by the Algerian army regarding its assault in Gharis now appear to have been a complete smokescreen. Indeed, that is more or less what the fourth source of information, RFI, confirmed. 'No assault, no Islamists, no victims and, for now, no ransom', it claimed, quoting sources close to the investigations into the kidnappings.[21] This was an extraordinary statement, and probably the reason why its author, a specialist on Algerian and Islamist terrorism, was soon after expelled from the country. It was also remarkably insightful. Let me take each of these four claims in turn.

First: no assault. The hostages obviously contradicted this statement as soon as they heard it, as they had witnessed the assault at first-hand. However, as I have shown, it was not long before it became clear that there was no proper assault, but simply a theatrical performance on the part of the Algerian army. None of the hostages was harmed, and all the terrorists except the four killed by the rocket(s) fired into the gulley, were allowed to escape.

To say that no 'Islamists' were involved is more problematic, and a subject to which I shall return later. At the time of the broadcast, immediately following the release of the first group of hostages, the point to which RFI was probably alluding is that, although the actual captors may have been genuine members of the GSPC, their leadership – the *emir*, El Para, as he was later to be identified – was almost certainly working in collaboration with or under the direction of Algeria's secret military intelligence service. Thus, while the hostage-takers themselves may have been members of the GSPC, the GSPC was not responsible for the kidnapping. In that sense, the RFI was correct in saying that no Islamists were involved. In fact, it is highly significant that the GSPC made no claim of responsibility for the kidnapping. When the tourists were taken hostage, their kidnappers issued no communiqué claiming responsibility. It was only on 12 April that the Algerian press first alleged, without offering any evidence, that the GSPC was responsible.[22]

At the time of its broadcast, RFI obviously did not have access to the hostages' testimonies. The first group of hostages' testimonies did not give conclusive evidence of their captors' identities. The one hostage who developed a relatively close relationship with some of his captors was the Austrian, Ingo Bleckmann. A French-speaker with an intellectual curiosity, he spent much time discussing and trying to learn more about his captors' faith and motives. He seemed convinced of their fundamental faith, that they were salafists and members of the GSPC. However, the testimonies of several members of the second group of hostages – who, it must be remembered, not only spent more than three times longer with their captors than the first group, but were joined by the captors of the first group on their way to Mali – were far more equivocal. They noted that many of their captors were at first uncertain of the name of their organisation – the Groupe Salafiste pour la Prédication de le Combat. Later, as the hostages talked more with their captors about the nature of their religious beliefs, the hostages gained the impression that the reasons that many of them gave for joining the GSPC were, in the hostages' own word, 'crazy', and bordered on the incredible.[23] This could, of course, be explained by the cultural divide that separated them, as well as the possibility that their captors were more familiar with the Arabic name for the GSPC, Dawa wa Jihad, than its French translation and acronym. Nevertheless, while the hostages' testimonies do raise doubts as to whether all their captors were genuine members of the GSPC, several of them had told the hostages how they had fled the repression after 1992, known the detention camps in the Sahara (from 1992 to 1995), seen summary executions and fought the regime, but did not want to harm the hostages.[24] In this context, they mentioned the abduction of 'religious Christians', in what was a clear reference to the seven French monks at Tibhirine who had been abducted and murdered in 1996.[25] Although this was attributed by the regime to Islamists, their captors told them that it was the army that had actually killed the monks.[26] My own view is that most of the hostage-takers, with the exception of El Para and possibly some of his lieutenants, were genuine salafists, and that if there was any confusion on their part as to the name of their organisation it was the result of a combination of cultural and linguistic confusion[27] and, quite possibly, because the name GSPC was not yet that widely known.

Who Ordered the Kidnapping?

The crucial question, however, is not whether the kidnappers, with the exception of El Para himself, were Salafists, as seems most likely, but whether the operation was ordered by the GSPC and its leader, Hassan Khattab, or by El Para and his masters, the DRS. As *Le Monde* later noted, many of the hostages, especially those in the Tamelrik group, subsequently testified that the operation was ordered by El Para rather than Hassan Khattab, the supposed head of the GSPC.[28] This conforms to the fax received by journalists in Algiers on 22 August, in which El Para claimed responsibility for the kidnapping.[29] Far more suspicious, however, is the fact that the Algerian media made much of alleged GSPC communiqués, especially that of 18 August 2002, following the release of the second group of hostages. The typewritten document in Arabic that was presented prominently on Algerian state television was recorded at the time by Susanne Sterzenbach, the Algiers-based North African correspondent for the German radio and television station Südwestrundfunk, and re-presented in her subsequent film on the affair.[30] The document was headed as being from the GSPC and signed by 'the *emir* of the 5th region [the Sahara], Abou Haidara Abderrezak Amari Al-Aurassi' (namely, El Para). It summed up the hostage-taking and confirmed the negotiations with the Algerian army over the liberation of the last hostages, as well as the fact that the army had been ready to liquidate the group along with the hostages, but had stopped short of that and had let them leave for Mali. El Para also went over the liberation of the first group of hostages at Gharis, saying that it had been the result not of a military assault but of a decision of his own men.

But why was such an important document not published on the GSPC's principal communication link – its website? Even more curious, why did the GSPC website not once mention the hostage-taking operation? Indeed, the only document on the

GSPC website which made any reference to the hostage-taking, and then only indirectly, was an appeal by the GSPC to the Chadian rebel movement, the MDJT, on 14 October 2004 – well over a year after the hostages' release.[31] Even more remarkable is that Mathieu Guidère,[32] in his analysis of GSPC documents and the organisation's mutation (in 2006–07) into the 'al-Qaeda of the Islamic Maghreb', made no mention of this most famous of hostage-takings, which, after all, has provided the entire basis for the Western world's myth of terrorist hideouts in the Sahara–Sahel, for the launch of a Saharan front in the GWOT, and for the creation of what was to become a military coalition of nine nations under the supreme command of the US to eradicate terrorism from the Sahara–Sahel. Indeed, the more we examine the evidence, the more difficult it becomes to ascribe El Para's kidnapping operation to the GSPC.

Although RFI's fourth claim – namely that no ransom had been paid; or, at least, not yet – was almost certainly correct, it opened up a number of crucial questions to which we will probably never have the answers. If we go back to the early weeks of the drama, one of its mysteries, frequently raised by the media, was why there had been no ransom demand – assuming that the motives for such kidnappings was either to kill the hostages for political reasons or to extract a ransom. However, in the week prior to the release of the first group of hostages, reports began circulating in the media that ransom demands had indeed been made and were being negotiated. The source of these reports seems to have been the journalist Richard Labévière. Writing in the Swiss weekly, L'Hebdo, on 8 May, under the headline 'Kidnappers hope for a million per hostage', Labévière reported that the Algerian authorities had received three ransom demands: one to the military commander in the south and two to the police in Algiers. The total price, he said, was between 30 million and 45 million francs.[33] Following the release of the first group of hostages, several media reports, citing RFI, indicated that 'the release was the outcome of negotiations over the payment of several million dollars'.[34] The Mouvement Algérien des Officiers Libres (MAOL), which is not known for its accuracy, even went so far as to accuse General

Smaïn Lamari, head of the DRS's counter-intelligence unit, of arranging the kidnapping and securing a US$15 million ransom for himself and his lieutenants.[35]

Whether a ransom was being negotiated, or was even on the table, is something we will probably never know. RFI, however, was probably correct in saying that no payment was made – at least at that time. Indeed, all three countries have strongly denied, as they would, that any ransom was paid.

What, then, lay behind the RFI story? Before even attempting to answer that question, I should make quite clear that we now know that the vast majority of information on the kidnapping sourced to Algerian authorities, or its media, was false and merely a smokescreen. The leakage of information from the Algerian authorities to Richard Labévière regarding the ransom demands must therefore be regarded, in all probability, as merely another example of Algerian disinformation.

My own inclination, however, is that Labévière's story contains more than just a grain of truth. The more we look at the media reports for that week – that is, the period from the release of the first group of hostages on 13 May to the fiasco at Tamelrik on 19 May – along with the testimonies of the hostages themselves and other information that is now available to us, the more likely it looks that things did not go according to plan.

The Journey from Tamelrik to Mali

The facts, as we now know them, are that on 19 May the Algerian authorities broadcast official reports, quoting General Lamari, Algeria's chief of staff, saying that the second group of hostages had been liberated in another military assault, and that they were all safe and sound. French and German reporters took this further, stating that the hostages were actually onboard flights heading for Algiers and home. By the evening of 19 May, these reports had been officially denied. We now know from the hostages' own accounts that they were not even in Tamelrik at that time – they had left their hideout in Tamelrik during the afternoon and early evening of 16 May,[36] believing, as one of their kidnappers told them, that they were going to Illizi and would be home the next day. They loaded their belongings and supplies on to their hidden vehicles, but instead of heading towards Illizi they crossed the Graveyard Piste and headed a short distance into the Issaouane dunes, where they met the kidnapper's leader, El Para, who told them that things had gone wrong and that their plans had changed. They camped in the dunes for five days, during which time they worked on repairs to the vehicles, including a broken gearbox for which they needed spare parts. The kidnappers used their radios to call Illizi for a range of spare parts and food supplies. Four Toyotas brought the supplies from Illizi, although the hostages could not identify either the vehicles or their drivers, as they parked some distance away and out of sight, obliging the kidnappers to fetch the supplies on foot.[37] With Illizi and the surrounding region, especially Tamelrik, allegedly swarming with troops, it is inconceivable that four vehicles could have left Illizi without the knowledge of the military authorities. We can only conclude that the spare parts were arranged and transported by the DRS, or elements working for the DRS. After five days, they set off in a northerly direction across Issaouane towards the oil installations of In Amenas and/or Ohanet, as if they were heading into Libya, before turning west towards Bordj Omar Driss, past Gara Khannfoussa, and south-west to the Immidir/ Iffetessen Mountains west of Amguid, where they picked up their colleagues who had escaped from the 'assault' that had liberated the first group of hostages in Gharis. We know from the hostages in that group that they holed up there until 26 June before setting off for Mali,[38] where they arrived in early July, some six weeks after leaving their hideout in Tamelrik.

What, if anything, went wrong between the 13 May and 16 May? One risible idea that held sway at the time among certain European 'security circles' was that elements within the Algerian army, still tied up with their former East German Stasi connections, thought that they could use the hostage drama to do a deal with Germany to acquire the European Tiger Attack-Helicopter (AH),[39] following the refusals of the Americans and the French to supply Apaches and the French-modified South African

Rooivalk[40] AHs, respectively. I shall say more later about the material needs of Algeria's military, when I look at the nature of the new Algerian–US alliance. For the moment, let me merely say that, as a result of the effective international boycott of arms sales to Algeria following its army's annulment of the 1992 elections, its army was becoming progressively under-equipped. It needed, as a matter of increasing urgency, a range of modern, high-tech weapon systems, notably night-vision devices, sophisticated radar systems, an integrated surveillance system, tactical communications equipment, and certain lethal weapon systems – especially attack helicopters.

A more plausible explanation relates to Labévière's suggestion that a ransom deal was in the offing. From interviews with key hostages, it seems that there was no talk of a ransom until after their departure from Tamelrik. If there were 'secret negotiations' over a ransom, as suggested by Labévière, then it was more likely a ruse by the Algerians to convince the Europeans of the authenticity of the kidnap than a real demand from the hostage-takers themselves. The deal, according to Labévière's implied suggestion, was that the freeing of the first group of hostages would be followed by the payment of a ransom of several million dollars, which would be followed by the freeing of the second group. Labévière suggests that the Swiss were not happy with this arrangement – partly because they were cross about having been kept in the dark about the liberation of the first group of hostages, and partly because they feared having to pay a disproportionate share of the final ransom.[41] Although this smacks of farce, the Swiss were rankled about not being informed of the assault plans on Gharis. This was confirmed by Simon Hubacher, a spokesman for Switzerland's federal department of foreign affairs, who said that none of the five Swiss liaison agents sent to the Algerian Sahara had been informed about or involved in the operation to free the first 17 hostages. He also confirmed that Switzerland had received no demands from the kidnappers for a ransom or anything else, and that nothing had been paid.[42] Both Germany and Austria also denied that any ransom had been paid.

We are thus left with the possibility that some sort of deal was afoot, but that there was a misunderstanding or failure to deliver by one or other party, whether it be over helicopters or a ransom, and the consequent abortion of whatever release may have been planned for the second group.

One other possibility, which should be mentioned, is that the Algerians may have felt that they could not keep the hostages' whereabouts secret for much longer. They therefore brought forward the planned liberation of the first group before any deal had been finalised. The reason for possibly having to do this involves yet another story of a 'passing nomad', although in this case the incident was corroborated by the hostages themselves. The story is that the kidnappers came across two camels, one of which they killed for meat, while the other they took with them for future use. The owner, however, on finding signs of one of his camels having been killed and the other missing, followed its tracks and, on coming across the hostages' whereabouts, told the army.[43] The DRS perhaps felt that it had to liberate the hostages before the nomad's story became common knowledge. This might explain why the kidnappers made the hostages travel on foot for several hours after dark each day during the last week or so of their captivity, so that they could reach the pre-selected rescue site ahead of schedule.

Further evidence that Algeria's secret military intelligence service, the DRS, planned the hostage-taking is revealed later. In the meantime, however, let me raise a few other aspects of the search for the hostages that also give grounds for suspicion.

The first, and perhaps most obvious, point is that it is inconceivable that 5,000 troops – and many more at the army's disposal – with aerial surveillance and nomad trackers-cum-guides, could not have found the hostages' location or locations within a relatively short period of time. Indeed, many of the troops involved in the search have subsequently let it be known that, whenever they got close to the hostage location, they were pulled back.[44] Further evidence that the Algerians knew the location(s) of the hostages almost from the outset comes from the hostages themselves, who stated that they regularly saw Algerian military helicopters overhead,[45] as well as planes they identified as US AWACS (Airborne Warning and Control System) on regular low-level patrol.[46] The hostages concluded that at least someone knew where they were. Indeed, the Algerian military authorities informed the hostages at their debriefing at Amguid that they had been located by air surveillance – especially that provided by the Americans.

We also now know that there was no truth in the information given to Austria's foreign minister, Benita Ferroro-Waldner, on her visit to Algiers in the second week of April, and subsequently leaked to the press, that the Algerians had found a message dated 8 April scratched on a rock, reading in German, 'We are alive'. The hostages never left such a message. This story, like most other information concerning the hostages' whereabouts, was just one of the many strands in the web of deception created by Algeria's DRS.[47]

The most skilful part of this deception concerns the two-month period from the time of the departure of the second group of hostages from their hideout in Tamelrik on 16 May until the German radio report of 18 July, which confirmed that the hostages and their captors were in Mali. Virtually every statement issued by Algerian government and army spokespersons and carried in its media during this two-month period was false. Whether the reported liberation of the hostages on 19 May, and the army's subsequent denial, was simply a misunderstanding between different branches of the army is something we will probably never know. But the stories relating to possible Libyan intervention; the official denial that the hostages and their captors had been seen moving north to Bordj Omar Driss; the encirclement of Tamelrik by Algerian troops; the prevalence of sandstorms and subsequent communication difficulties; and the note delivered by a passing nomad – all were lies; part of an elaborate deception which says much for the ingenuity of Algeria's DRS and its control over the media. The reason why the Algerians ordered the German drones to be grounded at Illizi is now clear: it was to ensure that the Germans did not see the departure of the hostages from the region and, perhaps, the signs of their absence once they had gone.

The Hostage Release in Mali

It is now obvious that this huge cavalcade of almost 80 people (15 hostages and some 60 or so terrorists) and their vehicles could not have made the 45-day[48] journey across such a vast expanse of the Algerian Sahara unless facilitated by Algeria's security forces. With Algeria's allegedly huge deployment of troops, and with its own aerial reconnaissance reinforced by US air and satellite surveillance, it would have been virtually impossible for anyone to travel far in the Algerian Sahara undetected. With fuel and other supplies dropped off for them along the way, the hostages realised that a corridor had been cleared and prepared for them. Only Algeria's security forces could have done this.

The fact that the Algerian security forces facilitated the transfer of the hostages and their captors from Tamelrik to Mali is not necessarily proof that they were collaborators in the hostage-taking. If they were confronted on this matter, the Algerians would almost certainly say that they were merely ensuring the hostages' safety. Be that as it may, the question arises as to why they did not liberate them along the way, as they had done with the first group in Gharis.[49] The answer is that the Algerians had already chosen Mali for the final release, and had prepared the ground there. We must therefore ask why Mali was so important. Moving the final release negotiations to Mali not only took the 'terrorist problem' into the Sahel – which, as I shall explain later, was one of the main objectives of the exercise; from a diplomatic point of view, it enabled Algeria both to shift and widen the whole footprint of the hostage drama: it would be remembered as a 'Saharan' or 'Malian', as much as an 'Algerian' incident.[50]

It is generally assumed that the hostages' release was secured by the payment of a 5-million-euro[51] ransom negotiated by mediators acting between the Malian authorities (who were in turn effectively acting on behalf of the German government, who, it is alleged, ultimately paid the ransom) and El Para's GSPC kidnappers. In practice, however, these negotiations, like most other aspects of this drawn-out saga, appear to have been arranged and orchestrated by Algeria's secret military intelligence services. Indeed, we know from local people that Algerians, later identified as agents of Algeria's intelligence services, were active in northern Mali and preparing for the arrival of the hostages.

After spending some time in the Tassili-n-Ahenet, the hostages crossed into Mali in the region of Timaiouine, before heading south towards Kidal.[52] At around the same time, an Algerian colonel, reportedly the Algerian defence attaché in Bamako, visited Kidal with several 'colleagues' for a number of days. Much of the colonel's time was spent with Iyad ag Ghali, one of the leaders of the Tuareg rebellion in the 1990s who had established particularly good relations with the Algerian services during the course of the subsequent peace negotiations.[53] Although he was still recognised as a significant Tuareg leader in the region, many of Iyad's former followers and peers now regard him as a little politically 'unreliable', partly because of his suspected Algerian DRS contacts, but also because of his recent following of the Tablighi Jamaat, an Islamic fundamentalist movement about which I shall say more later. The Algerian colonel visited several other Kidal notables at this time, but always, it seems, in the company of Iyad. It is believed that these meetings served to establish both the 'salaries' of the mediators, notably Iyad, and the direction that the negotiations would follow.[54]

During the course of these negotiations, which were spun out over the best part of a month, the hostages tried to compile CVs of the six mediators they believed to be involved in the negotiations: three for the kidnappers and three for the Malian state. Their data is obviously incomplete. Nevertheless, at least three and possibly four of the mediators, for both sides, are known to have been Algerian secret agents, or to have had close connections with the Algerian intelligence services. Moreover, none of the mediators was a sincere Islamist.

A week or so after their return home, the German hostages received a visit from agents of Germany's Bundeskriminalamt

(BKA), who interrogated them over the course of two days. The hostages were very surprised in the course of these debriefings to be shown photographs taken of both their captors and their hijacked vehicles while they were being held hostage. The photographs had been taken not from a plane, but at ground level.[55] Who could have taken them?

5

GROUNDS FOR SUSPICION IN THE SAHEL

When the hostages were finally released, on the afternoon of 17 August, they had no idea of how their six-month ordeal had been stage-managed from the moment of its inception, nor the key role they had played in enabling the Americans to establish a new Saharan–Sahelian front in their global war on terror (GWOT). But before turning to the nature of the Bush administration's relationship with the Algerians, and how the US became involved in the fabrication of this appalling human drama, let me continue by looking at the suspicions that emerged in the Sahelian Sahara in the months following the hostages' release, for, in a sense, the release of the hostages was only the halfway point in the fabrication of the narrative that was to legitimise the expansion of this new front in the GWOT across the entire Sahel.

My suspicions about the extent to which the GSPC terrorist threat across the Sahel was also fabricated by Algerian–US intelligence services focuses primarily on five main incidents or sequences of incidents, which I have already described, namely: (1) the alleged terrorist action in southern Algeria between the time of the hostage release in Mali in August 2003 and the military engagements against the GSPC in Mali at the beginning of 2004; (2) the nature and veracity of the military engagements in January 2004 that allegedly flushed the GSPC out of Mali and into Niger; (3) the hold-up of tourists in Aïr a few weeks later; (4) El Para's journey into Tibesti, his battle with Chad's security forces and his capture by Chad rebels; and (5) finally, to jump to the end of the story, his 'extradition' to Algeria and subsequent court trial. This chapter deals with the first four of these crucial stages of the fabrication. The fifth, his court trial in Algiers, is covered in the next chapter.

Alleged 'Terrorism' in Southern Algeria: August 2003 to Early 2004

In the wake of the final hostage release, Algeria's extreme south was awash with rumour and suspicion, especially that the Algerian government had been involved in the hostage-taking. With the local and regional government using the 'terrorist threat' to deflect attention from growing civil discontent, the name that began circulating in the region, particularly after the highway robbery near Amguid in early November, was that of Aboubacar Alembo. As I have mentioned, the Algerian authorities had identified the 'bandits' in the Amguid hold-up by their accents as Nigeriens, and Alembo was a Niger Tuareg who had come to prominence in the previous year for a string of criminal actions in Niger, including the killing of two policemen. Although we will probably never know for certain[1] whether Alembo was responsible for the Amguid robbery, he was identified as being in southern Algeria at around that time.[2] Following the incident, the Tamanrasset authorities closed the area to tourism. However, while it removed some tourists from the area, it allowed others to pass. This seemingly indiscriminate action aroused the suspicions of some of the Tuareg tourism agencies, who began to undertake their own research – in traditional anthropological manner – into the kinship ties of both Alembo and members of the local administration. A disturbing picture began to emerge. It revealed a complex network of family relationships linking many of the senior levels of the regional administration in both southern Algeria and Niger with both smuggling and local banditry networks, including that of Alembo. This Mafia-like network ramified through many of the most senior levels of southern Algeria's regional administration, including several of the *wali*'s main directorates, notably tourism and security, as well as the courts, police, the *daira*, and so on. The kinship links not only tied a number of these government officials to the favoured travel agencies whose clients had been allowed to continue on their travels, but to at least two well-known bandits, including Alembo, and to other agencies known to be implicated in smuggling and their counterparts in northern Niger.[3]

This 'revelation' not only conjured up the image of a local administration having its own pocket-size terrorist ready at hand, but raised the spectre of the most strategically important regional administration in the Sahara–Sahel zone being at the very heart of banditry and smuggling operations. It also begged the question of whether Algeria's endemic corruption had finally become so entrenched in the country's extreme south that the relevant authorities felt powerless to act, or whether this situation was being condoned, as many people believed, in order to destabilise the region and thus legitimise both the expansion of the US GWOT across the Sahara–Sahel and Algeria's own greater military presence in the country's extreme south.

Military Engagements Flush the GSPC out of Mali

Once Orwellian logic and disinformation become part of a regime's normal political discourse, so credibility, as both the Bush and Blair administrations have learned to their cost, becomes increasingly elusive. By the end of 2003, when it had been possible to reassess Algeria's official statements and media reports in the light of both the hostages' testimony and other evidence from the field, it was clear that almost every statement from the Algerian authorities about the hostage crisis over the course of the preceding year had been incorrect and deliberate disinformation. The Sahelian phase of El Para's campaign was no different.[4]

It is therefore extremely difficult to know whether military engagements really did flush El Para's GSPC out of northern Mali, as the Algerians and Americans claimed. There are five sources of information on what occurred during this phase of the saga, namely (i) the concurrent media reports of mostly Algerian origin; (ii) information received by European intelligence sources; (iii) US military intelligence sources; (iv) the Algerian gendarmerie's files on El Para and his men; and (v) interviews undertaken in 2007 by certain European broadcasters with senior members of the Niger army, the Forces Armées Nigeriennes (FAN).

(i) Algerian Media Reports

The impression given by the Algerian media was that El Para's men had been driven out of Mali around mid- to late January 2004, in a military sweep by some combination of Algerian, Malian and perhaps US forces. By that time, however, those who had been following the hostage drama in all its detail had proof that almost everything that had been said about it in the Algerian media had been disinformation. The Algerian coverage of subsequent events in the Sahel was therefore unlikely to be any different. Indeed, a careful reading of Algerian media reports of military engagements in the southern border regions around that time not only suggests that they may have been different reports of the same incident – namely, the killing of four Islamists and the capture of a large arms cache in the Tamanrasset area – but that the incident itself may have been fabricated.

The Algerian version of events is that its security forces intercepted a large cache of arms[5] near In Salah, which it claimed had been bought in Mali with the hostage ransom money and was destined for GSPC cells in the north of Algeria. Although the incident sounds quite plausible, foreign correspondents in Algiers at the time questioned why Algeria's high-profile media coverage of the event was managed so closely by the DRS. When I have tried to investigate this incident myself, most local people I have spoken to have questioned why the interception was made some 750km into Algerian territory (as the crow flies – nearer 1000km by recognised roads and pistes), and not nearer the border. One answer that has been suggested to me by several local people is that the military engagement was fabricated, and that the arms originated from the military barracks in Tamanrasset, not Mali.[6] Such rumours will abound until Algeria provides satisfactory verification.

I am now inclined to believe that this incident, or something along these lines happened. My change of mind comes from reading the Algerian gendarmerie files that I will mention presently. These police files were compiled, according to their date stamp, on 12 April 2004, but did not come into my possession until 2006. While it is almost certain that they were compiled to present the German media with the DRS's official version of events, most of the personal details that I have been able to check do appear to be accurate. Thus, although they make no mention of any incidents in the Sahel, which is surprising, they do mention that two of El Para's men met their death at In Salah on 13 February 2004.[7] One was apparently shot (*abattu*); the other is reported as having died from his wounds.[8] That there is an interval of a couple of weeks between the date of the incident, which happened on or before 31 January, and the deaths of the two men, is probably not significant and is likely to be explained by the bureaucracy surrounding the recording of the deaths. The reason why the DRS became so paranoid in managing the news of the event is, I believe, that they had set it up. By that I mean that they knew El Para's men were in Mali and that they had money; it is also reasonable to assume that they were buying arms to bring back to Algeria. More particularly, the Algerian army needed such an incident as supposed proof of GSPC terrorism and arms trafficking between the Sahel and the north. It is therefore quite likely that they knew of the passage of the men from Mali, and waited until they were in the In Salah region before attacking them. If that is what happened, the DRS would certainly want to manage the news and ensure there was no awkward questioning in public.

If I sound overly suspicious of Algeria's media, it is simply because almost all its reports on the hostages' capture, their movements and their release have subsequently been proved false. This manipulation of Algeria's media by its security forces was not limited to the hostage drama itself, but extended to virtually all news and information relating to terrorism in the Sahara around that time – especially if it was to do with El Para's GSPC and the border areas between Algeria, Mali and Niger. For example, on 17 August, the day before the hostages' release in Mali, the *Quotidien d'Oran*,[9] quoting Algerian military sources, reported that a skirmish had taken place between Mokhtar ben Mokhtar's GSPC men and the Algerian army near the border town of In

Guezzam on 15 August. On the following day, the same source changed its opinion, saying that the skirmish had been with arms traffickers transporting a huge quantity of Chinese-made AK47s. Both reports were incorrect. The incident involved neither the GSPC terrorists nor arms traffickers, but five Tuareg *ishomar*[10] from Niger and Mali, who were searching independently in a four-wheel-drive vehicle for tracks of the hostages and their captors when they were attacked by the Algerian army. They fled to Mali, three of them wounded.[11]

(ii) European Intelligence Sources

On 6 February 2004, I received information from the intelligence services of an EU country saying that 30 of the hostage-takers had been killed in an Algerian army offensive. I have received no corroboration of this incident from other sources, including local people familiar with the Malian–Algerian frontier zone. It is therefore very questionable that this incident actually took place. That is not to say that it was disinformation, for it is conceivable that the reference to 30 might have been a translation error whereby the number 13 *(treize, dreizehn)* was mistaken for 30 *(trente, dreißig)*. However, the general tone of the Algerian press at that time, and the lack of any immediate follow-up reports, would suggest that, in the unlikely event that this incident did take place, the lower number was more probable.

(iii) US Military Sources

A number of more recent articles which have been supported or encouraged by US military and intelligence services, or which have been based more or less exclusively on US military intelligence sources, have 'muddied the waters' and made any proper analysis of these events much more difficult.

Since I first published my suspicions and doubts about the nature and effectiveness of the alleged joint military action by US, Malian, Algerian and Nigerien forces in flushing El Para and his men out of northern Mali and pursuing them across the

Sahel to Chad[12], the Americans have used compliant journalists to try and give more credibility to the existence and effectiveness of such an operation.

A particularly good example of this sort of journalism is Raffi Khatchadourian's article in the New York *Village Voice*.[13] Although Khatchadourian admits that 'the full extent of Mali's counterterrorism coordination with the United States is unclear', he injects an ingenious spin by implying that the Pentagon had to deny the presence of US forces in the region. 'Publicly,' he writes, 'the Defense Department denies sending anyone into the Sahel for purposes other than military training.'[14] 'We didn't have any forces on the ground', a senior US commander in the region had told him.[15] However, as if to justify either the lies or incompetence of the US Defense Department, Khatchadourian then quotes a Niger defence official who confirms that US special operations forces, working with their Algerian counterparts, had tracked El Para in his race from Mali into Niger and Chad. To beef up the role of the US presence even more, he then appears to quote an unreferenced article in the *Boston Globe*: 'Meanwhile, just over the Malian border in Algeria, small teams of elite US troops hunted GSPC fighters, and "even put up some kind of infrastructure".'[16] 'In other parts of the Sahel', he writes, 'Peace Corps volunteers encountered American soldiers travelling in small units to remote villages, far from training bases.'[17] He then quotes a British firm, Africa Analysis Ltd,[18] which 'reported that there was "gossip" among intelligence experts in Washington that 200 US special-operations forces were in the Sahel for a range of clandestine missions, including "electronic surveillance, coordinating human intelligence with satellite data, and calling in computer-guided air strikes".' Khatchadourian continues:

> The report noted that the operatives were assisting in the hunt for Saifi [El Para], and that the Pan Sahel Initiative was at least partly 'cover' for such activities. It went on to say that some former Special Forces were 'adamant' that the 'public face [of the initiative] was only part of the story'. A former Bush administration official familiar with security issues in the Sahel told me that in late 2003 the US military engaged in 'a joint effort' with the

Malian army to ambush Islamic militants somewhere near the border with Algeria. This would have occurred when Saifi had just begun operating there. 'Our guys were advising', he explained ... 'Rumsfeld had his goons running all over the continent', he said.[19]

This sort of journalism gives the impression of US Special Forces playing a major and active role in driving El Para and his men out of Mali, across Niger and into Chad. However, when stripped down to its essentials, the article, like most of this genre, is a carefully crafted picture – an illusion – that is based on a combination of highly selective,[20] one-sided and unsubstantiated quotes and a mixture of largely unreferenced secondary and tertiary sources.[21]

(iv) Algerian Gendarmerie Files

The Algerian authorities were particularly cross that their version of events surrounding the hostage-taking was being met with so much scepticism by European intelligence services, especially in Germany. Indeed, suspicions of and evidence for US–Algerian complicity in the hostage-taking were being published even before El Para and his men had reportedly been flushed out of Mali and chased across the Sahel into Chad.[22] In order to convince the Germans that El Para and his men were 'real terrorists', and that the whole drama had not been fabricated, as these publications were suggesting, the Algerian intelligence services sought to leak a copy of their National Gendarmerie files on the hostage-taking and the hostage-takers to the Bundeskriminalamt (BKA), Germany's Federal Criminal Police Office.[23] The dossier, compiled by a Lieutenant-Colonel in the Bureau des Affaires Judiciaires de la Division de la Sécurité Publique on 12 April 2004, and destined for the Général-Major Commandant of the Gendarmerie Nationale, was compiled in such a way as to confirm all the information that the German intelligence services would have gleaned from their debriefing of the hostages, such as the names and personal details of their captors, but embellished with their previous 'terrorist' activities and 'criminal' records, along with additional information linking them to Algeria's own versions of El Para's and Mokhtar ben Mokhtar's alleged terrorist backgrounds. Thus, while the files containing the personal details of the hostage-takers appear to be correct, the information on both El Para's and Mokhtar's backgrounds is suspect.

Although the dossier was designed to convince the Germans that the hostage-takers were genuine GSPC terrorists and gives various details of their period of capture, as well as El Para's real or fictitious activities in northern Mali up to and following the hostages' release, there is no mention of any attacks on El Para and his men in northern Mali during or around January 2004, other than the killing of the two men at In Salah, mentioned earlier. Although that does not mean that they did not take place, one might have expected some reference to have been made to them if they had taken place in the way that the Algerian and US media-intelligence services have implied.

(v) Interviews with Niger Military Officers

In 2007 a German radio and television team interviewed the commanding officer of the Niger army at the time of the alleged pursuit of El Para and his men across the Sahel. While the officer could give no information about what happened in Mali, he was able to confirm that the Niger army lost contact with El Para's men after one skirmish with them soon after their entry into Niger,[24] and that there had been no further pursuit of them across Niger and into Chad, as claimed by the Algerians and Americans.

The 'Hold-up' of Tourists in Aïr

During the course of the last five years it has been possible to trace and interview many of the local witnesses and other people involved in the reported incidents relating to El Para's alleged escapade across the Sahel. As a result, we now know that the bandits who held up a group of tourists at Timia on 24–25 January were Tamashek-speakers – that is, local Tuareg, and not El Para's men. We also know a great deal more about the widely reported 'hold-up' of some 30 or more French and Austrian tourists at Temet on 23 February 2004 by El Para and his group of around 50 well-armed GSPC who, according to both Algerian and US sources, were being pursued from Mali across northern Niger by 'US Special Operational Forces in cooperation with North African militaries' and US air surveillance.[25]

The first point to make, before even examining the hold-up, is that there was no pursuit of El Para and his men by the US or any other militaries after the Niger army, as mentioned above, lost contact with them shortly after their crossing into Niger from Mali. Detailed and extensive interviews with local people, including local political leaders, from across much of northern Niger confirm that there was absolutely no sign of US or any other troops in the region at around that time. US-trained Niger troops passed through Aïr some six months later, for reasons that are explained in Chapter 17, and were severely embarrassed in the face of Tuareg resistance. A few US troops (Special Forces) were also spotted subsequently in the company of Algerian military detachments in the Emi Lulu region, approximately 100km south-west of Algeria's army base at In Ezzane.[26] US Special Forces have also been seen regularly in and around Agades. However, local people are adamant that the widely publicised chase simply did not happen.

It is also very interesting to note that Khatchadourian, who devotes much space to the alleged pursuit of El Para and his men across the Sahel, put El Para's men on a completely different trajectory across Niger from the one we know they took. He describes how El Para's convoy

> raced across Niger ... With the multinational force closing in and American reconnaissance planes observing from above ... During a recent battle, fire had damaged some gear, and certain electrical devices began to fail. One truck broke down near a forlorn place in Niger known as the Tree of Ténéré, where an ancient and solitary acacia once stood. The truck was abandoned.[27]

High drama in the middle of the world's greatest desert: the stuff of Hollywood movies, but now US disinformation. Unfortunately for Khatchadourian, or perhaps for the military intelligence sources who provided him with his disinformation, El Para's men did not pass by the Ténéré Tree. They travelled from Arlit, past Gougaram and across the Aïr to Temet, and then headed north-east to Adrar Bous and Tabarakaten. We know this because they took on a Tuareg guide from Arlit, whom I and my Tuareg colleagues have interviewed, and who took them as far as the Aïr. Further on in Aïr, at Temet, El Para's men discussed their onward route to Tabarakaten with several local Tuareg, whom we have also interviewed. Indeed, we even have photographs of El Para's group at Temet. Quite apart from the fact that the Ténéré Tree is precisely 300km south-east of Temet, as the crow flies, and much further by vehicle, it is not on the route that anyone heading across Ténéré from Temet would take. Nor is 'forlorn' a good adjective to describe the Ténéré Tree,[28] it being one of the Sahara's most visited spots on the much-travelled main piste from Agades to Bilma. It is the sort of place that any 'terrorist' worth the name, and on the run, would be wise to avoid.

So what did happen at Temet? The reader will perhaps get a better understanding of what took place there if I can provide a mental picture of what is one of the most extravagantly scenic places on earth. Temet is a small sand sea in the north-west corner of Niger's Ténéré desert. Its dunes – some of the highest in the Sahara, whose yellowy-gold would be the envy of van Gogh – ride up to the very edge of the dark, foreboding 6,400ft Greboun massif. Wind and water have somehow kept the two just far enough apart for a vehicle track to slither its way down between the massif and the dunes, so that travellers, whether they be tourists, bandits, military or El Para's GSPC, have a passage out of the Aïr mountains onto the vast, flat expanse of the Ténéré itself. It is the sort of place where tourists now come to play, sand-boarding down the dunes, searching for a rich archaeology along the adjoining terraces that was hoovered up several years ago, or simply to marvel at one of nature's most outrageously beautiful creations. Although remote, Temet is now the sort of place where it is difficult to be completely alone, especially in the winter tourist season. And so it was, on 23 February 2004, that 50 or so of El Para's men ran into two parties of 26 French tourists and a party of eight Austrians.

In Chapter 2 I described the Temet incident as a 'hold-up'. That is technically correct, in that the tourists were held up by the heavily armed 'bandits' and robbed of some 30,000 euros. However, the hold-up could not have been more high-profile. El Para, or someone identifying himself as El Para, allowed the tourists to photograph him, his men and their vehicles. He even drafted a bizarre contract, in English – which was signed by the eight Austrians, with partial addresses – in the name of Abu Haidara Abdul Razzaq al Ammari Al Arussi, a combination of his many aliases,[29] which read:

We the undersigned agree to:

1. pay the amount of two hundred millions (200,000,000) CFA – Francs within three weeks in cash to
Group Salafi for call and Holy War in Algeria
(Abu Haidara Abdul Razzaq al Ammari Al Arussi)

2. hold the guide, the driver and the cook free of any damage.

The high-profile nature of the hold-up, which received extensive global media coverage, was obviously intended to give maximum publicity to the presence of El Para and the GSPC in the region, and to draw attention to their journey to Chad.

We now know that the circumstances of the hold-up were rather different. El Para's GSPC men were not being chased across northern Niger by the American, Algerian or any other military, but were stumbling around – lost! Nor was El Para with them. I do not know their precise route or date of departure from Mali, but somewhere in Tamesna, or perhaps in the vicinity of the uranium-mining town of Arlit, they had taken on a Tuareg guide. The guide, who came from Arlit, was subsequently found and interviewed in the course of our research. He explained how he was taken on by El Para's men and paid a substantial sum of money to guide them to Tabarakaten, an extremely difficult place to find in the northern Ténéré, about 60km east-north-east from Adrar Bous.[30] They wanted to go to Tabarakaten because El Para had told them that it was the place where they would rendezvous with him. The Tuareg guide, however, realising who he was dealing with, took El Para's men into Aïr and, perhaps wisely, jumped ship – with his money. El Para's men would have been able to follow the track as far as Temet, but thereafter they would have been lost in the open desert with little chance of finding Tabarakaten without detailed GPS coordinates – which they appeared not to have – or a new guide. Their main concern at Temet, which they discussed at length with the local drivers and guides belonging to the tourist parties, was to find another guide.

El Para's Journey to Chad

This information not only throws a completely new light on the alleged 'spread of GSPC terrorism' across the Sahel, but enables us to ask some extremely pertinent questions – namely: Why did El Para leave his men to make their own way to Tabarakaten? What was he doing in the Tabarakaten area? Did they all make the journey to Chad, or did they split into two groups, one of which returned to Algeria? How did they manage to enter Tibesti when the region is so heavily mined, with only one safe route – well-known to the Chad army – into that part of Chad? How did they get fuel for the journey, when there is scarcely any available in this vast tract of the Sahara? Did they, we should perhaps now ask, actually go to Chad at all, or was this leg of their extraordinary journey across the Sahara and Sahel just a continuation of the imagination, deception and disinformation that had characterised their travels over the previous twelve months? And, if they really did go to Chad, was there ever a battle with the Chad forces, in which 43 members of the GSPC were killed, as America's military commanders were so quick to tell the world?

Let me cast some light on each of these questions, and begin with the hitherto overlooked matter of logistics, on which the Americans have curiously, but perhaps not surprisingly, made no comment. How did the GSPC obtain fuel? The distance from their starting point in Mali to their alleged battleground in Chad is some 2,000km as the crow flies, and almost certainly much further by whatever route they may have taken. El Para's men would therefore have needed to carry, or have had access to, several hundreds, more likely thousands, of litres of fuel, both petrol (gasoline) and diesel.[31] Fuel, however, is a precious commodity throughout most of the Sahel, and hard to come by. Apart from Arlit, which is a fairly heavily policed town, and one they would have been unlikely to enter, there were no other assured commercial supplies of fuel across their entire route. At the time of El Para's alleged journey, small stocks could sometimes be found at Iferouane in Aïr, at Dirkou, and occasionally at Chirfa (from the military) on the eastern side of Ténéré, but there is no evidence that they entered or obtained supplies from any of these towns, which, in any case, are garrisoned by Niger's security forces. Nor did the eyewitnesses at Temet notice them carrying sufficient supplies, which suggests that they were almost certainly reliant on fuel dumps – as they had been on their long journey from Tamelrik to Mali the previous year. These could have come from only three sources: the Niger army (which itself is nearly always short of fuel, and would hardly have been likely to assist them), smugglers, or the Algerian army.

Smugglers and the Algerian army were the only realistic sources. At any other time, it would have been conceivable for them to have arranged fuel supplies from smugglers. That is because fuel smuggling is a regular business between Algeria and Niger, especially by people-traffickers, who usually smuggle fuel, at a profit of about 500 euros per vehicle, on their return trip south. However, we have to ask whether it is likely that such security-sensitive and highly informed people would have engaged in such a high-risk arrangement. If, as the US and Algerian military intelligence spokespersons have been telling us, the militaries of the area, along with the air surveillance provided by an American P-3 Orion aircraft, were in pursuit of the GSPC, would the smugglers have engaged in what might have been a suicidal mission? Even if they had known that the pursuit was disinformation, they would have been aware of the prevailing state of military alert – at least on the Algerian side of the frontier – which would have made the venture extremely risky.

This leaves the question of whether Aboubacar Alembo, the most notorious bandit in that area, might have joined up with El Para. There have been many rumours and much speculation on this, but no confirming evidence. I first came across Alembo in July 2002, after he had killed two policemen in Niger, eluded the Niger army at Tamgak,[32] and escaped into Algeria.[33] By strange coincidence I was in the vicinity of Chirfa, on the eastern side of Ténéré, later in that year, when he and his gang undertook their vicious and highly publicised attack on French tourists. By this time he was beginning to stamp his mark on the Emi Lulu region of north-east Niger, which is something of a crossroads on the north–south track from Algeria's Djanet region to the Kaouar[34] region of Niger and the south-west–north-east route that carried mostly smugglers, people-traffickers and illegal migrants trying to make it on their own into Libya. It was this last category of people that became his main prey. Defenceless, both physically and in terms of having no legal protection from the countries through which they tried to pass, this pathetic trail of human desperation provided soft targets for Alembo. Although this wretched line of business earned him the disdain of other smugglers operating in the region, it was his attack on the French tourists in November 2002, and the damage it did to Niger's tourism industry, that finally made his activities intolerable to both the Niger government and his fellow Tuareg. Senior government ministers plotted with key Tuareg as to how they might capture him. With his whereabouts betrayed by other smugglers and members of his own family, who regarded him as 'dead', the posse tracked him down in November 2003, almost exactly one year after his attack on the French tourists.[35] Four of his gang were thought to have been killed in the attack, although their bodies have never been found. Alembo was captured, only to escape when the vehicle in which he was travelling was involved in an accident.

It is debatable whether our knowledge of this incident throws any light on El Para's situation, or merely adds another layer of mystery and intrigue. It is interesting that the attack on Alembo occurred within the same week as the reported robbery on the Amguid piste in Algeria, raising the question that he might have fled far to the north; or whether the Amguid hold-up was undertaken by other bandits from Niger; or whether, as is quite likely, it never happened at all. My belief at the time was that Alembo would have been likely to keep a low profile after such a narrow escape. However, reports of his being sighted in the region of Adrar Bous around 11 December and in the Djanet region a few weeks later suggest that he may have been 'back in business' – possibly trying to recoup his losses. It is, of course, quite conceivable, given his kinship links with tourism agents known also to be smugglers, as well as with prominent persons in the Algerian security services, that he was being afforded protection in Algeria, and possibly even being used by those elements of the Algerian security services involved with El Para. If Alembo was linked to the El Para business in this way, then an unverified report from normally reliable sources within the Niger government in mid-April 2004 is extremely interesting.[36] The basis of this report is that Alembo was believed to have had a meeting with the minister of the interior at which he was effectively given an amnesty in exchange for his pledge to renounce his outlaw ways.[37] The source was even under the impression that Alembo had received some 5–6 million CFA francs[38] from the minister. Whether this was a reward for his services in helping the GSPC on their way to their reported destruction in Chad, or compensation for the damages suffered at the hands of the posse, is a matter of conjecture.

If El Para, as now seems certain, was being run by Algeria's DRS, then the most likely source of fuel, as in the case of their long journey from Tamelrik to Mali, would have been the Algerian army. The Algerian army had fuel supplies just north of the border at its military bases at In Ezzane and In Azoua, and almost certainly at a number of other camps close to the border.

Why did El Para leave his men to make their own way to Tabarakaten? And what was he doing in the Tabarakaten area? The answer to the first of these questions is that El Para had business back in Algeria. Whether it was to arrange the fuel supplies or to sort out other matters with his handlers in the DRS is immaterial, as is the question of whether the army itself dropped off the fuel supplies or arranged for one of the smugglers, such as Alembo, to manage it for them. The reason for El Para choosing Tabarakaten for their rendezvous is that it was a convenient location for a fuel dump, having a good water supply, being roughly halfway along their route from Mali to Chad, and being conveniently accessible from Algeria.

Before turning to how El Para's men entered Chad, there is the question of whether all of the GSPC who were at Temet actually went on to Chad. We do not know. But there are several reasons for asking. One is that the Temet tourists, when questioned back in Europe, gave the impression that their hijackers may have been about to divide, with one group comprising four or five vehicles and perhaps 20 or 25 men going on to Chad, and the others heading back to Algeria.[39] Their evidence for this is very impressionistic. However, if they were correct, then 43 GSPC men could not have been killed in Chad by the Chadian forces, as US military intelligence services have asserted. If they were wrong, and all the GSPC did go with El Para to Chad, and if they were ambushed by Chadian forces, then the figure of 43 killed, with El Para escaping, perhaps with a handful of comrades, more or less accounts for the entirety of the party that passed through Temet and Tabarakaten. However, the initial reports on the alleged battle, which I shall mention presently, were highly equivocal, suggesting that far fewer than 43 had been killed.[40] Moreover, the French journalist Patrick Forestier, who entered the region and interviewed El Para in July 2004, filmed at least 14 GSPC men being held with El Para in the rebel camps of the Mouvement pour La Democratie et la Justice au Tchad (MDJT). That raises the question, which I address below, of whether any battle with the Chadian forces took place at all.

The only certain evidence that El Para actually went to Chad is in Patrick Forestier's filmed interviews with him, or someone purporting to be him. There are thus two outstanding questions. First, how did El Para's group, irrespective of its number, manage to enter Tibesti when the region and the access routes to it are heavily mined?[41] Second, was there a battle between the GSPC and the Chadian security forces?

According to the Algerian and other media reports, the alleged battle between the GSPC and the Chadian forces took place on 8 March. That means that their journey from Temet to the western side of Tibesti[42] was a remarkable achievement (especially if they were being chased by US Special Operations forces!), considering the difficulty of many of the passages and the prevalence of mines. The western scarps of the Djado and Mangeni plateaux are effectively impassable, which would have obliged the GSPC group to take either a northern route via Salvador, to the north of Mangeni and then across or around Tchigai, or a southern route heading east of Séguédine. Neither route would have been possible without a guide, which brings us back to the question of whether Alembo, or perhaps another guide, took them into Chad.

In a recent article, Baz Lecocq and Paul Schrijver, in commenting on El Para's move into Chad, say that he 'was undoubtedly seeking to procure arms, vehicles and other equipment at the arms market at the El Salvador Pass (on the Chad–Libyan–Niger border). It was there that they were finally caught by the Chadian rebel movement (MDJT).'[43] Lecocq and Schrijver provide no supporting evidence for this seemingly speculative claim. Nevertheless, I believe that this is the route (via El Salvador) by which El Para's group entered Chad. My belief is based on three sets of reasoning. The first is that the route via Séguédine would have been too close to the public eye of the Kaouar oases and their various police and army posts. Secondly, the access to the El Salvador Pass from the west runs within a stone's throw of Algeria's military base at In Ezzane. If El Para was really being chased across this part of the Sahara, the western approach to El Salvador, close to Algeria's In Ezzane military base, would have been one of the easiest places in the Sahara to cut him off. If, on the other hand, he was being ushered into Chad under the protective arm of Algeria's DRS, then this passage would have kept him close to his minders. Information provided by local smugglers suggests that US Special Forces may also have been based at In Ezzane around this time. My third reason for believing that El Salvador was El Para's chosen route is that it is the happy hunting ground of Alembo who, apart from knowing the area like the back of his hand, was under some sort of protection from the DRS, if not directly in their employ.[44]

This takes us to our last and perhaps most pertinent question: did El Para's men actually go to Chad at all? Or, in what amounts to almost the same thing, was there ever a battle with the Chadian forces in which 43 members of the GSPC were killed, as America's military commanders and their intelligence services have been so eager to tell the world?

One of the first reports on the incident was written on 10 March by Mounir B, a journalist for Algeria's *Quotidien d'Oran* and known to have good links with Algeria's security forces. He reported that Chadian forces had eliminated four members of El Para's group on the previous day.[45] The next day, 11 March, Reuters stated that 43 Islamist terrorists had been killed in Chad.[46] A few days later, on 15 March, a whole string of newspapers and agencies, including *L'Expression*, *El Watan* and AFP,[47] declared that El Para had been killed in Chad. *Jeune Afrique* – which stated that 49 had been killed in the battle with the Chadian forces, with five others being captured and taken to N'Djamena, and El Para and four others escaping to MDJT territory in the mountains of Tibesti – went so far as to report on how El Para's body had been extricated from the bottom of a gorge into which he had accidentally fallen on 15 March.[48] Four days later, AFP reported that El Para was not dead but in the Algerian desert.[49] The next day, *El Watan* stated that he was in Mali, 350km north of Timbuktu and 300km from the Algerian frontier![50] However, on 24 March, US Army Col. Vic Nelson, in a State Department interview, said that the Pentagon did not believe that El Para had been killed in the shoot-out with Chadian government forces.[51]

Over the next few weeks and months, reports began to emerge that El Para had escaped the carnage of the battle with the Chadian forces and had fallen into the hands of the rebel MDJT. By mid-summer the official story had been pretty well embedded in the world's media. It was that El Para's band of some 40 to 50 GSPC terrorists had been pursued from Mali, all the way through Niger and into Chad by US Special Operational Forces in cooperation with the militaries of Mali, Algeria and Niger, and supported by critical US air surveillance, and other intelligence and communications, before running into Chadian regular forces, who had eliminated all 43 terrorists except El Para, who had somehow escaped the carnage only to fall into the hands of the rebel MDJT.

Quite apart from the fact that there was, as we now know, no such pursuit, there are three serious problems with this official story. The first is that it lacks any verification. The second is that Patrick Forestier and his camera team from *Paris Match*,[52] who managed to visit the MDJT in July 2004 and interview El Para on film, found that he was being held with at least 14 of his men,[53] which is a pretty strong indication that 43 were not killed in the alleged battle.[54] The third problem is that MDJT leaders have stated that no such battle took place.[55] This assertion has been supported by local Tubu nomads, who also say that, after more than three years of searching, they have found no trace of any such battle.[56]

6

WHO WAS EL PARA?

The 'Truths' of El Para

Who was, or is, El Para? We know that he had an almost endless string of aliases, among which were Saifi Am[m]ari, alleged to be his proper name, El (Al) Para (Bara), Abderezak, Abou (Abu) Haidara, Ammane Abu Haidra, Abderezak Zaimeche, Abdul Razzaq, Abdul Rasak, Abdalrazak, al Ammari Al Arussi, El Ourassi and further combinations and alternative spellings of these.[1] Undoubtedly he had others, among which Qessah might be found to have been a military code-name for him.

There are many 'truths' about El Para. The question, which I attempt to answer a little further in the course of this chapter, is: Which one comes closest to 'reality'.

The least convincing 'truth', promulgated by Washington and its Algerian allies, is that El Para was second-in-command or, as claimed on occasion by Algeria's intelligence services, even leader of the Groupe Salafiste pour la Prédication de le Combat (GSPC),[2] rated by the US in its GWOT as one of the world's most dangerous terrorist groups. According to the Bush administration, he was Al Qaeda's representative – bin Laden's man – in the Sahel and, not surprisingly, high on the American president's list of the world's most-wanted terrorists. The US had declared him a 'Specially Designated Global Terrorist', a classification shared by bin Laden and his senior commanders, and put him on a roster known as the New Consolidated List of Individuals and Entities Belonging to or Associated With the Taliban and Al-Qaida.[3] With these credentials, he was the sort of man the Americans might have been expected to 'take out', at almost any cost. But El Para was not 'taken out'.

The US–Algerian media–intelligence services would have us believe, in spite of there still being no unequivocal proof, that El Para was held in captivity in Tibesti by the MDJT for seven months, from March 2004 until his highly questionable (and unverified) extradition to Algeria in October. I will throw a little more light on the mystery of El Para's sojourn in Chad presently. For the moment, let us stick with the official story, because it raises the highly pertinent question of why one of President Bush's most wanted terrorists was allowed to while away his time in a Saharan retreat, and not eliminated. The Americans had the military capacity to capture or kill him while he was in Tibesti. Why didn't they? From the Americans' point of view, there could not have been any serious questions about diplomatic niceties or sovereignty, neither of which have been much respected by the Bush administration, as the US military had already been in Chad since the beginning of the year as part of the Pan-Sahel Initiative (PSI), ostensibly a counterterrorism operation. Moreover, the country's dictatorially-minded president, Idriss Déby, who has been personally responsible for overseeing Chad's rise to the top of Transparency International's ranking of the world's most corrupt countries,[4] is propped up by a series of predominantly US interests headed by its largest oil company, ExxonMobil.[5]

As for the MDJT, the rebel group holding El Para, it had been split by factional disputes and severely weakened since the death of its leader, Youssouf Togoïmi, in 2002.[6] At the height of its powers around 2000, the MDJT is reckoned to have numbered about 1,500 men. By the time of El Para's arrival in Chad, estimates put its strength at as few as 200.[7] El Para was being held by one of these factions, possibly counting no more than a few dozen lightly armed men, in a remote but not unknown location in Tibesti. By US standards, his elimination would have required a relatively uncomplicated 'surgical strike'. But there was no such strike. Instead, El Para's name slowly dropped from the headlines, other than for the occasional story – part of the smokescreen – suggesting that he might already be back in Algeria, that the GSPC were going to pay, or had already paid, a ransom for him,[8] that he was still being held by the MDJT and that negotiations over his extradition were ongoing, and so on.

The same question as to why the Americans did not strike against El Para while he was in Tibesti must also apply to his flight across the Sahel. If, as the Americans claim, they were pursuing him on the ground across Mali and Niger and into Chad, and had him under their aerial surveillance, why did they not bring in an air strike against him? Unlike during his journey across the Algerian Sahara, he had no hostages with him: both he and his group could have been eliminated with one simple strike, without witnesses and literally 'in the middle of nowhere'. According to Raffi Khatchadourian, who had good connections with the US military, both the Pentagon and EUCOM had been pressing at various times for the use of air strikes in the region.[9]

From a technical point of view, such a strike would not have been impossible. If the Americans were discussing the use of air strikes in northern Niger, why did they also not use them in northern Mali? The fact that no such attempt was made suggests that either El Para was not there, or – more likely – that they did not want him killed.

The lack of effort by both the Americans and Algerians to kill or capture El Para during this period leads to a number of possible conclusions: that he was not in the hands of the MDJT, or perhaps not in Chad at all; that he was already dead or a 'phantom' who had never existed;[10] or, as most local residents in the Sahara had come to believe, that he was an agent of Algeria's secret military intelligence service, the DRS, and that his handlers, having created and managed this elaborate deception, were simply in the process of engineering a plausible exit strategy. Now that he had served his purpose as the key instrument in enabling the launch of a Sahara–Sahel front in the GWOT, he could be allowed to fade from the scene. Indeed, it is highly significant that the Algerian government's official position on El Para, six months after his reported capture by the MDJT, was, in the words of the country's interior minister Yazid Zerhouni, that "El Para is no longer of great importance to Algeria's fight against terrorism as he has been out of the country for over a year"![11]

El Para's Biographies

Algeria will obviously always deny that El Para was (and, as far as I know, still is) a DRS agent, and will have done everything possible to establish false identities, CVs and alibis, and to leave no obvious clues or evidence of his true identity. If we were to read the numerous articles on El Para in the Algerian media[12] between October 2002 and February 2003, as well as his alleged interview with *Paris Match* in July 2004,[13] we would learn that he was born at Kef el-Rih, near Guelma in the Aures region of eastern Algeria, on either 1 January 1968 or 2 April 1966,[14] to a Chaouia[15] father and, perhaps significantly, a French mother. Her name was Blanchet, and according to *Paris Match*, she was still living in Algiers at the time.[16] According to the same interview, he joined the army at the age of 15 or 16, and served in it from 1985 to 1991. The two most interesting features of his army career are that he trained as a parachutist and that he claims to have been head of the bodyguard of the former defence minister, Gen. Khaled Nezzar, from 1990 to 1993, with whom his friendship was such that the general apparently offered him his daughter in marriage.[17] Depending on whose version one believes, El Para left or deserted the army in either 1991, 1992 or 1993 – either for health or disciplinary reasons – and joined the Armed Islamic Group (GIA)[18] in 1992 or 1993.

These various articles tell us that El Para was then with the GIA until 1995, and was one of its 'strong men' in the *maquis* of eastern Algeria, along with Redouane Achir, Nabil Sahraoui (alias Abou Ibrahim Mustapha) and Droukdel Abdelmalek (alias Abou Moussaab Abdelwadoud).[19] In 1996 he participated in the creation of the GSPC (actually formed in 1998)[20] with Hassan Hattab, Abbi Abdelaziz (alias Okacha El Para), Abdelhamid Saadaoui (alias Abu Yahia), Abou El Bara, Mouffok, Amirouche Mazari, and others. According to *Le Matin*[21] and several other Algerian newspapers, El Para ousted Nabil Sahraoui as the *emir* of the GSPC's Zone 5 (south-eastern Algeria) and also became second-in-command to its founder, Hassan Hattab.

According to this popular biography, El Para was a 'terrorist' from the early 1990s, first with the GIA and then the GSPC. But was he? According to *Le Monde Diplomatique*,[22] which has spent some time digging into this question, none of the documents on the GSPC's website[23] mentioned Amari Saifi – alias Abou Haidara, alias El Para – until 2004. Nor do there seem to be many references to him in the press until 2002, which is surprising for such a high-ranking 'terrorist'.[24] Although the tourists abducted in 2003 identified him as one of their kidnappers, that is no proof of his actual identity. Moreover, as *Le Monde Diplomatique* noted, it is only his former employers, the Algerian general staff, who claim that El Para was acting on behalf of the GSPC. The GSPC itself, as I have already demonstrated, never actually claimed responsibility for kidnapping the tourists.[25] Indeed it is particularly significant that Hassan Hattab, leader of the GSPC at that time, never made such a claim, which leads us to conclude that the references in the Algerian and other media which claim GSPC responsibility for the kidnappings are highly suspect, as are most of the references linking the GSPC and El Para with Osama bin Laden and al-Qaeda. For instance, *Le Monde*'s investigation into El Para revealed that recordings played by the Algerian authorities to prove the link between the GSPC and al-Qaeda are now believed to be fakes, recorded by the GSPC's audiovisual unit.[26] Similarly, a video recording used by the DRS to try to persuade public opinion that El Para was a lieutenant of Osama bin Laden, charged with establishing al-Qaeda in the Sahel, is also now known to have been a forgery.[27] Indeed, if the GSPC and al-Qaeda were already linked in 2003, as Algeria claims, why did both organisations give so much publicity to their 'new' coming together at the end of 2006, and the changing of the GSPC's name in the beginning of 2007 to 'Al-Qaeda in the Islamic Maghreb'?

El Para as a DRS Agent

The most convincing evidence to suggest that El Para was one of the Algerian army's many infiltrators into the GIA is that there appear to be no records of his being a leading Islamist before around 2000.[28] If El Para was a DRS agent, when did he infiltrate the organisation? Or was he perhaps 'turned' fairly recently? We are unlikely ever to know, unless Algeria's secret intelligence service is one day forced to open its vast 'black' files.[29] As I explain below,[30] the GIA are known to have been heavily infiltrated by Algeria's secret military intelligence services. Indeed, a cruel witticism among many Algerians, but containing more than a grain of truth, is that the GIA were the creation of the Algerian military. We also know, from the reported testimonies of several GSPC members who have since taken advantage of President Bouteflika's various conciliatory amnesties,[31] that they were almost paranoid about being infiltrated by the DRS, and believed that their organisation had indeed been compromised in the same way as the GIA, from which they had broken away. However, having tried to investigate as far as is reasonably possible the question of when El Para infiltrated or was turned by the DRS, I believe there are three broad possibilities, which I present in order of increasing probability.

The first is only a rumour, but one which seems to have gained some credibility among Algeria-watchers since the hostage crisis. It is that El Para may have been 'turned' by the Algerian security forces as recently as January 2003. The background to this rumour is as follows. El Para was held responsible for an attack on an Algerian army convoy at Teniet El-Abed in the Aures Mountains on 4 January 2003, in which 43 to 49 soldiers were killed and 19 wounded.[32] Shortly afterwards, the Algerian media carried a report stating that the army had surrounded a mountain near Tebessa, a little to the east of the Teniet ambush, on which a group of GSPC was trapped. Surprisingly there appears to have been little media follow-up to this story, triggering the rumour that El Para had been captured on the mountain and persuaded to work for the intelligence services. It is also worth noting that this attack on Algerian troops took place, perhaps conveniently for the Algerians, on the day after a high-level US military delegation had arrived in Algiers to discuss the resumption of US arms sales to Algeria as part of the fight against terrorism.[33] El Para's first mission for his new masters, so this rumour would have us believe, was to make amends for their botched abduction of tourists in the Sahara four months earlier, and to organise a more successful one.[34] Although that is plausible, there are inconsistencies in the dates of press reports.[35] Nor does it explain the suspicious lack of records after 1994, suggesting that El Para is more likely to have been a long-term 'sleeper', perhaps going back to his days as Gen. Nezzar's bodyguard, than recently 'turned'.

The second possibility relates to a set of links which might explain the way in which El Para infiltrated the GSPC in the eastern region (Zone 5). It relates to his reported involvement in contraband business, known as *trabendo*, along the Tunisian frontier, and especially to livestock trafficking. A number of recent press reports have referred to his control of much of the racketeering and contraband in this, his home region. It is widely believed that arms trafficking, especially by the GIA, is closely tied to such smuggling businesses. Indeed the ideological interests of these groups are often subordinated to their financial interests and operations.[36] It is also common knowledge throughout Algeria that many of the generals and clans who effectively run Algeria from behind the scenes – *le pouvoir*, as they are known – have a major financial stake in *trabendo*. *Trabendo* touches on almost every aspect of commerce in Algeria, ranging from such things as arms and drug trafficking at the more extreme end of the spectrum, through cigarette and people trafficking, car theft and exportation, to the control of food and livestock markets, cement and construction materials, container trafficking, and so on. If El Para was controlling much of the *trabendo* in Zone 5, he would almost certainly have had links with both the GSPC, or other armed groups, and corrupted elements within the country's military establishment – almost certainly including the DRS. In the same way that Mokhtar ben Mokhtar is alleged to have done many favours for states in the region, it would be quite conceivable for El Para to have managed such a favour for the DRS. It is highly plausible, and indeed quite likely, that he may have been turned (or awakened if he was a sleeper) by the threat of withdrawal of protection, or the promise of a stake in other *trabendo* business, in order to use his GSPC network to effect the hostage abduction on behalf of the DRS.[37]

El Para as a US Green Beret?

The third and most likely possibility, considering the evidence now coming to light, is that El Para is not simply a DRS agent, but was trained for three years as a Green Beret by US Special Forces at Fort Bragg in North Carolina.[38] His biography should perhaps be amended as follows.

El Para (Qessah?) was trained in 1987 at the Algerian army's Special Forces college at Biskra, some 350km to the south-east of Algiers, passing out with the rank of sergeant. He was then transferred to the 12th Regiment of the Para-Commandos, an elite unit in the Algerian army. Those who claim to have known him at this time say that he gave no indications of any religious leanings.[39] Indeed, he was noted for his participation in drinking sessions with his comrades – hardly the sort of behaviour suggesting that he was about to desert and join the Islamists. But desert he reportedly did. In 1992 he left the Beni Messous barracks in Algiers for the *maquis*. During the following two years, however, he was reportedly seen on several occasions in the CPMI (Centre Principal Militaire d'Investigation) at Ben Aknoun (the headquarters of the DRS in Algiers) in the company of its boss, Col., later Gen., Bachir Tartague (alias Col. Athmane), who was soon to acquire a certain infamy for his proficiency in torture, and who came directly under the command of Gen. Smaïn Lamari.

In 1994 El Para, now with the rank of lieutenant, was reportedly sent on a three-year training course to Fort Bragg, home of America's Green Berets (Special Forces). On his return to Algeria in 1997, he was promoted to captain, and later in the year 'deserted' once again to rejoin the *maquis*.

This amendment to El Para's biography would explain why there was little or no trace of him for so many years. It also raises serious questions for both the Algerians and the Americans, should it be proved, implying that a highly-trained Algerian DRS agent, who was one of the American forces' own Green Berets, masqueraded as a top al-Qaeda terrorist to justify the extension of America's GWOT into Africa.

The senior military officers believed to be behind this affair are Gen. Mohamed Mediène ('Toufik'), head of the DRS, and his second-in-command, Gen. Smaïn Lamari, head of its counter-insurgency unit. They have long track-records of involvement in similar 'dirty tricks', going back as far as the assassination in 1992 of Algeria's president, Mohammed Boudiaf.[40] Since then, their names have been indelibly linked to almost all the 'dirty tricks' associated with the Algerian army's long war against the Islamists (outlined in Chapter 9). There is no doubt that these two men were intimately involved in both the hostage-taking of 2003 and the orchestration of the war on terror across the Sahara–Sahel since then. Both Gen. Mediène and Gen. Smaïn Lamari would almost certainly have been involved in El Para's secondment to Fort Bragg.[41] Which of them has been El Para's direct handler during the course of the hostage drama is conjectural, but it is most likely to have been Smaïn, who personally handled the debriefing of the first group of hostages released.

We are unlikely ever to know how far down the Algerian military – or perhaps more precisely the DRS – chain of command knowledge of El Para's role went. In time it will probably leak out, as these things are inclined to do; for the moment, we must rely largely on conjecture. Gen. Bachir Tartague, El Para's former minder at Ben Aknoun, would almost certainly have been in the picture. It is also likely that Gen. Kamel Abderrahmane – head of the second military region and in charge of media relations during the course of the hostage drama, who was a former colonel in the DRS and Tartague's immediate superior – would have known what was going on. Gen. Abderrahmane is also believed to have bought the *Quotidien d'Oran* newspaper through a front name, which explains why so many of the key pieces of disinformation have been run through it. It is also likely that Gen. Abdelmajid Sahab[42] – commander of the fourth military region, which extends from Ouargla to Djanet and incorporates the Illizi area and Tamelrik – was also aware of the situation. Why else would the military at Illizi have ignored the nomads' warnings of the kidnappers' preparations in Tamelrik (see Chapter 10)?

Some of my Algerian informants have suggested that a handful of foreign mercenaries associated with the DRS may also have been involved in the project. The names that have been suggested are all those of figures who worked for Executive Outcomes – a private company registered in the Isle of Man, but with 'head offices' in Pretoria, South Africa,[43] that was involved mostly in commercial–mercenary operations throughout much of Africa. Most of its personnel came out of the more unsavoury branches of the apartheid regime's defence forces, with skills in counter-espionage, torture, chemical warfare and similar areas of expertise. The company was already well-connected with the Algerian army, so that it was not surprising for many of its more 'talented' personnel to gravitate towards Algeria's DRS following its official closure in South Africa on 1 January 1999. After all, torture is torture, no matter at what end of the continent it is being practised. The names disclosed by the Mouvement Algérien des Officiers Libres[44] are Emanuel Damink, who was reported to be attached directly to Gen. Mediène; Stefan Desmond, who was reportedly close to Gen. Tartague; and Uri Barsony, a member of Israel's Shin Bet counter-espionage organisation, and reportedly a close friend of Gen. Fodil Cherif. All three excelled in the more reprehensible practices of South Africa's apartheid regime, and at the time of the hostage affair were reported to have been located in the Ben Aknoun barracks, where they were working in close association with the DRS.

Phantasmal Terrorists

Are all of Algeria's more infamous 'terrorists', such as Mokhtar ben Mokhtar, El Para, and many others who are not mentioned in this book, 'real people' or just fabricated identities? Do they actually exist, or are they merely phantoms created by Algeria's secret intelligence services to be reeled in and out as and when needed? I first came across this cynical notion of 'phantoms' during my initial investigations into Mokhtar ben Mokhtar. By the time El Para came on the scene, Mokhtar's death had already been reported in the Algerian media on at least six occasions. And yet he, or his identity, still has an uncanny knack of turning up in the most outlandish places, and at the most convenient times for Algeria's media–intelligence services. If El Para was a DRS agent, as is now widely believed, then we might expect the DRS to have used the same mechanism – namely his reported death – for reeling him in and out of the *maquis*. Lo and behold, a search through Algeria's media reveals that El Para had undergone at least two reincarnations prior to his involvement in the 2003 hostage-taking. On 18 February 2001, Agence France-Presse, citing Algerian press reports, stated that a leader of the GSPC, Abderrazak 'El Para', and four of his men had been killed at Maadid, 250km south-east of Algiers, as they headed for a GSPC meeting in the Bouira region. Less than three weeks later, according to the Arabic-language Algerian newspaper *El-Khabar*, El Para (spelled 'Bara') was again reported killed by the security services. On this occasion, the sources quoted by *El-Khabar* said that a large number of GSPC 'terrorists' had been trapped and surrounded by the security forces in an abandoned cave in the Boutaleb mountains, in the south of Setif province. The terrorists in the cave rejected the surrender offer, and the siege ended with the security forces blowing up the cave entrance. The sources quoted by *El-Khabar* stated that at least 50 terrorists, including Abderrazak Bara (Hattab's right-hand man) and eleven more commanding elements of the GSPC, would have been killed inside the cave – 'from which the smell of decomposed bodies was emanating...'[45]

Many other emblematic figures in Algeria's 'terrorist' leadership have received similar reincarnations. Nabil Sahraoui, the alleged GSPC *emir* until his death in June 2004, would have been one of the GIA elements who organised the famous escape of 1,200 prisoners from the Tazoult prison in March 1994, an operation which is known to have been arranged by the DRS both to eliminate certain Islamists and to infiltrate the underground.[46] According to the military communiqué reporting the *emir*'s death, several of his most important deputies would also have been killed with him.[47] Yet eight months later the Algerian press announced that one of these murdered lieutenants, Abdelmalek Droukdel, may have been designated to be Nabil Sahraoui's successor as head of the GSPC.[48] In May 2005, the same press once more announced Droukdel's death.[49] Soon after, he was resurrected at the head of the GSPC – a position which he still held at the end of 2008. As François Gèze and Salima Mellah recently commented:

> This media pantomime, designed solely to sustain confusion, reminds us of the cases of the GIA 'national emirs' Djamel Zitouni and Antar Zouabri, who were also killed several times and resurrected, according to 'security sources', and later discovered to be DRS agents.[50]

The reference to El Para's death in February 2001 is not quite the first media reference to him. That appears to have been on the *El-Khabar* website, in Arabic, on 3 June 2000. The article refers twice to 'the so-called Abderrazak El Bara' being in command of the GSPC's fifth region (eastern Algeria), and being responsible for a terrorist attack on a Tunisian border post.[51] The same story was syndicated to other newspapers and journals, being reported, for example, in *Africa News* four days latter, with reference again being made to the responsibility of Abderrazak El Para (now spelled with a P) for the attack.[52] June 2000 would have been at least two years after El Para's return from Fort Bragg – a reasonable time-span in which to reinsert him into the *maquis* and enable him to infiltrate the GSPC. With killings ascribed to terrorists in Algeria still running at around 2,500 per annum, an attack on a border post may have been conceived as a good way of winning press attention over and above that gained by the run-of-the-mill attacks within Algeria, which were now quite widespread and given little prominence in the press.

El Para's Communications

If, as seems certain, El Para was managing the hostage abduction on behalf of the DRS, he would have had to have a means of regular communication with his handlers, and also between the two teams of hostage-takers. Obviously, such information is not going to be forthcoming from his handlers. We are therefore dependent on the hostages' observations, which, fortunately, were acute in this regard. El Para and his group were equipped with both short-wave radio and Thuraya satellite phones. From the hostages' descriptions of the antennae, the kidnappers appear to have been using 40m short-wave Warsaw Pact radio equipment, probably manufactured in the former East Germany – an example of the Algerian army's outdated equipment.

The hostages soon realised that the two groups were unable to communicate with each other on the short-wave radios unless they were at least 300km apart. When both groups were to the east of Amguid, one in the Tamelrik area and the other around the southern end of Tifernine, they were unable to contact each other. It was for this reason that the Tifernine group worked its way progressively westwards, towards the Immidir Mountains to the west of Amguid and into the Gharis region. There, between 320km and 350km from the Tamelrik group, they found the best distance at which to communicate with each other. According to the hostages, the two groups communicated about three times a week. Not surprisingly, the hostages kept a close eye on their captors' use of their radios. To begin with, when the two groups were less than 200km apart, El Para would regularly take the radio onto relatively high ground, such as the dune summits in Tifernine, to communicate. But, as the hostages asked themselves, with whom was he communicating? They knew it could not have been the other group, as they were not far enough away. They realised it could only be his handlers.

Another interesting feature of El Para's use of the radio that the hostages noted was that he frequently used it, or fiddled with it, when the rest of the captors were at prayer. Indeed, the hostages noted that he was remarkably lax in his prayers – an observation that conformed with the lack of religiosity noted by his former army colleagues at the military school at Biskra.

If El Para was a genuine terrorist, we would expect him to have exercised considerable caution in ensuring that communications between the two groups could not be overheard. By the same token, if he was a DRS agent, he would not have needed to be so careful, although of course there was always the possibility of third parties – such as the Libyans, who were not so far away, or the western oil companies – picking up his frequency. Again, not surprisingly, the hostages cannot throw much light on the use of satellite phones, for the simple reason that they would probably not have seen their captors using them. However, the impression given by the hostages is that satellite phones were not used in the early stages of the drama. That is quite understandable, since all sorts of outside parties could have intercepted them. Later, they do not appear to have been so cautious in their use of satellite phones. To begin with, though, communication was by short-wave radio and in code.

It is almost certain that the Americans would have been able to intercept these communications through their use of AWACS, which the hostages frequently saw flying low overhead. Furthermore, in view of their close working relations with Algeria's intelligence services, it is conceivable that they would have had access to the codebook. Thus, if we assume for the moment that El Para was a genuine terrorist and not working with the DRS, it is almost certain that the Americans were intercepting his radio communications. However, the Tamelrik group lost its codebook; in spite of a massive hunt it was never found, obliging him to communicate in un-coded language. Again, it is inconceivable that the Americans would not have had access to translators. It is therefore fairly safe to assume that at all times, before and after the loss of the codebook, the Americans would have been fully conversant with the communications between the two hostage groups and between El Para and his handlers.

This also raises questions about the role of the German authorities in the affair. As mentioned in Chapter 4, the hostages released in August were debriefed by Germany's Bundeskriminalamt (BKA) Federal Criminal Investigation Bureau a week or so after their return home, during the course of which the BKA mentioned that they had been able to decipher the terrorists' code and had therefore been able to pinpoint their location continuously.[53] The BKA had also said this to the group that had been liberated in May. Why did the BKA mention this to the hostages? Was it to demonstrate how the BKA had been trying to help them? Or was it to impress the hostages with how smart their intelligence and code-breaking methods were?[54] Why did the BKA feel it necessary to mention the code when we know that the codebook was lost fairly early at the Tamelrik camp, and that radio communications were in plain language from that point onwards? Was it because the BKA was lying to the hostages? Could it be that it was not in fact listening in on the communications, did not know that the codebook was lost, and was merely accepting what it was being told by the Algerians? That is almost certainly how the Algerians would have tried to manage the situation, just as they stopped German drones flying over Tamelrik when the hostages were being moved out. If that was the case, then the BKA is guilty of serious dissemblement. If, on the other hand, the Germans were listening to the communications, whether coded or un-coded, they would surely have been aware of El Para's relationship with the DRS. This question goes beyond the scope of this book, but it relates to many other curious aspects of the behaviour of the German authorities during the course of this affair which in turn raise questions about their competence and/or complicity that still need to be investigated.

When I discussed the US interception of these communications with a senior Pentagon official in Washington, it was suggested to me that the US probably did not have translators, and that the AWACS team might simply have given the tapes to the Algerians. However, if El Para really was the terrorist that the Bush administration claimed him to be, it is inconceivable that the Americans would not have retained copies of the tapes and translated them. If, however, El Para was an agent for the DRS, and thus indirectly (and perhaps directly) for the Americans, then the main concern about communications security would have been to keep such an incriminating secret secure from any outside party – such as the Libyans, private security firms working for the foreign oil companies, and especially the intelligence services of the European countries involved. That, I believe, is the reason why Algeria closed its air space during much of March, April and May 2003 to all but Algeria's own aircraft and the US AWACS.[55]

In the Sahel, it seems that El Para's group was unconcerned about surveillance and used its satellite phones quite freely. It is perhaps significant that Gen. Mediène, boss of the DRS, was in possession of El Para's satellite phone number. In April, a few weeks after the beginning of El Para's alleged sojourn in Tibesti, three representatives of the Chadian rebels in France were discreetly invited to Algeria to meet with Mediène. Mohamed Mehdi, vice-chairman of the MDJT abroad, recounted the meeting to *Le Monde Diplomatique*:

> When we described the leader of the prisoners to him, he [Mediène] confirmed that it was Amari Saifi, alias Abderrazak El Para. The DRS officers were very well informed. They even pointed out a mistake in El Para's satellite phone number, which we had written down on a piece of paper. They had the real number. We dialled it together and El Para's phone, which had been recovered by our men, rang in Tibesti.[56]

This anecdotal account assumed that the phone in question really was El Para's. But there is also the question of whether the person presumed to be El Para at both Temet and in the Tibesti might have been an impersonator, perhaps Abdelhak Abou Ibrahim,[57] who reportedly bore a close resemblance to El Para. Nor is such a revelation that surprising, for if the DRS and US intelligence services were really hunting down a terrorist network in the Sahara, they might be expected to have intercepted their satellite phone communications, and thus be in possession of their phone numbers. But, by the same token, if El Para really were a seasoned terrorist, he would surely have taken more care to ensure that his number was not in the hands of his pursuers!

Most Algerians with whom I have discussed the 'El Para story' are aware of their army's proclivity for disinformation and 'dirty tricks', its infiltration of the Armed Islamic Groups and its creation of phantasmal bogeymen. Not surprisingly, they are highly sceptical about El Para's identity, and about whether there has even been such a person, other than as a construct of the military intelligence services. Indeed, one of the most extraordinary aspects of this entire story is that, although he was almost continuously in the headlines for the best part of three years, there were very few sightings of him. During the course of the hostage drama, he actually spent very little time in the company of the hostages. For example, after their first couple of weeks of capture he visited the Gharis group only twice, both times after dark.[58] During his time with this group, he remained distant from the hostages and always insisted on conversations in French being translated to him in Arabic, in spite of his seeming fluency in French.[59] As he was veiled or partly veiled for most of the time, it would be surprising if any of this group were able to identify him positively. Neither did he ever give his name to the hostages, being referred to always as *emir*.[60] Nor did he spend a great deal of time with the Tamelrik group. After spending a few days with them at the beginning of their capture, he disappeared until 19 May. During the intervening time, his men thought he was negotiating, which we now know not to have been the case. Similarly, while the Tamelrik group remained holed up after leaving Tamelrik in the Immidir/Iffetessen Mountains until 26 June, El Para was again away for most of that time, presumably arranging fuel dumps and other preparations for their ultimate release in Mali.

El Para's two visits to the Gharis group, as well as his other comings and goings, raise another very pertinent question. How was he able to drive between the two hostage locations, Gharis and Tamelrik, which were known to both the Algerians and Americans, when they were reportedly surrounded by some 5,000 troops, and when vehicle tracks not only last for a long time but can be identified and tracked with ease? The same question must be asked of his access to the later camp in the Mouydir/Iffetessen Mountains. There can be only two possible answers: either the DRS stood the army patrols down on the key routes on those nights, thus allowing him safe passage, or there were no army patrols in the area.[61] Following on from this question is another: If, as we now know, El Para spent so little time with his hostages, where did he spend his time? The answer must surely be: with his handlers in the DRS.

Since the release of the hostages in Mali in August 2003, there have been only three reported sightings of El Para. The first was in mid-December 2003, when a party of German tourists in Mali stumbled across a group of 'bandits' north-east of Timbuktu. They were later identified by the former hostages, who saw their photographs, as being some of the group that had abducted them earlier in the year. One of them was identified as El Para. The second sighting was at the Temet hold-up in Aïr on 24 February 2004. Once again, the hostages identified El Para in the tourists' photographs. The third sighting was in July–August 2004, when Patrick Forestier, a journalist from *Paris Match*, along with a photographer and cameraman,[62] entered Chad clandestinely, located the MDJT and undertook a photo-interview with El Para.[63] Once again, the hostages identified the photos as being of El Para. [64]

The fact that the hostages identified El Para from the photographs as being at all three locations (Timbuktu, Temet and Tibesti) raises a serious question, for the simple reason that we know from interviews with the local Tuareg who spoke with El Para's men at Temet that he was not with them, but waiting for them at Tabarakaten. We can only speculate as to whether El Para had an impersonator – perhaps Abdelhak Abou Ibrahim, or someone else – and whether Forestier's interview was actually with El Para or with someone else. We will almost certainly never know.

El Para was the key instrument in fabricating and justifying a new Saharan–Sahelian front in the GWOT. The biggest problem for his handlers, Algeria's DRS, was probably the concoction of a plausible exit strategy, or at least one that would provide America's military-intelligence services with a sufficient degree of credibility to enable them to stamp 'closure' on the issue for the world's media.

El Para's Extradition to Algeria and Trial

Good stories have a beginning, a middle and an end. In El Para's case, I have so far focused largely on the middle. That is because the beginning will be explained more fully in Chapters 9–11.[65] The end of the El Para story, especially when so much of it has been a fiction, requires a definitive closure: verifiable death in the course of action, or due legal process resulting, for those who still believe in 'an eye for eye', in public execution; or, for those less fundamentally inclined, in a lengthy prison sentence. In El Para's case, death in Chad might only have been acceptable if his body could have been publicly presented and identified – something that was probably impossible for the DRS to arrange. The alternative was therefore extradition and a judicial hearing, followed by either execution or long imprisonment. From a legal perspective, El Para could have faced a court trial in Germany, where the Karlsruhe public prosecutor had earlier issued a warrant for his arrest;[66] any one of the Sahelian countries (Mali, Niger, Chad) in which he had allegedly committed crimes; or Algeria, the country of his birth, and where he reputedly had to answer a number of terrorism charges.

A trial in Karlsruhe would have been highly embarrassing for Germany for a number of reasons. Not only would it have exposed Germany's payment of a ransom, which it has always denied; it would also have raised questions of its inept intelligence and possible collusion. All three countries – Austria, Germany and Switzerland – had very little intelligence on Algeria and its machinations, which is not surprising since Algeria is not within their rather limited spheres of influence and interest. However, in Germany's case there seems to have been a determination 'not to know'. For example, the best informed Germans on this affair were two German journalists whose insights and evidence have been persistently ignored by the German authorities. I myself made two approaches to the German Embassy in London,[67] requesting a meeting with the appropriate German authority in order to disclose key information on the hostage-taking.[68] The request was rejected. Several Germans with whom I have discussed this matter have proffered the view that the German authorities, especially the Foreign Ministry, preferred not to press the Algerian authorities, for fear of damaging the rapid growth of new German business in Algeria in the wake of Bouteflika's attempts to 'normalise' the country. Whether we are talking about collusion or incompetence[69] is something that only time may tell.[70]

A trial in Germany was therefore never really on the cards. Quite apart from the difficulties it would have caused to Germany, neither the US nor Algeria would have countenanced it: neither could have afforded the sort of revelations contained in this book being revealed in open court. Indeed, with the US publicly advocating that El Para face justice in Algeria, there was never much likelihood of Algeria losing control of the exit strategy.

On 27 October 2004, seven months after his alleged arrival in Chad, the Algerian press reported that El Para had been returned to Algeria,[71] thanks to the good offices of the Libyans. How El Para reached Algeria from Chad, via Libya, is not at all clear. Accounts in the Algerian press were brief and low-key. Nor did the Algerian media show much further interest in El Para, other than in a few brief articles questioning whether he would appear before a civil or military tribunal. The US State Department's response was also low-key. The Department's Daily Press Briefing,[72] with spokesman Richard Boucher, reads as follows:

Q: All right. Do you have anything about the extradition by Libya to Algeria of this guy who is –

Mr B: Mr Al Para?

Q: Yeah, the kidnapper.

Mr B: Yeah.

Q: Or alleged kidnapper.

Mr B: Well, we welcome the news that the Algerian authorities now have custody of the wanted terrorist, Abderrezak Al Para. The pursuit of Al Para took place across North Africa for many months, and his capture and return to Algeria to face justice for his crimes demonstrates the commitment of several countries in the region to work together to fight terrorism. That's our guidance.

Q: That's it?

Mr B: That's it.

However, for those analysts who had been following El Para's case, his alleged extradition from Chad brought the question of his identity, even of his existence, into even sharper focus. Since his reported return to Algerian custody, he has never been seen in public. Nor were the Algerian authorities prepared to divulge where he was being held. Finally, on 25 June 2005, eight months after his return, he was convicted of 'creating an armed terrorist group and spreading terror among the population' and sentenced in absentia to life imprisonment. The trial was notable for its brevity, and for El Para's absence.[73] Local media questions about El Para's whereabouts were brushed off by 'security experts' explaining that the authorities were reluctant to bring him to court as he was linked to so many terrorism cases, and believed to hold 'national security–sensitive information'. The media were also told that El Para was in custody at an undisclosed location, and under interrogation for several other terrorism-related charges that were being prepared against him, including kidnappings and numerous killings of soldiers and civilians spanning more than a decade. The court's vapid justification for trying him in absentia was that 'the case was brought to court before his extradition to Algeria last October'.[74] While the authorities explained that he was in custody at an undisclosed location and under interrogation for other terrorism charges, the presiding judge made the most revealing comment of the entire trial, namely: 'For us there are no indications that he is under arrest'![75]

Irrespective of what other cases may be prepared against El Para, it is unlikely that he will ever make an appearance in court. That is not because he has already been sentenced to life imprisonment, nor because of the precedent that has been set for sentencing in absentia, but because he really does hold 'national security–sensitive information' that could never be revealed in court.[76]

The Last Word on El Para?

When will we be able to write the last word on El Para? In December 2005, the German newspaper *Muenchner Merkur* wrote: "If US armed forces are correct, Berlin paid five million Euros for the release of the German Sahara hostages in 2003. Today, the kidnapper Ammari Saifi is regarded as one of the richest businessmen in North Africa."[77] When I tried to follow up on the *Muenchner Merkur* report, I heard in the Algiers rumour-mill that El Para had become the adviser to those directing the activities of the US forces in the Sahara. A parody of the truth? Quite possibly. What is certain is that El Para, in the space of 12 months, has done more than anyone to secure the Bush admin-istration's imperialist designs in Africa.

But that is by no means the end of the El Para story. On 11 April 2007 two massive suicide car bombs exploded in Algiers, killing 33 people and wounding many others. The attack was attributed to Al-Qaeda in the Islamic Maghreb (AQIM), the new name for the GSPC. Shortly after the attack, it was reported that the bombs had been detonated externally and not by the vehicle drivers themselves, leading to widespread speculation as to whether the attack was the work of elements within Algeria's security services.[78] The names of the three bombers were also released. One, Abou Doudjana, was with El Para in the Sahel.[79]

In February 2008, two Austrian tourists were kidnapped in Tunisia and taken to Mali (where they were released on 30 October 2008). El Para's name has been associated with the kidnapping, and at least two of his accomplices from 2003/04 have been identified as the abductors.[80]

Thus, apart from El Para, we know for certain that at least three of his accomplices returned safely to Algeria.

7
OIL AND EMPIRE*

What were the US imperialist designs on Africa that El Para did so much to secure? The answer, which US government officials are becoming increasingly less coy in admitting, was oil: oil and empire.

There are two statistics which almost anyone who knows anything about oil will recognise: they are that the US has only 5 per cent of the world's population but consumes 25 per cent of its oil. As President George W. Bush reminded his countrymen in his 2006 State of the Union address, '[W]e have a serious problem: America is addicted to oil, which is often imported from unstable parts of the world.'[1]

America's Energy Crisis

America's dependency on imported energy is not breaking news. As long ago as World War II, when the US was the world's leading oil producer,[2] President Roosevelt feared that the accelerated wartime production would precipitate the exhaustion of America's own reserves and hasten reliance on imported supplies – a situation which he realised would have serious implications for America's long-term security.[3] Successive US administrations since Roosevelt have consequently tended to view foreign oil from a national-security perspective. Both Presidents Truman and Eisenhower regarded the protection of the Persian Gulf as a key element in Cold War strategy. In 1963, President Kennedy built on the precedents of the Truman and Eisenhower Doctrines when he

---

* A longer version of this chapter, containing more detail and notes, has been placed on the publisher's website (www.plutobooks.com/), and can be downloaded free of charge.

sent US war planes to the region when Yemeni forces, attached to President Nasser of Egypt, attacked Saudi Arabia.[4] In 1963, US dependency on foreign oil supplies was still relatively modest, being only 20 per cent of consumption. But it was to grow quickly – to 30 per cent in the early 1970s, 40 per cent by the mid-1970s, and to the psychologically critical 50 per cent in 1998.

As this dependency has increased, so US policy on securing the vital supply of Gulf oil has hardened. Prior to the Iranian Revolution and Russia's invasion of Afghanistan, US policy in the Gulf involved little more than supporting and looking after the interests of the Shah of Persia and the Saudi Royal Family. This was seen most spectacularly in the 1970s, when President Nixon transferred billions of dollars to both regimes in the form of a panoply of military equipment and support, including fighter aircraft.[5] In the context of the Gulf, Nixon told Congress: 'We shall furnish military and economic assistance when requested, but we shall look to the nation directly threatened to assume the primary responsibility of providing the manpower for its defence.'[6] US policy towards the Gulf region received a rude wake-up call with the almost simultaneous events of the Iranian Revolution and Russia's invasion of Afghanistan. Both posed major threats to US national security interests. The US response was almost immediate, President Jimmy Carter telling Congress on 23 January 1980, in an expression of what has since become known as the 'Carter Doctrine', that the secure flow of Persian Gulf oil was a 'vital interest' of the US, and that Washington would use 'any means necessary, including military force' to keep the oil flowing. As the US had few forces in the Gulf at that time, President Carter established the Rapid Deployment Joint Task Force (RDJTF) at MacDill Air Force base near Tampa, Florida, and gave it responsibility for combat operations in the Gulf. Three years later, in 1983, President Reagan elevated the RDJTF and renamed it the 'Central Command' (because it was in the 'central region' between Asia and Europe). Prior to George W. Bush's policy of pre-emption, the Carter Doctrine was the bedrock of US policy in the Gulf Region.

For many years, successive US administrations have been aware of the country's growing imbalance between energy supply and demand, and the critical importance of foreign oil supplies, especially from the Persian Gulf. Although the breach of the 50 per cent dependency level in 1998 went some way to drawing attention to the impending dangers facing America as it lurched, like a drunkard, towards an ever more serious energy crisis, its gas-guzzling lifestyle caused little soul-searching. And as far as the country's policy-makers were concerned, the answer still lay in the same old recipe mix: the Persian Gulf and military force. Indeed, the high-level task force established in 2000 by the Centre for Strategic and International Studies, headed by former Secretary of Defense James Schlesinger and former Senator Sam Nunn, placed special emphasis on the need to use force to ensure 'open access' to the Persian Gulf.[7]

The threat of America's oil dependency to national security became an election issue for the first time in 2000, as George W. Bush, himself an oil-man, pledged to make energy security a top priority. Within two weeks of taking office, he established a National Energy Policy Development (NEPD) group under the Chairmanship of his Vice-President and former Halliburton CEO Dick Cheney.

The Cheney Report

The group's report, known as the Cheney Report,[8] was presented in May 2001, less than four months before the 9/11 terrorist attacks. Its findings were stark: between 1991 and 2000, Americans had used 17 per cent more energy than in the previous decade, while domestic energy production had risen by only 2.3 per cent. It projected that US energy consumption over the next twenty years (2000–2020) would increase by about 32 per cent, with the domestic oil share remaining at around 40 per cent.[9] In 2000 that share represented an average of 19.5 million barrels per day (mb/d), more than a quarter of the world's total consumption. Thus, although the share of oil in total energy consumption might remain the same, the absolute amount of oil being consumed would rise by 33 per cent by 2020.[10]

These figures would not be so critical if domestic oil production were on the rise. But that has not been the case for over 30 years: domestic production peaked in the early 1970s, at 11.3mb/d and has been declining ever since, standing at 5.7mb/d in 2003, with the result that US dependence on oil imports has grown sharply from about 4.3mb/d in 1985 to 10mb/d in 2000.[11] In spite of technological advances transforming exploration and production, the US produced 39 per cent less oil in 2000 than in 1970.[12]

The picture for natural gas is similar. While consumption of natural gas, which grew from 16.2 trillion cubic feet (tcf) in 1986 to 23.2tcf in 2000, before easing to 21.95tcf in 2003, is projected to rise to 30.9tcf in 2025 (an increase of just over 40 per cent), domestic production is forecast to increase from 19.13tcf in 2003 to just 22.19tcf in 2025 (an increase of only 16 per cent). Between 2003 and 2025, the shortfall between domestic production and consumption will therefore increase from 2.9tcf to 10.2tcf, requiring an increase in net imports from 3.24tcf in 2003 to 8.60tcf in 2025. In 2003 almost all of the US's natural gas imports (3.1tcf out of a total of 3.5tcf) came from Canada. The small balance of 0.4tcf was in the form of liquefied natural gas (LNG).[13] By 2025, Canadian imports are forecast to have fallen to 2.6tcf, from 3.1tcf in 2003, which means that the US will have to import some 6.0tcf – roughly 20 per cent of its consumption – from elsewhere. It is forecast that this gap will be filled by imported LNG. Although the report of the Energy Information Administration (EIA) makes no reference to the source of the LNG imported in 2003, nor to that of the huge amount required by 2025, much of it will be sourced from Africa – especially Algeria and Nigeria.

The main conclusion of the Cheney Report was that US oil consumption would grow by more than 6.0mb/d between 2000 and 2020. At the same time, if US oil production follows the same historical pattern of the last ten years, it will decline by 1.5mb/d. In other words, by 2020 domestic oil production would be supplying less than 30 per cent of US oil needs. Thus, to meet

US oil demand, oil and product imports would have to grow by a combined 7.5mb/d, from around 10mb/d in 2000 to some 17.7mb/d in 2020. That means that US imports, already at over 50 per cent of US consumption (58 per cent in 2004), would increase by more than another 50 per cent by 2020, with the result that the US would be importing nearly two of every three barrels of oil that it used.[14]

Critics of the Bush administration and the Cheney Report have argued that the Report was written by the oil industry for its own benefit. To some extent, that was true.[15] Nevertheless, its statistics and findings were laid out for the nation to read. The fact that they did not make a greater impact on the national psyche was partly because many Americans were aware that the primary agenda of the Bush–Cheney regime was to serve the interests of the US oil industry and its associated military–industrial complex, and partly because debate over the Cheney Report was overtaken by the events of 9/11. However, for the Bush administration, and especially the neo-conservatives who dominated it, the Cheney Report justified the urgency and provided the legitimacy for much of the subsequent US foreign policy associated with the neocon global agenda that has evolved since 1997 through its 'Project for the New American Century' (PNAC).[16] As I will show presently, aside from Iraq, this has been nowhere more apparent than in Africa.

The Cheney Report enabled Bush to beat the neocon drum. On the publication day of the Cheney Report,[17] he highlighted the threat posed to the country's security by its increasing oil dependency: 'If we fail to act, our country will become more reliant on foreign crude oil, putting our national energy security into the hands of foreign nations, some of whom do not share our interests.'[18]

With no simple fixes available on the domestic front, Cheney looked around the globe. His report concluded that the only way to satisfy the growing demand of American consumers and producers for energy was to ensure that the US had reliable access to increasing quantities of oil and natural gas from foreign sources. Like the domestic front, however, the global front also offered no simple fixes. The world oil scene, especially when viewed from an American perspective, was becoming increasingly problematic.

The Bush administration's major concern on taking office in 2000 was the 'policy challenge' posed by the 'concentration of world oil production in any one region of the world'.[19] The 'any one region' was, of course, the Middle East, and more specifically the Persian Gulf countries of Saudi Arabia, Iraq, the United Arab Emirates, Kuwait and Iran – which together produce close to 30 per cent of global output and, more significantly, contain nearly two-thirds of the world's proven reserves.[20] Compounding the problem of geographical concentration is the fact that this region is one of high political risk. The Persian Gulf has long been an area of turbulence, seeing wars that have periodically interrupted oil exports. The longstanding US concern about the security of oil supplies from the region has been heightened since George W. Bush came to office by the events of 11 September 2001, the associated threat of political upheaval in Saudi Arabia, and the US invasion of Iraq in March 2003.

Until recently it has been widely believed that Saudi Arabia is the one country which can, if necessary, increase production to meet the US shortfall, or to compensate for any cut-offs in supplies from other major producers of the kind that occurred in 1990, when Iraq invaded Kuwait. However, whether the Persian Gulf producers are capable of meeting the projected increased demand from the US and the rest of the world is now looking increasingly doubtful.[21] Meeting that demand over the next two decades would require a doubling of the region's output from just over 22mb/d to just over 45mb/d,[22] with the Saudi contribution requiring an increase in output from 11.4mb/d to 23.1mb/d.[23] While Saudi Arabia might have sufficient reserves, it almost certainly does not have the capacity to make the necessary infrastructural improvements that would be required to facilitate such an increase in production without massive foreign financial assistance – something which the Saudi leadership would be loath to incur. Analysts are also casting doubt on whether the Saudis can increase their production significantly. An article in the *New York Times* in early 2004 raised a number of concerns over the state of Saudi oil fields, and whether they could lift production much above 12mb/d. Even this figure could, in the opinion of one Saudi Aramco official, 'wreak havoc within a decade', by causing damage to the oil fields.[24] Some analysts are questioning whether some of Saudi Arabia's big fields have not already been pushed too hard, thus accelerating their depletion and bringing nearer the point when their production drops dramatically. Some of the biggest fields, such as Ghawar, are already becoming very costly to maintain, and are now running at an average decline rate of 8 per cent per year.[25]

Irrespective of what the oil industry and the politicians may tell us publicly, they know that the amount of oil remaining in the world is both unknowable and finite. Even if reserves are still plentiful, they know that the recent trend of production capacity growing more slowly than demand is almost certainly irreversible, and is something that the world – and most of all America, the world's greatest consumer of oil – will have to live with.

The Importance of African Oil to the US

As far as the Bush administration was concerned, the solution to meeting the country's long-range energy needs, as Energy Secretary Spencer Abraham told the House International Relations Committee on 20 June 2002, was to 'maintain a diversity of fuels from a multiplicity of sources'.[26] In particular, he meant actively encouraging and facilitating greater oil production in diverse parts of the world, such as the Caspian Sea region, Latin America, and especially Africa.

Dick Cheney, thanks largely to his experience as CEO of Halliburton, had had his eye on Africa for some time and, not surprisingly, it was singled out in his Report. Sub-Saharan Africa was a region which, as US Deputy Assistant Secretary of Defense for African Affairs Michael A. Westphal highlighted in June 2002, was already supplying 14 per cent of US oil imports,[27] and, more importantly, had the potential for increasing that amount substantially over the next decade. The following month, US Assistant Secretary of State for Africa Walter Kansteiner, while visiting Nigeria, declared that 'African oil is of strategic national interest to us' and that 'it will increase and become very important as we go forward'.[28]

Kansteiner's visit to Nigeria reflected the African country's increasingly important position in the US's future security plans. Nigeria is Africa's[29] largest oil producer and the fifth-largest source of US-imported oil. At the time of the publication of the Cheney Report, the US was already Nigeria's largest customer for crude oil, accounting for 40 per cent of Nigeria's oil exports, amounting to 900,000mb/d out of 2.1mb/d – and, as the Cheney Report noted, Nigeria 'has set ambitious production goals as high as 5mb/d over the coming decade'.[30] The Cheney Report envisaged US investments of US$10 billion in Nigeria, rising substantially over the current decade in line with increasing exploration both offshore and in the interior, and an anticipated increase in the country's established reserves, which stood at 22.5 billion barrels. These increased investments have paid off: by the end of 2006, Nigeria's proven reserves had already increased to 36.2 billion barrels, 60 per cent up on the beginning of the decade. Particularly important as far as the US is concerned is that roughly two thirds of Nigerian oil is 'light' and 'sweet'[31] – the right type of crude for the US market.

African oil, however, is not limited to Nigeria. Other sub-Saharan African countries on which the Bush administration was fixing its sights in 2001 were Angola, Gabon, Congo-Brazzaville, Chad and Equatorial Guinea, and especially the offshore deposits in the Gulf of Guinea between Nigeria and São Tomé and Principe.

At the time of the Cheney Report,[32] Angola was the second-largest sub-Saharan African producer, and already the ninth-largest supplier of oil to the US. Between 2001 and 2006 Angola's reserves rose from 5.7 to 9.0 billion barrels. During the same period, oil production, which is located mostly in the enclave of Cabinda, increased from around 0.75mb/d to 1.41mb/d, of which some 40 per cent or more was exported to the US. Production is set to increase to 2.1mb/d by 2010 and to 3.3mb/d by 2020.[33]

Gabon is the third-largest oil producer in sub-Saharan Africa. With reserves approaching 2.5 billion barrels, current production is running at 232,000 barrels per day (bpd), down slightly from the 301,000bpd of 2001. Almost half Gabon's crude is exported to the US.[34] Gabon is particularly attractive to the US in that it left OPEC in 1996, and is therefore not subject to quota restrictions, while its oil, like most West African crudes, is mostly 'light' and 'sweet'.

In 2001 Congo–Brazzaville was sub-Saharan Africa's fourth-largest oil producer, with production of 231,000bpd and proven reserves of 1.5 billion barrels, but has now overtaken Gabon, with production at 262,000bpd and proven reserves at 1.9 billion barrels. Although most of its output goes to Europe, exports to the US are around 40,000bpd. As in Gabon, its crudes are generally 'medium-to-light' and 'sweet'.[35]

Chad has proven reserves of around 1 billion barrels in its southern Doba field, which came on line in 2003, 14 months ahead of schedule, following a US$4.2 billion investment by a consortium led by ExxonMobil and ChevronTexaco, and including the World Bank. Production of around 225,000bpd is exported via a 1,070km pipeline across Cameroon to an offshore terminal at Kribi.[36]

Equatorial Guinea, whose proven reserves (mostly offshore) have tripled from 0.6 billion barrels in 1996 to 1.8 billion barrels in 2006, has also become a major exporter. Production has risen from 173,000bpd in 2001 to 358,000bpd in 2006, of which some two-thirds is exported to the US.[37]

Both the Democratic Republic of Congo (DRC) and Cameroon produce small amounts of oil. In Cameroon's case, production is 60,000–70,000 bpd, with comparatively small reserves of 200,000 million barrels. The DRC, with production of only 24,000bpd, has proven reserves of just over 1.5 billion barrels.

It has been widely believed over the last few years that the biggest oil strikes in the region are likely to be made in the offshore waters of the Gulf of Guinea, off the coasts of Equatorial Guinea and Nigeria, and especially in the continental shelf deposits to the north of São Tomé and Principe, whose reserves have been estimated as being in the region of 8–24 billion barrels, and possibly more. However, while the coastal waters off both Nigeria and Equatorial Guinea hold substantial reserves, no oil has yet been found off São Tomé and Principe, and recent reports suggest that the predictions of vast oil finds there may be part of an elaborate hoax.[38]

While Nigeria is the jewel in the West African crown, the whole of that crown, from Washington's perspective, is shining increasingly brightly: between 2000 and 2006, proven oil reserves have grown by 46 per cent, and production increased by 34 per cent. Proven reserves of 51.9 billion barrels and production of 4.94mb/d[39] may not seem huge by Persian Gulf standards, but they are becoming of critical strategic importance to the US. Not only are many of its streams the lighter, higher-valued crude that are a ready substitute for Middle East oil supplies, but they have the additional advantage of being geographically close to the markets of the US east coast, and its main Very Large Crude Carrier terminal, the Louisiana Offshore Oil Port. If that was not enough, West Africa, at least at the time of the Cheney Report, was seen as a region of comparatively low political risk. US agencies and think tanks, including the CIA, project that one in every five new barrels of oil entering the global economy in the latter half of this decade will come from the Gulf of Guinea, which by 2015 will be providing America with 25 per cent of its imported oil.[40]

The Cheney Report focused attention predominantly on sub-Saharan Africa. But when the North African countries of Algeria and Libya are included, Africa as a whole assumes an even greater importance in America's national security considerations. At the time President Reagan imposed an import ban on Libya in 1982,[41] Libyan oil production had been as high as 3.3mb/d, with 700,000bpd being exported to the US.[42] By the time President Bush lifted sanctions in early 2004, for reasons which had much to do with America's need for oil and – as in Iraq – very little to do with weapons of mass destruction, Libya's fields had fallen into such disrepair that output had dropped to around 1.5mb/d.[43] Exports recommenced in April 2004, initially at around 33,000bpd, but with the pick-up in production reaching 1.83mb/d by the end of 2006. This suggests that the production target of 2.0mb/d by

2010 may well be doubled, if US and other foreign companies make sufficient investments and new discoveries are made. With Col. Gaddafi short of cash and the US short of oil, oil activity is picking up at a rapid pace.[44]

Libya holds a number of crucially important advantages as far as the US is concerned. Firstly, its potential reserves are massive – possibly larger than any country other than Saudi Arabia.[45] In 2007, proven reserves were put at 41.5 billion barrels, which amounts to 3.5 per cent of the world's proven reserves. Secondly, most of Libya's oil is of the highest low-density–low-sulphur quality, making it ideal for the US market.[46] It is also extremely low-cost to lift, and easily transported to the US.

In this overview of Africa's strategic importance to the US, I have rather glossed over Algeria. That is because Algeria is more than just a major player in the world's hydrocarbons markets, being the world's thirteenth-largest oil producer (producing 2.01mb/d) and sixth-largest gas producer (84.5 billion cubic metres per annum);[47] in 2003 it became the Bush administration's 'partner in crime' in fabricating the Sahara–Sahelian front in America's controversial war on terror – a role that will be discussed in more detail in succeeding chapters, and in *The Dying Sahara*.

Africa's strategic importance to the US is accelerating. In 2005, Richard Haass, president of the Council on Foreign Relations, predicted that '[b]y the end of the decade sub-Saharan Africa[48] is likely to become as important a source of US energy imports as the Middle East'.[49] In 2006, 22 per cent of US crude oil imports came from Africa, compared to only 15 per cent in 2004 – a rate which now slightly exceeds US imports from Kuwait and Saudi Arabia. In 2007, the Heritage Foundation confirmed this trend, reporting that 'currently, over 18 percent of US crude oil imports comes from Africa, compared to 17 percent from the Persian Gulf'.[50] Incredible as it may seem, Nigeria overtook Saudi Arabia in March 2007 as the third-largest oil exporter to the US.

Since the publication of the Cheney Report in 2001, US oil imports from Africa have nearly doubled. Indeed, some estimates now claim that African oil imports will account for 35 per cent of total US imports by 2015 – substantially more than the National

Intelligence Council's 2004 estimate of 25 per cent.[51] Analysts such as John Daly, for ISN Security Watch, believe this figure is quite conceivable when it is appreciated that African oil production climbed from 7.0mb/d to 9.5mb/d between 2004 and 2007, and that the US Department of Energy estimates that African oil production will rise by 91 per cent between 2002 and 2025.[52]

It was the recognition of this potential increase in African oil supplies to the US during the first years of this, the 'New American Century', that led the Bush administration, shortly after coming to power, to define African oil as a 'strategic national interest', and thus a resource that the US might choose military force to control.[53] It was the main reason – so US Deputy Assistant Secretary of Defense for African Affairs, Michael Westphal, explained in a Pentagon press briefing in early 2002 – that Africa matters to the US, and why 'we do follow it very carefully' at the Pentagon.[54] It is the reason why the chairman of the US Congress African sub-committee, the influential Republican senator from California, Ed Royce, called in early 2002 for African oil to 'be treated as a priority for US national security post 9/11'.[55] It is also the reason, five years later, following the announcement of a new, dedicated US military command for Africa (AFRICOM), why US European Command (USEUCOM) commander General Bantz Craddock told journalists in Washington, '[When] you look at West Africa and the Gulf of Guinea, it becomes more focused because of the energy situation', with the result that protecting energy assets 'obviously is out in front'.[56] And if we still have any doubts that the current US militarisation of Africa is not primarily about oil, Ryan Henry, the Principal Deputy Under Secretary of Defense for Policy, reassured journalists at a Foreign Press Centre briefing in Washington on June 2007 that the new US African Command 'is about resources, specifically oil, specifically the oil in the Gulf of Guinea and that's what this command is about'.

While the main reason why Africa has become so strategically important to the US is oil, US policy towards Africa cannot be reduced to, or explained solely by, America's increasingly serious energy crisis. Africa has much else to offer the US. For instance, besides oil, the US is dependent on Africa for many other raw materials such as manganese (for steel production), cobalt and chrome (both vital for alloys, especially in aeronautics), vanadium, metals in the platinum group, antimony, gold, fluorspar, germanium, industrial diamonds, and many other lesser-known materials such as columbite-tantalite (coltan, for short), a key component in everything from mobile phones and computer chips to stereos and VCRs.

Another important but often overlooked factor in the current US administration's policies towards Africa is the pressure within the Republican Party from the religious right, which, in its own fundamentally extremist way, sees Africa as the battleground for its brand of Christianity against Islam.

Africa has also become the scene for a few uniquely American turf wars. The most apparent during the Bush–Cheney years have been those between elements within the State and Defense Departments, and between the many intelligence agencies, the White House and the National Security Council. However, as far as Africa is concerned, the most significant of these has possibly been the determination of USEUCOM to carve out a new role for itself and its commanders in the wake of the ending of the Cold War. With its main arena of operations, the former Soviet Union, drastically reduced, USEUCOM has been switching its focus of activity increasingly to Africa. Indeed, by 2006, USEUCOM was devoting 70 per cent of its time to African affairs, up from almost nothing as recently as 2003.[57] This redirection of USEUCOM's energy towards Africa is associated with the emergence of the new US operational military command for Africa (AFRICOM), which was authorised by President Bush on 18 December 2006, and which became a new, independent, fully autonomous command on 1 October 2008.[58] Without El Para and such gung-ho commanders as General Charles Wald (now retired), who used El Para's activities in the Sahel to exaggerate greatly the terrorist threat in Africa, it is most unlikely that the promotion of AFRICOM would have got beyond first base.

And, of course, there is China. When the neocons envisaged their 'New American Century', they viewed Third World nations as 'strategic assets' within a larger global geopolitical struggle. The

White House's 'National Security Strategy of the United States' of 2002 declared that 'combating global terror' and ensuring US energy security required that the US increase its commitments to Africa, and called upon 'coalitions of the willing' to generate regional security arrangements on that continent.[59] That was in 2002, just before El Para came on the scene, and when the US was considering ways in which to carry its war on terror – the vehicle for its imperial expansion – into Africa. At that time, China was still relatively low on the US radar, with few in the US considering it a major threat to Western imperialist control of Africa. That is no longer the case. Since before the start of the 'New American Century', China, as the *Wall Street Journal* noted in 2006,

> has made Africa a front line in its pursuit of more global influence, tripling trade with the continent to some $37 billion over the last five years and locking up energy assets, closing trade deals ... and educating Africa's future elites at Chinese universities and military schools.[60]

By 2006, the Council on Foreign Relations was also depicting the leading threat as coming from China:

> China has altered the strategic context in Africa. All across Africa today, China is acquiring control of natural resource assets, outbidding Western contractors on major infrastructure projects, and providing soft loans and other incentives to bolster its competitive advantage.[61]

As a key *Monthly Review* commentary noted in 2006,

> China imports more than a quarter of its oil from Africa, primarily Angola, Sudan, and Congo. It is Sudan's largest foreign investor. It has provided heavy subsidies to Nigeria to increase its influence and has been selling fighter jets there. Most threatening from the standpoint of US grand strategists is China's $2 billion low-interest loan to Angola in 2004, which has allowed Angola to withstand IMF demands to reshape its economy and society along neoliberal lines.[62]

For the Council on Foreign Relations, China's incursions into Africa are a threat to Western imperialist control of that continent. As its report states, the United States and Europe cannot consider Africa their *chasse gardé* [private hunting ground], as the French once saw francophone Africa. The rules are changing as China seeks not only to gain access to resources, but also to control resource production and distribution, perhaps positioning itself for priority access as these resources become scarcer.[63]

The US's 'total militarisation' of Africa is epitomised by AFRICOM,[64] the new US military command structure that was unveiled on 6 February 2007 and became an operational military command on 1 October 2008. Its primary function, notwithstanding all the rhetoric about bringing development and other such good things to Africa, is to secure US 'national security interests': Africa's oil. George W. Bush, like all his predecessors, showed no originality in his response to the Cheney Report: he turned, as Michael Klare commented, to the US military 'to provide insurance against the hazards associated with dependency'.[65] His administration simply designated African oil a 'strategic national interest', and thus a resource that the US might choose to use military force to control.[66] But the process of US militarisation of Africa has taken on changing and increasingly complex dimensions over the last five years. From securing African oil, AFRICOM, as the Council on Foreign Relations urged, is now also about combating China's designs on Africa through the expansion of US military operations in the region.

Militarising an entire continent is not easy, especially if you are not much loved or welcomed. The US has therefore desperately sought ideological justification for its militarisation – or 'invasion', as many local people have called call it – of Africa. The Bush administration has sought ideological legitimacy to secure what it refers to ominously as its 'national strategic interests', or, in Noam Chomsky's terms, its imperial grand strategy[67] in Africa, by invoking the GWOT. That, however, has not been easy, for the simple reason that Africa – despite pockets of terrorist activity in the Maghreb,[68] especially Algeria, and the 1998 US embassy bombings in Dar es Salaam and Nairobi – has been relatively free of terrorism. How do you make war on terror where none exists? This is where El Para was such a godsend to the Americans. His role in the fabrication of GSPC terrorism in the Sahara and Sahel during 2003/04 enabled the US to open a second,[69] Saharan–Sahelian front in the war on terror, which, in turn, created the ideological conditions for the US militarisation of Africa.[70]

8

ALGERIA'S 'BLACK DECADE'*

While America's strategic interests in Africa can be explained primarily in terms of its need to secure oil resources, Algeria's reasons for its post-9/11 involvements with the US are rooted in the inordinately complex and murky politics and violence of what is often referred to somewhat euphemistically as Algeria's 'failed democratic transition'.

Algeria's tortured history is punctuated by two huge human tragedies: its eight years of brutal war with France (1954–62), through which it gained its independence, but at the cost of at least one million dead; and the equally long and perhaps even more ruthless violence of the 1990s, during which as many as 200,000 Algerians are now estimated to have been killed. Algeria's needs at the time of 9/11 can only be understood in the context of this second violence, from which it was just beginning to emerge.

However, for those readers who do not know Algeria well, the violence of the 1990s becomes even more incomprehensible without an understanding of the 'crises' of the decade which preceded it. That presents both me, as the writer, and those readers unfamiliar with Algeria with a problem, for the simple reason that this book is not intended to be either a history or analysis of Algeria. And yet, an understanding of what Algeria

---

* Full-length versions of this chapter and Chapter 9, on the violence of the 1990s, have been placed on the publisher's website (www.plutobooks.com/) and can be downloaded, free of charge. This summary version provides a quick glimpse into the roots of the political, economic, social and religious forces at play in contemporary Algeria, notably the crisis that exploded into violent street-fighting in October 1988 and the rise of the Islamic fundamentalism, in the form of the Front Islamique de Salut (FIS), which led almost inexorably, in January 1992, to a *coup d'état* and the onset of a ruthless and bloody struggle, ostensibly between Islamists and the state. It is the aftershocks of this struggle, still traumatising the country, which explain why Algeria has come to play such a duplicitous role in America's GWOT.

has experienced in the last two decades is essential if we are to make sense of the country's singular post-9/11 relationship with the US.

The Economic Crisis of the Mid 1980s

The crisis that overwhelmed Algeria in 1988 was fundamentally economic, but it had profound social and political consequences.

In late 1978, Algeria's president, Colonel Houari Boumédiène, died unexpectedly, and without a designated successor, from a rare kidney disease. Following the army's 'recommendation', the national congress of the country's single legal political party, the Front de Libération Nationale (FLN), named Colonel Chadli Benjedid as secretary-general of the party and its candidate for president in January 1979. He was duly confirmed as president in a national election one week later.

Boumédiène's socialist economic policy had focused almost entirely on channelling the country's substantial rents from the hydrocarbon sector into inefficient and over-sized, state-controlled industrial complexes. Chadli's presidency, at least in its first term, was a period of 'de-Boumédiènisation'. While cautiously consolidating his power and gradually taking full control of the state, the party and the military apparatus, he also took advantage of the high oil price to introduce tentative steps towards economic liberalisation and the beginnings of a free market, with his first moves being to prioritise agriculture, which had been largely ignored by Boumédiène, as well as light industry and social infrastructure. He also sought to increase the productivity and efficiency of the big state industrial sectors by restructuring them into smaller subsidiaries and more manageable regional entities.

Following his re-election in 1984, Chadli took his economic liberalisation policies further – freeing more state enterprises from socialist central planning, reducing subsidies, lifting price controls and reducing the fiscal deficit by cutting government expenditure. These reforms, combined with his opening of the economy to limited foreign investment, his strategic reorientation of the country away from the Soviet Union, and his lowering of the country's profile as a revolutionary state and champion of the Third World, endeared him more than his predecessors to the US, and in 1985 he made the first visit by an Algerian head of state to Washington. On the home front, however, the Chadli era was soon to become known as *la décennie noire* (the black decade), as social unrest, stemming from these hesitant steps towards economic liberalisation, became increasingly more frequent and violent from 1985 onwards.[1]

Algeria is a classic *rentier* state, in that it is heavily reliant on the revenues derived from its oil and gas production. The hydrocarbons sector is responsible for approximately two-thirds of budget revenues, some 40 per cent of GDP and over 97 per cent of export earnings. It was Algeria's misfortune that Chadli's reforms coincided with a collapse in world oil prices.[2] Between 1985 and 1987, Algeria's oil revenues fell by 40 per cent, from US$13 billion to US$8 billion.

The sharp drop in oil prices took the country into a substantial deficit and made it increasingly difficult to service the foreign debt Boumédiène had incurred to finance the country's industrialisation programme. Drastic cutbacks in state expenditure led to a reduction or elimination of many social services and welfare capacities, along with the removal of state subsidies and price controls. Unemployment and inflation soared. By the end of the decade the official rate of unemployment was well over 20 per cent, while the price of many basic foodstuffs had doubled.

The main consequence of Chadli's reform process was that it accentuated and consolidated the fundamental division of Algerian society between the 'elites' and the 'masses'. Two inter-related processes worked towards this end. The first was that the reforms were riddled with mismanagement and corruption, enabling the political, economic and military elites – *le pouvoir* – to profit rapaciously from the economic liberalisation process.

The formative strands of Algeria's corrupted political–military elite can be traced to earlier political eras. However, it was Chadli's mismanaged attempts to liberalise the economy that provided them with their first big opportunity to accelerate their means and processes of accumulation, and to entrench the structures that enabled the military to expand its economic interests and infiltrate the economic fabric of the country. The initial break-up of the big state industrial complexes and the first steps towards privatisation enabled senior military figures and party officials to gain control of a number of state-owned assets, especially large amounts of formerly state-owned land. Much of this land was used to construct luxury villas and private factories, or simply sold on at substantial profits.[3] Some of the best agricultural land was acquired in this way, only to be used for uncontrolled urban development and consequent declines in the nation's already neglected food supply. By the end of the 1980s, two-thirds of the country's food had to be imported. As the economic situation worsened, so corruption among state officials – the *nomenklatura* – became rife. For example, the highly profitable food distribution system came under the control of a small but totally corrupt handful of individuals. It was also during this period that prominent elements within *le pouvoir*, and especially the military, moved decisively into the rapidly expanding black markets in what Stone aptly describes as 'difficult-to-obtain goods'.[4]

The second process – and the scandal of the Chadli era – was the transfer of the burden almost exclusively to the masses, the majority of whom were under the age of 30 and unemployed. This deepening of the country's social division, whereby a minuscule domestic elite controlled the bulk of the population, made Algeria a dangerously polarised society. There was, however, another and perhaps more inflammable ingredient being added to this already combustible socio-economic and political mix. This was the naked corruption through which the elites were accelerating their accumulation, and thus reinforcing their ideological, political and military elitism with raw economic muscle.

Since independence, this fundamental division of Algerian society had been masked by the various politics of nationalism, populism, personalisation and socialism; but the blatant corruption unleashed by Chadli's liberalisation dispelled any such ideological veneers. Instead, the reforms merely enhanced the hostility and mistrust between the elites and the masses and, not surprisingly, strengthened the elites' distrust of any form of political opposition.[5]

From Economic to Political Crisis: 1988–1992

Unrest, which had been increasingly frequent from 1985 onwards, reached a zenith in October 1988. Nationwide protest demonstrations saw symbols of the state coming under attack in cities and towns across the country. In probably the worst single incident, the security forces opened fire on a crowd being addressed by the Islamist leader, Ali Belhadj, in Algiers' Place des Martyrs, killing at least 40.[6] In the first week of October, as many as 500 people are estimated to have been killed by the security forces,[7] with at least 3,500 arrested, including many children, and a large number tortured.

State repression, however, failed to silence the opposition, but rather empowered it, the most popular slogans combining Islamic, populist and democratic demands. 'Black October', as it became known, had shaken the regime. Algerians had also been shocked by the extent of the unrest and the brutality of the security forces, who, in the slaughter of the Place des Martyrs, lost whatever remained of their largely mythologized role as the 'honourable guarantor of the revolution'.[8]

Chadli knew that the massacre was likely to propel the country into even greater violence. Accordingly, on 10 October he addressed the nation on television, accepting blame for the suppression and promising to introduce a wide-ranging programme of economic and political reforms. Chadli's political reforms were described by one commentator as setting off 'the most promising and inspiring phase of political life since Algerian independence. Civil society burst into life ... and the world watched fascinated as Chadli appeared set to establish the first genuinely pluralistic society in the Arab world.'[9] For a short time, Algeria experienced heady days. Almost everyone who could write became a writer. Freed from state control, newspapers sprang up everywhere. Chadli's new Constitution heralded dramatic and potentially far-reaching political reform. Above all, it replaced the one-party state with a commitment to a multi-party democracy by allowing the creation and participation of independent political parties and associations. The political classes were beside themselves with the regime's apparent commitment to democracy: 28 new political parties were ready to apply for registration before the new law had even been passed.

The most significant of the new political parties was the Front Islamique de Salut (FIS).[10] The FIS, which encompassed a range of Islamist positions, emerged from the wave of renewed focus on Islam and Islamic values that had spread through Algeria during the 1980s. Its two main leaders were Ali Belhadj, a high school teacher who had been rallying the masses in the Place des Martyrs on 7 October when the security forces had opened fire on them, and Abassi Madani, a professor of psychology.

The first real test of Algeria's democratic credentials, and more especially of the strength of the FIS, were the municipal and provincial elections of 12 June 1990. The outcome was a decisive blow to the FLN and the old guard, with the FIS taking 55 per cent of the popular vote and winning 853 of the 1,539 municipalities, and 32 of the 48 *wilayas*. The FIS victory was disquieting for Chadli, the FLN and the elite, especially as the FIS now claimed to be the legitimate rulers of Algeria, and was demanding that both parliamentary and presidential elections be brought forward. But the government drew some comfort from two mitigating factors: the 65 per cent turnout and the fact that many voted for the FIS as a protest against a hated regime and 30 years of FLN misgovernment and corruption. The turnout, although seemingly high by many western standards, indicated to the regime that roughly a third of registered voters had not bothered to vote. As for the protest vote, this was the lesser of two evils for the regime. Knowing that much of the FIS vote was a protest against the regime was less worrying for the regime than if the FIS vote had indicated a clear wish by the public for Islamist rule.

The 1990 elections were a humiliation for the government. But instead of annulling the results, as many expected, the government allowed them to stand, thus reinforcing its apparent commitment to political liberalisation. The next step in this bold transition towards Algeria's democratisation was parliamentary elections. Again, the regime thought it could fix the result, this time by massive and blatant gerrymandering.[11]

However, despite the FIS leadership being in gaol, the government's grotesque gerrymandering, and almost 50 parties participating in the elections, the first round of voting, on 26 December 1991, gave the FIS 188 of the 231 parliamentary seats. It needed only 28 of the 199 seats being taken to the second round on 16 January – a certainty – to become the world's first ever democratically elected Islamist government. Algeria faced its greatest political crisis. What to do?

A Military Coup by Any Other Name

The FIS stood on the brink of power. Nothing, it seemed, bar the annulment of the elections, stood in the way of certain confirmation of a massive FIS victory on 16 January, very probably granting it something like 75 per cent of the seats.[12]

The regime had less than three weeks to make up its mind on whether to continue with the experiment of political liberalisation, and thus relinquish control of the state to the FIS, or to annul the elections. For the best part of two weeks, a 'will they, won't they?' atmosphere prevailed in the media, among the political classes, and on the streets. Although surprised by the unfavourable first round of voting, many political leaders still seemed convinced that the democratic experiment should be allowed to continue, and even expressed the view that they could work with the FIS in some sort of coalition. The popular view was probably best expressed by the slogan of 300,000 demonstrators at an FFS[13] rally in Algiers, which called for 'Neither a police state, nor an Islamic state, but a democratic state'.[14] Interestingly, even the prime minister, Sid Ahmed Ghozali, indicated publicly that his government would adhere to the electoral process when, in a televised address on 5 January, he encouraged Algerians to participate massively in the second round, saying that this was the sole guarantee of a free and fair democratic process.[15] Especially significant, in view of the role that he was to play as the nominal head of government within a few days' time, was the view of Mohamed Boudiaf, a highly respected FLN veteran of the Revolution who was living in exile in Morocco. In an interview given to an Algerian newspaper, he declared:

> Now the FIS is here, they have the majority, they have to lead the country ... Either it is a democracy, or we turn against the FIS and jeopardise everything ... To argue that we can stop the FIS experiment and still keep on being a democracy is to contradict oneself ... For what should we do next? Are we to dissolve the FLN? The other parties? Are we to leave them as they are? In 1988 it was time for change and we did not do it.[16]

On the international front, too, the general response, at least in public, was that foreign governments would accept the results of the elections.

Ghozali's stated views were not shared by all members of the government – especially those belonging to the FLN old guard and the military establishment. Khaled Nezzar, former chief of staff and now minister of defence – along with many other senior military officers, several ministers, such as Maj. Gen. Larbi Belkheir, minister of the interior, and many from the Westernised political and economic elite – were in favour of cancelling the results. To that end, the government, or at least Nezzar, had taken soundings among both neighbouring states and key Western democracies, which, almost certainly reinforced his decision to move against the FIS. Neighbouring Arab countries – notably Tunisia, Libya and Egypt – were distinctly unenthusiastic about the prospect of a democratically elected Islamic government in Algeria, as it would galvanise Islamic opposition in their own countries. Among Western democracies, the issue was more sensitive. While welcoming this unique move towards democracy, they too were not enchanted about the prospect of a FIS government. The two key countries, France and the US, said little in public to encourage Nezzar, although it is now widely accepted that they gave him and his plotters more than a few nods and winks behind the scenes.

The army's mechanism for effectively taking power was complex, ingenious and illegal. Nezzar and his plotters contrived a constitutional crisis that enabled them to regard the constitution as suspended, and thus (temporarily) transfer all legislative and executive powers to a pre-existing consultative body – the Haut Conseil de Sécurité (HCS). The HCS immediately declared that it was impossible to continue with the electoral process under these circumstances, and accordingly suspended the second round of the elections. Two days later, on 14 January, the HCS officially handed over presidential powers to a newly created five-man institution, the Haut Comité d'Etat (HCE) (High State Committee). The most powerful member of the HCE was Gen. Khaled Nezzar, who, through his office as minister of defence, maintained the army's grip on power. Its chairman was Mohamed Boudiaf, who was called back from more than 20 years in exile to chair the HCE, and thus effectively act as the country's makeshift president.

The army's and HCE's justification for the cancellation of the elections required the demonising of the FIS as being fundamentally opposed to democracy and determined to seize power by whatever means possible. They asserted that Islamism per se rejected democracy, and that once the FIS had used this opportunity to obtain power it would change the Constitution to ensure the entrenchment of an Islamist and undemocratic state.

If the army's assertions sounded questionable at the time, they were shown to be even more unjustified three years later, when the FIS signed a communiqué entitled the National Contract with most of the country's other main political parties, in which it gave public undertakings to accept the democratic principles of 'political pluralism'. The Contract, signed in Rome on 13 January 1995 under the auspices of the Catholic Sant' Egidio Community, was the outcome of talks between most of Algeria's political parties, with the notable exception of the government.

It is conceivable, if the Sant' Egidio talks had been held a year or so earlier, that the government might have attended. But, by the end of 1994, as we shall see in the next chapter, Algeria had been bailed out of its financial bankruptcy by the

IMF and knew, from then on, that it had the financial means to win its war against the Islamists. The regime had also been emboldened in 1994 by a number of American reassurances, the most significant of which – especially in the context of post-9/11 US–Algerian relations – was a financial tie-up with the US Halliburton Company.

9

ISLAMISTS AND ERADICATORS: ALGERIA'S 'DIRTY WAR'*

Who is Killing Who?

The annulment of the elections and the effective military coup of January 1992 plunged Algeria into what Habib Souaïdia famously described as *La Sale Guerre* (the Dirty War).[1] Once in a while, there is a book which turns history. Habib Souaïdia's *La Sale Guerre*, published in 2001, was one of them, not just because of what it revealed about the role of Algeria's military regime in that war, but because its subsequent passage through the French courts gave Algeria's peoples a reaffirmation of the truth, and of the sense and knowledge of justice that may one day enable them to fight just one more battle against the repression under which they live. Whether that battle will be fought in the streets, suburbs and maquis of Algeria, as has so often been the case, or in the International Criminal Court is still a matter of speculation.

Souaïdia was not the first to accuse the Algerian army of being responsible for many of the atrocities in Algeria's 'civil war'. That credit should perhaps be given to Nesroulah Yous, whose book,[2] published the previous year, provides what Hugh Roberts described as 'a harrowing eyewitness account of the massacre at Bentalha, a township in the Mitidja plain some ten miles south of Algiers, on the night of September 22, 1997, in which over 400 people – men, women and children – were pitilessly slaughtered'.[3] This massacre followed several others of a similar nature, such

---

* A longer version of this chapter, containing much more detail and notes, has been placed on the publisher's website (www.plutobooks.com/) and can be downloaded free of charge.

as those at Raïs and Beni Messous a few weeks earlier, which prompted calls for an international inquiry into the question: 'qui tue qui? (who is killing who?)'.[4] Roberts concluded that the Algerian authorities' thesis that the massacres were perpetrated by Islamists 'does not survive a reading of Yous's book'.[5]

Yous recounts the massacre in detail, as well as the events which preceded it. He was convinced that the Bentalha massacre was undertaken by elements of the Algerian army. However, the weak link in his testimony, at least to Roberts's keen sense of justice, is that, while it 'provided the basis of a *prima facie* case for the charge of complicity [by the Algerian army], as accessories before and after the fact, in mass murder', it did not establish for a fact that the assailants, as Yous and his fellow-victims were convinced, were members – a special commando or death squad – of the Algerian army.[6]

That weak spot in Yous's testimony was bridged by Habib Souaïdia. He was a whistle-blower par excellence, an officer in Algeria's Special Forces who had served for two-and-a-half years in and around the country's nastier areas of violence, especially in the Mitijda Plane and around Lakhardia.[7] His book was potentially devastating for the Algerian regime and its generals – especially the former army chief and defence minister, General Khaled Nezzar – as Souaïdia detailed the names, places and dates of the massacres of civilians undertaken by Algerian soldiers disguised as Islamist rebels, of suspects shot dead by the army in cold blood, and of rebels and civilians tortured to death in the army's torture chambers.

Although Souaïdia's best-seller was a massive indictment of the Algerian army, it was Souaïdia who was to find himself in court. In August 2001, Nezzar announced his intention to sue Souaïdia for defamation, following an interview of Souaïdia on France's Channel 5 in May in which he accused Nezzar of 'being responsible for the assassination of thousands of people'. But in the eyes of most Algerians and many others around the world, it was the Algerian army, not Souaïdia, that stood on trial in the Paris court. Three months after its commencement, in July 2002, Nezzar's case was dismissed.

Nezzar's defence was completely destroyed by the most compelling evidence of Mohammed Samraoui, a star witness whose testimony[8] removed whatever doubts all but the most vehement supporters of Algeria's ruthless brand of state terrorism may have harboured over the veracity of either Yous's or Souaïdia's publications.

Samraoui, unlike Yous and Souaïdia, was a big fish. Trained by the KGB, he had risen through Algeria's intelligence services to the rank of colonel and deputy head of the regime's deadly counter-intelligence service, the Sécurité Militaire (SM), or Direction des Renseignements et de la Sécurité (DRS) as it was renamed. Until 1996 he served as the regime's top counter-intelligence officer in Europe, where he was in charge of monitoring the activities of the entire FIS leadership in Europe. His testimony provided detailed confirmation of all that Souaïdia had said and implied. He detailed which massacres and other atrocities had been undertaken by the army and its various ancillary forces, and which had been undertaken by the Islamists. He also gave detailed information on the regime's plan to 'eradicate' the Islamists, and on the key roles of those in charge of the DRS – especially the extent to which they had infiltrated the various Islamist movements and effectively controlled several of their leaders (*emirs*).

Long before Yous, Souaïdia and Samraoui published their books, credible evidence was emerging that pointed 'inescapably to the conclusion that the GIA [was], in fact, a creature of the Algerian secret services'.[9] For example, as early as June 1997, the former Algerian prime minister (1984–88), Dr Abdel Hameed Al Ibrahimi, disclosed in an interview with the *Palestine Times* that Islamic armed groups [GIA]

> are penetrated by the military intelligence service ... It is known that most of the mass killings and bombings are [carried out] by the government itself whether through special forces or through the local militias (about 200,000 armed men), but the government accuses the Islamists of the violence.

The purpose of these killings, he explained, was so that the regime could 'obtain additional financial, political and diplomatic support from France and other Western countries [by posing as] the defender of the West against fundamentalism in Algeria and as an acclaimed partner in defending the French and Western interests in the region.'[10] A few months later, Dr Hamoue Amirouche, a former fellow of the Institut National d'Etudes de Strategie Globale in Algiers, noted that

> the military regime is perpetuating itself by fabricating and nourishing a mysterious monster to fight, but it is demonstrating daily its failure to perform its most elementary duty: providing security for the population. In October 1997, troubling reports suggested that a faction of the army, dubbed the 'land mafia,' might actually be responsible for some of last summer's massacres, which ... continued even after the Islamic Salvation Army, the armed wing of the FIS, called for a truce, in effect as of October 1, 1997.[11]

The French magazine *Paris Match* reported that this 'land mafia', consisting of elements of the Algerian military regime, was cleansing premium lands of peasant occupants in anticipation of the privatisation of all the land in 1998.[12] Robert Fisk, writing in the *Independent*, referred to 'evidence that the massacred villagers were themselves Islamists, and increasing proof that the Algerian security forces remained – at best – incapable of coming to their rescue,' thus 'casting grave doubt on the government's role in Algeria's dirty war'.[13] The *Independent* also cited the testimony of an Algerian army conscript who spoke of 'watching officers torture suspected "Islamist" prisoners by boring holes in their legs – and in one case, stomach – with electric drills in a dungeon called the "killing room".' More pertinently, 'he claimed that he found a false beard amid the clothing of soldiers who had returned from a raid on a village where 28 civilians were later found beheaded; the soldier suspects that his comrades had dressed up as Muslim rebels to carry out the atrocity.'[14] The *Sunday Times* similarly noted that the genocidal massacre of over 1,000 villagers in the first three weeks of 1998 occurred 'within 500 yards of an army base that did not deploy a single soldier, despite the fact that the gunfire and screams would have been clearly audible. Villagers said that some of the attackers wore army uniforms.'[15] In November 1997, the secretary-general of Amnesty International, Pierre Sane, reported that 'Algerians have been slain in their thousands with unspeakable brutality ... decapitated, mutilated and burnt alive in their homes ... with torture, "disappearances" and extrajudicial executions becoming part of the daily reality of Algerian life.' More importantly, he noted that 'many of the massacres have been within shouting distance of army barracks, yet cries for help have gone unanswered, the killers allowed to walk away unscathed', with the majority of massacres taking place

> in areas around the capital Algiers, in the most militarized region of the country ... Yet the army and security forces did not intervene, neither to stop the massacres nor to arrest the killers – who were able to leave undisturbed on each occasion.[16]

According to 'Yussuf-Joseph', a career secret agent in Algeria's SM/DRS who defected to Britain, 'All the intelligence services in Europe know the [Algerian] government is doing it, but they are keeping quiet because they want to protect their supplies of oil.'[17] At the time of Algeria's 'dirty war', as now, the extent of this secret network of complicity extending throughout European governments and their intelligence services is kept well hidden from the their unwitting electorates. As the *Observer* noted in 1997, Algeria

> squats on huge oil and gas deposits worth billions. It supplies the gas that warms Madrid and Rome. It has a 31.8 billion pounds contract with British Petroleum. No Western government wants to make trouble with the state of Algeria. Its wealth buys silence, buys complicity.[18]

By any standard, what took place in Algeria in the 1990s was an exceptionally dirty war. Among contemporaneous atrocities, it was surpassed in killing, violence and obscenity only by Rwanda's frenzied genocide of 1994. Estimates of the numbers killed in the almost daily massacres of civilians range from around 150,000 to more than 200,000 – 70 per cent of them, as I was chillingly reminded on my return there, being by what the French-language press calls *l'arme blanche* – cold steel, a collective term for knives, axes, machetes and the like.[19]

The Beginning of Armed Conflict

In the run-up to the elections, the FIS had threatened to overthrow the regime by force if it interfered with the elections. However, when the regime chose to call its bluff by annulling the elections in January 1992, proclaiming a state of emergency in February, dissolving the FIS in March and its municipal and departmental authorities in April, there was no spontaneous reaction from the 3 million or so FIS voter-sympathisers.

Why not? Why did resistance not begin immediately? The answer, perhaps – as Luis Martinez postulated – is because voting for a cause, in this case an Islamic state, like supporting a trade union, involves little cost, whereas defending it and being prepared to die for it are quite another matter.[20] As most analysts and commentators on the war have pointed out, however, the FIS was not the only Islamist organisation in Algeria at the time of the annulment of the elections. A number of small, militant Islamist organisations, founded mostly in 1990/91, such as Al Takfir wa'l Hijra ('Excommunication and Flight'), the Kataeb el Qods ('Jerusalem Brigades'), the Algerian Hezbollah and the Mouvement Islamique Armé (MIA), whose leaders were mostly in disagreement with those of the FIS over the direction of the struggle, emerged publicly after the military coup and started a jihad with attacks on police, soldiers and other elements of the security forces. In fact, some of these small groups, belonging to the most radical minority fringe of the Islamist movement, had been responsible for militant actions before the 1991 elections. However, with the exception of the MIA, they were quickly neutralised by the security forces during the course of 1992.

At least, that is what most commentators on the war supposed, until Habib Souaïdia's trial in 2002. From Samraoui's testimony, we now know that 'the armed factions were in fact created by the Sécurité Militaire during the first months of 1991 under the umbrella project "global action plan" drafted in December 1990' to impede FIS access to power.

Nezzar's Plan was hatched by the power behind the regime, Larbi Belkheir, the principal private secretary of the President of the Republic Chadli Benjedid, while Generals Mohamed Touati, Abdelmadjid Taright and Mohamed Lamari drafted the plan which was then handed over to the DRS.[21]

According to Samraoui, in early 1991 Gen. (then Col.) Smaïn Lamari of the DRS ordered the reactivation of the armed Islamic opposition that had emerged in the 1980s under Mustapha Bouyali, but which by 1987 had been effectively suppressed by the security forces. It thus seems that many of the small militant organisations that sprang up in 1991 may well have been nothing more than the products of these reactivated Bouyalists, now operating as *agents provocateurs* and activists, supplied, directed and protected by the DRS. Indeed, Samraoui even confirms that the MIA, the only armed opposition through 1992 and early 1993, was given communications and other technical support by the SM during this period, and that he had personally handed over four vehicles to the MIA.[22] Samraoui believes that many of these Islamists believed they were serving the Islamic cause.

This category of manipulated Islamists', he wrote, 'no doubt implemented the criminal plans of Smaïn Lamari ... and his consorts, by attacking the targets their officers-in-charge designated for them, who generally selected the people who needed to be eliminated; journalists, enemies, problematic individuals in the military, all potential people who could jeopardize the Nezzar plan.[23]

While the response of most FIS supporters to the coup was to wait and see what would happen, that of the regime and its security forces was to take the initiative by launching a massive campaign to eradicate Islamism in Algeria. Indeed, with the FIS leadership of Abassi Madani and Ali Belhadj imprisoned, the party dissolved, and no signs of a general uprising, the regime expected an easy victory. The security forces occupied mosques and seized documents that gave details of the FIS organisation. Mass arrests of known or suspected Islamists followed. Islamists, in turn, attacked police stations, notably the central police intelligence offices at El Harrech, to get the names and addresses of civilian employees of the police. Thousands of young militants or FIS sympathisers who had played no part in the armed struggle were tortured, killed or sent to internment camps in the Sahara, where perhaps as many as 20,000 were interned. Many of them were tried and condemned to summary execution by military tribunal outside the legal process.[24]

It was these mass arrests, the scale of the repression and the violence of the security forces that provoked the initial resistance. The regime's repression activated a big pool of FIS and other sympathisers in support of jihad, especially in those *communes* that had supported the FIS. With increasingly less likelihood of a general uprising, the three armed Islamist factions – the MIA, GIA and MEI (Mouvement pour l'Etat Islamique) – concentrated increasingly on recruitment, and on consolidating themselves as Islamist military organisations. The response of the government was to train its own specialist counter-guerrilla force, initially numbering 15,000 (but to be increased substantially), and special units under the command of General Mohamed Lamari.

General Lamari, soon to be appointed chief of the general staff[25] – whose voice I was to hear on national radio ten years later declaring that the second group of hostages had been released from their captivity in Tamelrik – was the most powerful of the military officers among the dominant faction in the regime that was known as *les éradicateurs*. From late 1992 onwards, this group pressed for the all-out and extremely brutal suppression – the eradication – of the Islamist movement. Its main supporters were a coterie of powerful army officers who had been trained by the French and who had served in the French army, the French-educated wing of the political class and, not surprisingly, Paris, which provided them with constant support.

By around late 1993 and early 1994, the struggle had reached something of a stalemate. Neither the mass arrests nor the banning of the FIS had put an end to the Islamist alternative. Yet neither had the *jihad* aroused the 3 million FIS voters on whom the Islamist leaders had counted. With no chance of victory in a frontal battle, both sides began to settle in for what Martinez described as 'total war', in which the 'the two sides ... decided to use all varieties of strategic attack to weaken each other's position ... [N]ot only fighters but also economic assets and networks of support – financial and political, national and international – were declared as targets.'[26]

An analysis of Algeria's expansion into 'total war' goes far beyond the scope of this book. Nevertheless, three aspects of it need highlighting, in so far as they provide key insights into the nature of contemporary Algeria and, more especially, the post-9/11 US–Algerian relationship.

These are the role of international support – especially that of the IMF, the USA and France – for the Algerian regime; the 'non-ideological' or 'financial' nature of the war as it developed after 1994; and the central role of the secret military intelligence service, the DRS, in Algerian affairs.

International Support for the Algerian Regime

Aside from the Islamists, the biggest problem facing the regime in 1992 was the servicing of its international debt, which stood at US$26 billion. By 1993 the country was close to bankruptcy, with no alternative but to go cap-in-hand to the IMF. With strong support from both the US and France, the IMF came to the regime's rescue on 9–10 April 1994 with a debt-rescheduling package generating a windfall of some $10 billion per annum,[27] which it could now use to finance and prosecute its war: the 'total eradication' of the Islamists.

In addition to this critical support from the IMF, Chadli's reform of the oil sector had opened the way for partnerships with international oil companies whose investment became increasingly important to the regime. A particularly significant but scarcely publicised contribution to the regime at this critical time in its survival, not least because of its potential political and military–strategic implications, came from the involvement in the state-controlled end of the Algerian economy of the US Halliburton Company. In 1994 Halliburton's engineering branch, Kellogg Brown & Root created a joint venture company with Sonatrach (Algeria's national oil company), called Brown & Root

Condor (BRC), in which they held 49 per cent and 51 per cent stakes, respectively. With US Vice President Dick Cheney being parachuted in as Halliburton's CEO in the following year, BRC embarked on at least 26 major state contracts through what many now regard as thoroughly corrupt and illegal arrangements, but which only came to light in 2006 – with disastrous consequences, as revealed in *The Dying Sahara*, for US relations with Algeria and its 'Saharan front'.

This international backing for the regime made the Islamists more bitter and determined – so much so that militants of the former FIS formed their own armed organisation, the Armée Islamique du Salut (AIS). Its aim, quite simply, was to topple the regime and replace it with an Islamic state.

The Non-ideological, 'Financial' Dimension of 'Total War'

It is conceivable that, if the IMF had not been so accommodating, the regime might have been obliged to attend the Sant' Egidio talks in Rome, and might even have become a party to the National Contract. However, with the diversion of international foreign aid into the modernisation and strengthening of the repressive apparatus, the regime took on a renewed confidence, knowing that it now had the means to reverse the balance of forces with the Islamists.

Winning the war, however, was more than just a matter of buying arms and munitions. The IMF windfall, combined with the conditions of its accompanying Structural Adjustment Programme (SAP), brought an entirely new dimension to the war. The conditions of the SAP – namely, the liberalisation of trade, the ending of state subsidies to consumer goods, the devaluation of the currency, and the privatisation of state enterprises – were designed, as in other countries that fell into the IMF's clutches, to create a liberal market economy. At least, that was the theory. In Algeria, however, the creation and control of this market economy became another dimension of 'total warfare'. The privatisation policy created a 'plunder economy'[28] in which both military personnel and the *emirs* had their hands on resources, thus enabling both sides to finance and maintain the violence.

The war became increasingly lucrative for both the *emirs* and senior army personnel. Indeed, the irony of the IMF bailout was that its encouragement of privatisation and a market economy strengthened both the regime and the Islamists. It boosted the regime through its increased means and use of various forms of patronage – especially by its having the resources to favour elements in the private sector – but it also let the *emirs* into the market. The e*mirs*' main entrée into the market economy was through their creation of export–import companies,[29] along with their rapidly expanding control over *trabendo* – the black market. They became military entrepreneurs – warlords who gradually distanced themselves from the struggle against the regime to concentrate their attention increasingly on running their local areas and on the pursuit of considerable wealth. Through this economic dimension of the war, the politico-military elites not only became further corrupted, but also used this opportunity to further embed themselves within both the more formal aspects of the economy and its rents, as well as in the *trabendo* sector. It was also during this period, through the way in which these openings in the economy sustained the 'total war', that the *emirs* rose to their positions of regional political and economic power. It is in this milieu of the plunder economy and its affiliated *trabendo* sector that we can find the roots of the Mokhtar ben Mokhtars and the El Paras of the society that Algeria was to become over the course of the subsequent decade.

It must be understood that such figures necessarily worked closely with those elements of the military that had also immersed themselves in this lucrative and rapidly expanding sector of the economy. Thus, in trying to unravel the complex and murky networks that today link Algeria's supposed terrorist *emirs* to the security forces, they can nearly always be traced back into the interstices of the economy that opened up and flourished through the conditions, needs and opportunities created by the IMF's SAP, and the associated nature of the 'total war'.

State Terrorism and 'Dirty Tricks'

The third aspect of Algeria's dirty war that is central to our understanding of the Saharan front in America's GWOT is the key role that has been played by Algeria's secret military intelligence service (SM/DRS). In itself, that is not at all surprising, especially in a society that has long been characterised by the repressive nature of its regime. What is extraordinary – indeed unique – about Algeria's DRS is that both its command and modus operandi have remained unchanged for almost two decades. Its two top generals – Mohammed Mediene (a.k.a. Toufik, also spelled Tewfik) and the same Smaïn[30] Lamari who debriefed the first hostages liberated at Amguid in May 2003 – became the two most feared names in Algeria. The service was in their control from the point when they came together in September 1990, until Smaïn Lamari's death on 28 August 2007. Throughout that time, their modus operandi – namely 'terrorism', torture and an almost unlimited panoply of dirty tricks – has also remained firmly in place.

Toufik and Smaïn had a good war. Their commitment to the 'eradication of Islamism' was absolute and, some have said, 'flawless'.[31] In early January 1992, Smaïn, referring implicitly to the number of FIS voters and sympathisers, told his subordinates: 'I am ready and determined to eliminate 3 million Algerians if necessary to maintain the order threatened by the Islamists.'[32] Although the apex of Algeria's military hierarchy was the chief of the general staff, the conduct and operation of the war was largely in the hands of Toufik and Smaïn, who, to all intents and purposes, had the Algerian army and the regime's other forces (gendarmerie, police, and so on) at their disposal. Of the two, Smaïn, as head of both the DRS's most important counter-espionage unit (Direction du contre-espionnage – DCE) and its operational headquarters, was probably the most hands-on. He was directly responsible for the infiltration of the GIA and the other Islamist groups, including later the GSPC. He was responsible for many of the most grotesque massacres allegedly conducted by the GIA in the 1990s, such as those of Bentalha, Rais, Beni-messous and many others, in which thousands of civilians were butchered by his men.

By the beginning of this millennium, Toufik and Smaïn's power was almost impregnable, and they consolidated and extended it by placing and maintaining their own men in key positions of control within the DRS. The fingerprints of Toufik and Smaïn are smeared over almost every incident in Algeria's dirty war. Although Smaïn's genocidal enterprise fortunately resulted in far fewer than his oft-quoted 3 million deaths, his entire working life was dedicated to murder. Canonised in the Algerian media upon his death, Smaïn was one of the greatest mass murderers of the modern era.

The first major test of Smaïn's flawless loyalty came with the assassination of Algeria's president (Chairman of the HCE), Mohammed Boudiaf, in June 1992. The official account is that he was shot by one of his bodyguards, Lembarek Boumaarafi, a supposed Islamist sympathiser, while making a speech at the opening of a cultural centre in Annaba. The truth is rather different. Bravely, but perhaps unwisely, Boudiaf had set out on 'mission impossible' – namely, to rid the country of the corruption that was rooted at the very heart of its military regime. His confidant, Kasdi Merbah, a former head of Algeria's secret services, whom Boudiaf trusted intimately, provided him with a dossier detailing the activities of certain members of the regime, including details of their bank accounts, mostly in Switzerland and France, through which they had laundered and embezzled massive state funds. Merbah also provided Boudiaf with the names of a few officers who could be trusted implicitly in this delicate mission. From these, Boudiaf chose another DRS officer, Col. Mourad, whom he sent to Paris, along with three aides, to investigate these misappropriations.

Boudiaf's mission set alarm bells ringing on both sides of the Mediterranean. In Algiers, elements at the heart of the regime realised that they had to take drastic action. A week after his return from France, Mourad was found shot dead; his three aides were also eliminated, officially by terrorists. Boudiaf had disturbed the Algerian mafia: he had to be stopped. According to the MAOL,[33] the murder plotters were Khaled Nezzar, Larbi Belkheir, Mohamed Mediene (Toufik), Smaïn Lamari and

Mohamed Lamari. Toufik entrusted Smaïn Lamari with the planning and execution of the murder.

France's Direction Générale de la Sécurité Extérieure (DGSE) would almost certainly have been aware of Mourad's mission, and of Toufik and Smaïn's roles in Boudiaf's assassination. Indeed, there is an increasing amount of evidence of collaboration between the Algerian and French secret intelligence services in a number of 'projects' in Algeria's dirty war. Their aim was to make both the French government and public more supportive of the Algerian regime's war against the Islamists.

The first well known example of this strategy was in 1993, when the DRS leadership of Toufik and Smaïn, in collaboration with Jean-Charles Marchiana, advisor to France's right-wing interior minister, Charles Pasqua, arranged the suspicious kidnapping of three officials from the French embassy in Algiers. Algeria's secret services successfully mounted a phoney operation to convince public opinion that they had freed the French hostages from 'Islamist terrorists'.[34]

In September 1994, the GIA leader Ahmed Abu Abdullah (a.k.a. Sherif Ghousmi) was killed by security forces and replaced as 'national emir' by Djamel Zitouni. Zitouni, however, was soon suspected and later confirmed by Samraoui as being Smaïn's man. Thereafter, the DRS's strategy of running false flag operations was bound up increasingly with this successful infiltration of the GIA. From September 1994 to his death in July 1996, Djamel Zitouni, at the head of the GIA, enabled the eradicators to pull the strings on both sides of the divide. Nezzar himself more or less admitted the infiltration of the GIA and other armed factions by the DRS when he stated in his Paris trial that 'infiltrations are the job of any service'.[35]

Many of the 'terrorist incidents' directed against France at this time are now known to have been conducted by or under the direction of Zitouni as part of the Algerian regime's attempt to discredit the Islamists in the eyes of French and world opinion.[36] For example, on 24 December 1994, a death-squad of four GIA terrorists hijacked an Air France Flight in Algiers en route to Paris. During a two-day drama that moved from Algiers to

Marseilles, three passengers were murdered and all four hijackers eventually shot dead. In the action, eleven French commandos, thirteen passengers and three crew members were wounded, and the plane so badly damaged that it had to be scrapped.

A few weeks later, following the conclusion of the Sant'Egidio peace talks in Rome on 14 January 1995, French politicians lent their weight to the Sant'Egidio platform which, among other things, called for an enquiry into the violence in Algeria, the end of the Algerian army's involvement in political affairs, multi-party democracy, and the return of constitutional rule. This was anathema to Algeria's generals, and they determined never again to allow France's politicians to consider withdrawing their support from their regime. The DRS began diverting its agents in France from their initial task of infiltrating Islamist networks to becoming *agents provocateurs*.[37] Algeria's key agent in this operation was Ali Touchent. Working with Zitouni, Touchent began gathering together and inciting a network of disaffected young men from North Africa to undertake terrorist attacks in France. Between July and October 1995, ten French citizens were killed and more than 200 injured in a series of rudimentary bomb attacks. The campaign was successful: the French government, faced with public hysteria against Islam, abandoned its support for the Rome accord.

The incident that caused the greatest public revulsion in France was undoubtedly the abduction and murder of seven Trappist monks of the Cistercian Order of the Strict Observance from their hilltop monastery in Tibéhirine, near Medea, in 1996. The monks were abducted in March; their severed heads were found in a sack two months later. The precise details of their murder have still not been made clear, partly because of the reluctance of the French legal system to pursue the case. While the Algerian regime has always tried to blame the GIA, there is overwhelming evidence of the involvement of Zitouni and the DRS in the murders, including the testimony of former Warrant Officer Tigha Abdelkader, a DRS agent, who claims to have seen the monks in the hands of the DRS in the Blida barracks, where he worked between the time of their abduction and murder.[38]

In November 1997, a serving officer with the Algerian military known as 'Hakim' contacted the French newspaper *Le Monde* to express the feelings of a group of officers who were sickened by their work. Hakim said:

We have become assassins, working for a caste of crooks who infest the military. They want everything: oil, control of imports, property ... I confirm that the outrages of St Michel [The attack on the Paris Metro that killed eight and wounded more than 130 people] and that of Maison Blanche (when 13 were wounded) were committed at the instigation of the Infiltration and Manipulation Directorate (DIM) of the Directorate of the Intelligence Services (DRS), controlled by Mohammed Mediene, better known under the name 'Toufik' and General Smaïn Lamari.[39]

10

THE 'BANANA THEORY' OF TERRORISM

After murdering the president, bombing Paris, hijacking an Airbus, butchering seven monks, infiltrating the armed Islamic groups and slaughtering tens of thousands of innocent civilians in cold blood, arranging the abduction of a few tourists in the Sahara would have seemed like very small beer for Smaïn and Toufik. And the same would have been true for their American counterparts. Indeed, when it comes to the promotion of state terrorism, in all its insidious forms, there is little that the Americans could learn from the Algerians.

The Reagan Administration's 'War on International Terrorism'

The events of 9/11 did not mark the beginning of the war on terrorism for the Americans; they marked, rather, the beginning of a 'new' war on terror. In 1981, President Reagan came into office declaring that the core of his administration's foreign policy would be the war against 'international terrorism'. The ideological basis of the Reagan administration's war on international terrorism, which justified its shift to a 'renewed interventionist foreign policy' and a 'new alliance between right-wing dictatorships everywhere' had been promoted and established in the summer of 1979, at what became known as the Jerusalem Conference on International Terrorism (JCIT). The JCIT's defining theme was 'that international terrorism constituted an organised political movement whose ultimate origin was in the Soviet Union'.[1] More significantly, it established the ideological foundations for both the 'war on terror' promulgated by the Reagan administration and the 'new' war on terror that followed 9/11, the sole difference being that the threat posed by the former Soviet Union had been replaced by that of a 'new transnational Islamism'.[2]

There were, however, remarkable similarities between the war on terror launched in 1981 and the 'new' war on terror launched twenty years later. In 1982, a masters thesis, submitted by Philip Paull at San Francisco State University, revealed that the JCIT's literature and use of source documentation was

'profoundly flawed'. For instance, the JCIT literature heavily cited 'statistics purporting to demonstrate a drastic ten-fold increase in incidents of international terrorism between 1968–78 [which] were deliberately concocted and inflated, and contradicted original CIA data illustrating a decline in terrorist incidents'.[3]

Even more reminiscent of the Bush–Cheney war on terror, 'it routinely relied on techniques of blatant disinformation, misquoting and misrepresenting Western intelligence reports, as well as recycling government-sponsored disinformation published in the mainstream media'.[4] In his conclusion – which could just as well have been the conclusion to this book – Paull wrote that the 1979 JCIT was

a successful propaganda operation ... the entire notion of 'international terrorism' as promoted by the Jerusalem Conference rests on a faulty, dishonest, and ultimately corrupt information base ... The issue of international terrorism has little to do with fact, or with any objective legal definition of international terrorism. The issue, as promoted by the Jerusalem Conference and used by the Regan administration, is an ideological and instrumental issue. It is the ideology, rather than the reality, that dominates US foreign policy today.[5]

Paull's words are likely to haunt the reader through the remainder of this book.

In mulling over other similarities between the 1981 and 2001 wars on terror, we should not lose sight of the fact that one result of Reagan's war on terror – notably his war against Nicaragua and the associated illegal Iran–Contra deals – was to leave the US with the unique credential of being 'the only state on record which has both been condemned by the World Court for international terrorism and has vetoed a Security Council resolution calling on states to observe international law.'[6]

Significant though comparisons between 1981 and 2001 may be, the US's advocacy of state terrorism and support for terrorist organisations long predate the Reagan administration's flouting of international law and conventions. A cursory glance at the controversial history of the School of the Americas,[7] and the records of its alumni, gives just one insight into US support for state terrorism and human rights abuses in Latin America. Beyond its own backyard of the Americas, there are countless examples of US support for state terrorism of one sort or another – ranging from the backing given to Pol Pot's genocidaires, to the specialist tortures of Philippine dictator Ferdinand Marcos, to interventions – mostly through the CIA – in Indonesia, Iraq, Iran, much of Southeast Asia, Greece, South Africa, Angola, Libya and a host of other countries; not to mention the roles of US agencies in planning and/or carrying out the assassinations of some 40 prominent foreign individuals since World War II alone.[8]

Examples of US support for terrorism are countless, and many books have been written on the subject. The point I am making here is simply that we should not be surprised at the relationship that has been forged between the Algerian and US military intelligence services in their launching and orchestration of the Saharan front in the new war on terror. Algeria's military regime and successive US administrations have long been soul-mates in their shared belief in the practice of terrorism – or, to be more precise, 'state terrorism' – including torture, to achieve their political goals. The only thing that is perhaps surprising about this relationship, which I shall examine in this and subsequent chapters, is the speed with which the two countries became 'partners in crime' – in little more than that short space of time, after the departure from office of the Clinton administration, that it took George W. Bush to settle himself into the White House.

As we have seen, the US backed the IMF bailout of the Algerian regime in 1994; US oil companies and Halliburton made politically significant investments in the country in the late 1980s and 1990s, and by the mid-1990s the US had become a significant importer of Algerian liquid natural gas. There were also reports that the CIA maintained what appear to have been indirect but effective links with the Algerian army's secret intelligence services during the course of that country's 'dirty war'.[9]

Although these links are important for this narrative, they were of relatively little significance within the global context of America's international relations during the Clinton era, throughout which Algeria remained low on Washington's radar. Clinton's foreign policy was orientated more to the Pacific region, with Middle East and North African interests confined almost exclusively to the Israel–PLO peace process. While Washington naturally welcomed initiatives that might herald Algeria's return to 'normality', such as the Sant' Egidio proposal of 1995 and the presidential and parliamentary elections of 1995 and 1997, respectively,[10] the Clinton administration was aware of the Algerian regime's rapidly deteriorating human rights record, and followed the international community in distancing itself from the country.[11] The low point in contemporary US–Algerian relations was most plainly reached at the funeral of Morocco's King Hassan II in Rabat, in July 1999, where President Clinton avoided any public contact with Algeria's newly elected president, Abdelaziz Bouteflika.[12] In the wake of that fortuitous meeting, it is safe to assume that the Algerian president prayed long and hard for a Republican victory in November 2000.[13]

New, Post-2000, US–Algerian Relations

With his prayers answered, Bouteflika quickly made his sentiments known to the White House. This, too, paid off with relations at both the military and intelligence levels warming up almost as soon as the Bush administration had established itself in office. In February 2001, General Carlton W. Fulford, deputy commander of US forces in Europe, received General Mohamed Lamari, chief of staff of the Algerian army, in Germany, while the director of the FBI was reported to have made a 48-hour secret visit to Algiers at around the same time.[14] Bouteflika himself was rewarded with an invitation to a summit meeting with President Bush in July 2001. Their meeting in the White House, which lasted 80 minutes, was only the second visit of an Algerian president to Washington. Over the next four years, Presidents Bush and Bouteflika were to meet on six occasions.

At that stage, still almost two months before 9/11, and notwithstanding the developing interests of US oil companies in Algeria, it is probably true to say that Algeria had a greater need for US support than vice versa. At the time of Bouteflika's election to the presidency in April 1999, there was a widespread feeling that Algeria's political crisis might be approaching an end. The number of killings had fallen considerably, while among the country's long-suffering population, traumatised and exhausted after so many years of conflict, fear and gratuitous killing, there was increasing talk of peace, perhaps even reconciliation, and of a 'new beginning'. Aside from the question of how the country would achieve such internal peace and reconciliation, the Algerian state that emerged from the crisis of the 1990s faced two major problems: the decrepit state of its armed forces, and its status as an international pariah.

As we have seen, Algeria's army has played a decisive role in the development of the post-colonial Algerian state, with its security establishment – the *mukhabarat* – holding the country in an iron grip. As the Algerian historian, Mohamed Harbi, remarked, 'Algeria has an army with a state at its service, rather than an army at the service of the state'.[15] Following the cancellation of the 1992 elections and the ensuing 'dirty war', the US, as well as European and other Western countries, were reluctant to sell arms to Algeria for fear of Islamist reprisals, as were experienced in France,[16] and criticisms from human rights groups. The result was that the Algerian army became increasingly under-equipped during the course of the 1990s. As the door of international recognition creaked slightly ajar, the Algerian army and its state preoccupied themselves with trying to acquire those modern, high-tech weapons systems that it lacked – notably night-vision devices, sophisticated radar systems, an integrated surveillance system, tactical communications equipment, and certain lethal weapons systems. President Bouteflika, a former foreign minister with considerable international standing in his own right, also sought to overcome Algeria's pariah status and re-establish the country's position and reputation in international affairs – perhaps even at the US 'high table'. The Bush administration was seen as likely to be able to deliver both prizes.

With the ink scarcely dry on the Cheney Report,[17] Bouteflika said everything that the Americans wanted to hear. He told George Bush that, while European companies had fled his country in times of trouble, American ones, by contrast, had 'gambled on the future of Algeria'. He stressed that, in US–Algerian relations, 'oil is oil and politics is politics'. That was music to the ears of the American oil industry, and especially to Dick Cheney, whose Halliburton Company was one of those that had made such a 'gamble'. Cheney had long sought to build closer ties with Algeria, and had previously met Bouteflika in Algiers, in his former role as Halliburton CEO. There he had promoted the concept of stronger bilateral ties, including American military cooperation. With both presidents now expressing a general desire to expand US investment in Algeria's energy sector, Algeria's foreign minister, Abdelaziz Belkhadem, told attendant journalists that the target was 'to increase the size of American investments in the oil sector from the current [2001] level of $4 billion to $8 billion in the next four years'.[18]

Bouteflika, pleased though he evidently was with such developments in the oil sector, did not lose sight of what he really wanted from Washington. Almost as a harbinger of what was to befall America precisely 59 days later, in the events of 9/11, he told President Bush that his country had dealt with the fight against terrorists and that he was now 'seeking specific equipment which would enable us to maintain peace, security and stability in Algeria'.[19] Less than three weeks after Bouteflika's Washington visit, the Algerian army chief of staff, General Lamari, visited the military headquarters of US EUCOM (European Command) in Stuttgart, where he sought further support for his army's modernisation effort.

The Opportunity of 9/11

Although it was the realisation of America's energy needs, highlighted by the Cheney Report, that underpinned this new warming in US–Algerian relations at the start of the Bush administration, it was the 9/11 attacks on the World Trade Center in New York and the Pentagon Building in Washington DC that inaugurated a new era in US–Algerian relations.

The events of 9/11 provided a heaven-sent opportunity for Algeria. Bouteflika, not one to miss a political trick, was going to take maximum advantage of it. After ensuring that he was almost the first Muslim leader to offer help and support to the US in its 'war on terror', it was down to business. For Algeria, America's tragedy offered several opportunities. In terms of trying to overthrow its pariah status, 9/11 provided Algiers with the horrifically real imagery with which to persuade the world of the correctness of its policy of 'eradication' in its dirty war against Islamists.[20] It was the chance to say 'We told you so!'[21] To show its willingness to help the US in its war on terror, Algiers provided the Americans with a list of 1,350 names of Algerians abroad with alleged links to Osama bin Laden, and a list of alleged Islamist militants inside Algeria.[22] Neither the US State Department nor US intelligence services have been willing to comment on these lists. That is not surprising, as we now know that many of the links with al-Qaeda that the Algerians attached to those on the list it provided to the US were false. We also have good reason to believe that many of the names handed to the US were the Algerian regime's own enemies: not necessarily 'terrorists', but innocent Algerians who, for the most part, had done nothing more than vote for a religious party and then flee their country for their own safety. We will probably never know how many of them have been 'disappeared' through US rendition services, or simply eliminated along the way.

Above all, 9/11 provided Algeria with a golden opportunity to push for the high-tech weaponry that had been denied its army for years. It was with such a shopping list in mind, and in a spirit of opportunism, that Bouteflika made his second visit to

Washington, in November 2001. His meeting with President Bush was scheduled for 5 November. Three days before the meeting, Bouteflika started beating the terrorist drum. While reaffirming his country's support for America, he reminded the US administration that 'the Algerian people had had to confront terrorism alone, amongst general indifference'.[23] He hoped that the US would now see Algeria's struggle against Islamic militants as comparable to its own war against al-Qaeda, and thus be more willing to provide the sophisticated weaponry that his army needed so badly.

Although the US made no public comment about what the two presidents had discussed in their meeting, Algeria Interface was able to quote State Department sources confirming that Algerian demands for military equipment were at the centre of the discussions between the two presidents.[24, 25]

US Tardy on Algerian Arms Sales

However, behind the diplomatic niceties, smiles and hand-shaking, Bouteflika was to find that the new US administration was not quite the soft touch that Algeria had been hoping for. Only four days after Bouteflika's meeting with Bush, a spokesman for the National Security Council told Human Rights Watch that Algeria had been asking the US 'to be more forthcoming'. He also explained that the US was maintaining its 'go-slow' approach and had not changed its opposition to selling night-vision equipment – an item Algeria has long sought for counter-insurgency use.[26]

In spite of all the post-9/11 'war on terror' rhetoric, and Washington's announcement that it was planning to expand military and security aid to Algeria through the transfer of equipment and accelerated training, the transfers were mostly of a symbolic nature, in the form of frequent visits to Algiers by senior US officials,[27] regular visits by US naval ships, and a doubling of the International Military Education and Training Program (IMET).[28] The weapons systems that Algeria sought were not forthcoming.[29]

There were two main reasons for America's tardiness on arms sales to Algeria. The first was Washington's expressed fear of criticism by human rights groups[30] – although, given the Bush–Cheney regime's complete lack of concern for human rights,[31] this should be interpreted merely as a euphemistic way for the US to say that it was worried about provoking further Islamist attacks on the US. The second was the decline of terrorism in Algeria. By 2000, average monthly killings had fallen to around 200 – a marked drop since the 1990s, when killings averaged some 1,500 per month. By 2002, Algeria appeared to have further reduced the number of killings and largely contained terrorist activities to the more remote and mountainous parts of northern and north-eastern Algeria. This much-improved situation undoubtedly led the American administration to think that the Algerian army was on top of the terrorist situation, and could manage without US military equipment.[32] Indeed, this marked improvement in security was reflected in a doubling of tourists visiting the Algerian Sahara in both 2001 and 2002, following a complete absence of tourism between 1991 and 1999.[33]

Although Bouteflika paid another visit to Washington, in June 2002, at which the sale of night-vision military systems was reportedly agreed, little military equipment actually seems to have been transferred to Algeria during the course of the year. This is borne out in several statements made by US officials on arms sales to Algeria in late 2002. Although seemingly positive on the subject of military collaboration, the statements reflect America's caution on the sale of lethal weapons systems. In fact, Washington even went so far as to state publicly that no approval of the sale of lethal weapons systems to Algeria had been given. One US official was reported as saying that the US would proceed slowly on the military aid package, partly because of criticism by human rights groups. Another, when pushed, said: 'down the road we might consider it. We will consider requests if we believe they contribute to the counter-terrorism effort'.[34] It was also noticeable that William Burns, assistant secretary of state for Near East affairs, made no reference to lethal weapons systems when he said 'We are putting the finishing touches to an agreement to sell Algeria equipment to fight terrorism.'[35]

Origins of the 'Banana Theory'

If there was any single moment in time over the entire duration of this narrative when a number of circumstances and events came together in such a way as to provide those crucial clues that enable an understanding of this extraordinary story, then it was through the later months of 2002, from September onwards. The circumstances and events that I recount below have not been documented before. Each one, taken on its own, might seem insignificant; but when brought together and examined in the round, this string of seemingly unrelated incidents provide us with the trailer for the full, wide-screen, Technicolor whole.

Let me start at the global level. The immediate US response to 9/11 was to declare a new 'war on terror', with a massive attack on Afghanistan, named Operation Enduring Freedom (OEF). The combined objectives of OEF were, as President Bush explained in his address to a joint session of Congress on 20 September and in his 7 October address to the country, to capture Osama bin Laden; to destroy al-Qaeda, along with its terrorist training camps and infrastructure; and to remove the Taliban regime. As we now know only too well, none of these objectives was achieved. Nevertheless, in the wake of its prematurely proclaimed 'victory' in Afghanistan, from around midsummer 2002 the US began to develop what I have called the 'banana theory of terrorism'.

The banana theory of terrorism is a reference not to the state of Washington's intelligence, which, as I explain below, belonged more to the realm of imagination than reality, but to the banana-shaped route that Washington imagined the terrorists it had dislodged from Afghanistan were taking into Africa. The fact that most of them appear to have moved little further than across the border, into Pakistan, is another story. The route Washington presumed or imagined they had taken in their flight from US forces in Central Asia was to the Horn of Africa and into Sudan – a country already well-tarred with the bin Laden brush – and then across the Sahelian countries of Chad, Niger, Mali and Mauritania, from whence they headed north to link up with Islamic militants in the Maghreb.[36]

There was absolutely no hard evidence to support this theory. As a report on Islamic terrorism in the Sahel by the highly respected International Crisis Group was to conclude in 2005, 'there was little or no Islamic extremism and no terrorism in the Sahel at that time'.[37] Neither was there any firm evidence that terrorists from Afghanistan, Pakistan or the Middle East were taking this route. And yet, as we have seen,[38] by the time the hostage crisis was over, the banana theory was the official Washington line, as expressed in statements such as that of EUCOM's Maj. Gen. Jeff Kohler in January 2004: 'As terrorist cells were uprooted from Afghanistan and elsewhere by US Central Command ... they shifted to ... the wide-open, relatively desolate areas of Africa ... an easy back door into Europe through Algeria, Morocco and Tunisia.'[39] Or, as one of his colleagues opined, 'If you squeeze the terrorists in Afghanistan, Pakistan, Iraq and other places, they will find new places to operate, and one of those places is the Sahel/Maghreb.'[40]

If there was no hard evidence for the banana theory, on what was US intelligence being based? And how and when did the idea begin to take root? Let me stay with the big, global picture for just a moment longer. While 9/11 may have diverted public attention away from the Cheney Report,[41] the Pentagon, now effectively driving US foreign policy, had certainly not taken its eyes off the ball. Indeed, 9/11 and the launch of a global war on terror (GWOT) was just the sort of opportunity that the Project for the New American Century sought. It provided the ideological pretext to secure the militarisation of those regions, such as Africa, that US imperial interests required. The Bush administration had already defined African oil as a 'strategic national interest', and thus a resource that the US might choose military force to control.[42] It was the reason why Ed Royce, the chairman of the US Congress African sub-committee, called in January 2002 for African oil to 'be treated as a priority for US national security post 9/11';[43] and, as US Deputy Assistant Secretary of Defense for African Affairs, Michael Westphal, explained in a Pentagon press briefing in April 2002, why 'Africa matters to the United States'.[44] Westphal reiterated the point two

months later, stressing that Africa was already supplying 14 per
cent of US oil imports, and had the potential to increase that
amount substantially over the next decade. In June, with the
Afghanistan 'victory' over his shoulder, and the war on terror
on its way to Africa, US Assistant Secretary of State for Africa
Walter Kansteiner told his audience in Nigeria that 'African oil
is of strategic national interest to us' and that 'it will increase
and become very important as we go forward'.[45]

Unfortunately for the new US administration, Africa was not
prolific in terror. Indeed, insurance rates on big projects in Africa,
always a good measure of such risk, were about the lowest in
the world at that time. The only serious terrorist attacks on
the continent in sub-Saharan Africa at that time had been the
almost contemporaneous bombings in 1998 of the US Embassies
in Nairobi and Dar es Salaam, both of which were attributed to
Osama bin Laden's al-Qaeda network.[46] Later, in November 2002,
the bombing of a hotel in Mombasa, believed to have been targeted
at Israelis and also attributed to al-Qaeda, killed more than a
dozen. These attacks were not only specifically targeted against the
US and Israel, but were on the other side of the continent, far from
West Africa's crucial oil resources and hardly enough to justify the
launch of a whole new front in the GWOT. On the other hand,
the idea of terrorists swarming across the continent, from the
Horn to the Atlantic and Mediterranean coasts, and hiding in the
vast, little-government and open spaces of the Sahara–Sahel, was
something that US intelligence could work with. Thus, in the wake
of Afghanistan, Washington's philosophers began to formulate
seriously their banana theory of world terrorism – of terrorists,
dislodged from Afghanistan, using the Sahel as a conduit and
then fanning out northwards into the Maghreb and Europe, and
southwards into the strategic oil-producing countries of West
Africa and the Gulf of Guinea.

Until the later months of 2002, US intelligence services had
their banana theory, but no facts with which to substantiate it.
After extensive enquiry, I believe that US intelligence agencies
may have been relying on little more than two or three snippets of
intelligence. These were certainly not enough to substantiate the

notion of the Sahel as a conduit for terrorists from Central Asia to north-west Africa and Europe. Their fragments of information consisted of an unpublished memo that I had sent to colleagues in the US regarding the funding of a Saharan research programme in the UK, and its research project into banditry and trafficking in the Sahel, which found its way into the hands of intelligence agencies in Washington in June or July 2002. Secondly, both that memo and the Algerian press provided US intelligence services with references to the trans-Saharan smuggling activities of the outlaw Mokhtar ben Mokhtar. Finally, the CIA seems to have misinterpreted the nature of the Islamic Tablighi Jamaat movement in Mali.[47] The movement's 200 or so members in Mali were often referred to simply as 'the Pakistanis', because their sect's headquarters were in Pakistan.[48] This reference to Pakistan seems to have convinced members of the US intelligence community that Mali was on the route that terrorists from Afghanistan and Pakistan were taking across the Sahel to the Maghreb and Europe.

There are also indications that the very limited US intelligence-gathering facilities in the region relied heavily on local army officers telling the US what it wanted to hear.[49]

A New Era in US–Algerian Intelligence Relations

A whole new phase in US–Algerian relations opened up after the end of July. On 31 July 2002, Marion E. ('Spike') Bowman, deputy general counsel for the FBI, presented evidence to the Senate Select Committee on Intelligence in regard to proposed amendments concerning the Foreign Intelligence Surveillance Act. Until this moment, the American intelligence community was anxious about working too closely with its Algerian counterparts, for fear that they would pass sensitive information to Palestinian organisations. However, Bowman's statement, in which he presented the background and present nature of what the FBI calls the 'International Jihad Movement', dispelled many of the anxieties about collaborating with the Algerians by showing how close Algeria was to the US in its fight against al-Qaeda and terrorism.[50] From that moment, especially as the summer moved to autumn, collaboration between US and Algerian intelligence services moved onto a new level.

But this new level of US–Algerian collaboration was not plain sailing – on the contrary, by the last few months of 2002, US–Algerian relations had become a little tetchy. Algeria was beginning to complain publicly that US assistance was both minimal and slow in arriving, while behind the scenes it seems that senior Algerian officials were more vociferous in expressing their anger at being 'let down'. They felt that they had opened themselves and their country to the Americans and done everything possible to collaborate with them in their war on terror – in which they were both victims – but had received little or none of the weaponry they wanted in return.

It looked as if the wheels might be about to come off the developing US–Algerian relationship. And yet, as we know, the hostage drama that began only a few months later, in February–March 2003, was to lead the two countries into what has become one of the closest international relationships in the entire GWOT. What put the show back on the road? It was almost as if a fairy-godmother had suddenly intervened. Or was it the touch of evil genius? Careful exploration of what happened in the Sahara, and elsewhere in Algeria and the Sahel, during the winter of 2002/03 yields a very strong sense that pure evil may have been at work – which brings me be back to the question of who instigated the abduction of the 32 European tourists in the Algerian Sahara in February–March 2003. The Algerians? The Americans? Or both?

In the weeks and months of post-Bowman collaboration between the US and Algerian intelligence services, the Algerians were conscious of two key issues. One was that they needed to demonstrate to the Americans, if they were to get any new military hardware from them, that terrorism within Algeria was not, in fact, under control. Secondly, they were aware of the US's larger designs on Africa, and that their 'banana theory' would not hold up unless it could be based on hard facts in the form of real, headline-grabbing terrorism in the Sahel. The Algerians realised that they were in a position to kill two birds with one stone: they had the means to fabricate the terrorism, and thus to help themselves and the Americans at the same time. The stone required was to be unearthed in the depths of the Sahara. It was there, in October 2002, in a remote and little-known corner of the Algerian Sahara, that the bigger picture began to take form.

Arak, October 2002: the First Attempt at Hostage-taking

The autumn of 2002 was exceptional in that persistent, penetrating rains fell over much of the central Sahara. Tourists might well have wondered if they were really in the Sahara, as sand seas turned green almost before their eyes, *pistes* and roads became impassable to vehicles, or in some cases washed away altogether, *oueds* flowed, *shotts* filled, and plastic covers and umbrellas became almost de rigueur. But for four Swiss tourists travelling back home from Tamanrasset, the Sahara was far more traumatic. Because the main road south to Tamanrasset had been washed out in the floods, there were fuel shortages throughout the region. However, the four Swiss tourists managed to obtain special permission from the authorities in Tamanrasset to purchase 100 litres of fuel for their Isuzu Trooper.

While negotiating the fuel purchase from the local authorities, the Swiss asked if they had to join a convoy, as had been required three years earlier when Mokhtar ben Mokhtar held much of the extreme south to ransom. 'Non, non vous voyagez ici en sécurité' (No – you travel here in safety), they were told. They left Tamanrasset on Thursday 17 October, reaching Arak by nightfall. The following morning they continued north on the road to In Salah, only to find the road blocked 40km north of Arak by a Nissan Pickup and five men with Kalashnikovs trained on them. Three other vehicles, including one lorry, all belonging to Algerians, were stopped over the next hour or so, before the four Swiss and the Algerians were taken 15km to a base camp where other bandits – twelve in all – were holding another 17 Algerians hostage. The bandits claimed to be 'soldiers of Allah' seeking revenge for the unjustified killing of their families by the Algerian army.[51]

Negotiations, the substance of which is not at all clear, continued throughout the day. Just when the hostages thought the situation was becoming less tense, a Kalashnikov was mounted on a vehicle 10 metres in front of them. They were photographed with the gun trained on them. One of the tourists, thinking that their last moment had come, plucked up his courage and walked towards the gun. He put his index finger into the barrel and pushed it away with the words: 'Never point guns at people'. The hijackers, seemingly baffled and surprised, burst out laughing. The tension immediately eased and the bandits, for reasons we will never know, began organising their own departure, taking with them the tourists' vehicle and all their possessions except the clothes they were wearing and their passports. As they left the camp, they ordered everyone to remain where they were for two hours, warning that they would otherwise be shot. The whole group later made its way back to Arak in the lorry that had been held up, but not taken.

The tourists claim that the police at Arak treated them extremely badly, failing to take proper statements or to investigate. The gendarmerie, however, picked up the trail and tracked the hijackers across 600km of desert, before finding them at the well at Tin Ghergoh, two-thirds of the way to Mali. The hijackers' tracks zigzagged all over the desert, giving the impression that they were unfamiliar with the region, which meant that they almost certainly came from the north. When the gendarmes finally caught up with them, their commanding officer called the head of military security in Tamanrasset to request instructions.[52] Two hours later the gendarmes were ordered by the DRS in Tamanrasset to let their captives go free.[53] This and other aspects of the incident[54] convinced local people that it had been planned and carried out by members of Algeria's DRS. At that stage, however, they could not understand why.

Whether the Arak 'hijack' was a botched attempt to kidnap European hostages, and thus demonstrate that Islamic terrorism had spread into the Sahara, or a test-run for the hostage-taking four months later, will probably never be known. Neither do I know if US intelligence services were aware of it. However, with the US now turning its attention to the Sahel, its intelligence services, even if not informed by their Algerian counterparts, would surely have picked up the report of the incident on a Swiss travel website.

Perhaps the most crucial piece of information, which never came to light during the hostage drama of 2003, is that preparatory work for that kidnapping – in the form of locating, preparing the access to and stocking the cave system in the Tamelrik mountains in which the hostages were to be held – was begun shortly after the Arak incident. The reason we know this is that Kel Ajjer (Tuareg) nomads in the Tamelrik area came across a number of bearded and heavily armed men working in the region. The men first approached the nomads in November, some three to four weeks after the Tin Ghergoh release, to buy goats and sheep from them for meat. This was not a one-off incident. The men remained in the Tamelrik region, and had several further such contacts with the nomads over a number of weeks. The Kel Ajjer, being experienced with the arms purchases and trafficking of fellow Tuareg in Niger, recognised the nature of their arms and became increasingly suspicious of their presence and activities, to the extent that the nomads notified the military authorities in Illizi.[55] The military took no action at all. From subsequent interviews with these nomads, it is clear that these men were scouting out the maze of caves and shelters in Tamelrik, and installing the sort of rudimentary infrastructure required to hold a large number of hostages for a considerable period of time.

Although the circumstantial evidence is strong, it will probably never be known for certain whether the men preparing the Tamelrik caves were the same as those who had hijacked the tourists at Arak. But what we do know, thanks to these Kel Ajjer nomads, is that plans to kidnap tourists and hold them in Tamelrik were in place within less than a month of the Arak incident – that is, by November – and that the Algerian military authorities, although warned, did absolutely nothing to investigate.

Planning for the Pan-Sahel Initiative (PSI)

The clearest indication we have that the Americans were aware of what the Algerians were planning is that, at some point between

Bowman's testimony at the end of July and the Arak hold-up in October, the Bush administration had decided to take its GWOT into the Sahel. We know this because in October, at the time that the Swiss tourists were being hi-jacked, two officials from the US Office of Counterterrorism – namely 'AF DAS Robert Perry' and 'S/CT Deputy Coordinator Stephanie Kinney' – were traversing the Sahel, briefing the governments of Mali, Niger, Chad and Mauritania on the Bush administration's Pan Sahel Initiative (PSI).[56] The State Department explained the PSI as

> a program designed to protect borders, track movement of people, combat terrorism, and enhance regional cooperation and stability. It is a State-led effort to assist Mali, Niger, Chad, and Mauritania in detecting and responding to suspicious movement of people and goods across and within their borders through training, equipment and cooperation. Its goals support two US national security interests in Africa: waging the war on terrorism and enhancing regional peace and security.[57]

How could the US Office of Counterterrorism have been so confident in proselytizing the PSI if it did not have advance knowledge of the terrorism that was going to befall the region?[58]

Moreover, while the armed *mujahideen*, undisturbed by Algeria's security forces, were busy burrowing into the gorges and caves of Tamelrik, the US State Department was beginning its technical assessment of the situation on the southern side of Algeria's borders. In Mali, this involved a visit to Timbuktu in November by the US ambassador. For an ambassador to visit Timbuktu is not unusual. In this instance, however, the trip went a little further. Local people reported that the ambassador, travelling with 20 men whom they described as 'CIA' in two helicopters, got lost in the desert for about ten days. It is less likely that the helicopters either crashed or 'got lost' than that that the locals were simply surprised at how long they spent in the area. Local residents, interviewed shortly after the mission, were asked if they knew its purpose. They said that the American party was checking out terrorist training facilities known – or rather thought – to be in the area. They also thought the party was reconnoitring a possible site for establishing a military base for what the local people, possibly quoting the Americans, referred to as 'anti-al-Qaeda purposes'.

11

PREPARING THE DISINFORMATION

By the end of November 2002, some three months before the disappearance of the first of the 32 hostages, the Algerian and Malian Sahara were hives of activity. In Algeria, *mujahideen* were busy preparing the Tamelrik site. Across the border, the Americans were busy reconnoitring the north-east Malian corner of the Sahara that was later to become pivotal in the so-called 'war on terror' in the region.

In Algiers, in the meantime, Generals Mohammed Mediene (Toufik) and Smaïn Lamari were almost certainly pondering General Khaled Nezzar's failed defamation case. While the shock of 9/11 diverted world attention from the revelations of Habib Souaïdia's *La Sale Guerre*, the DRS bosses knew precisely what the implications of the Paris court judgement could be. Effectively proved guilty of crimes against humanity, their best protection from the International Criminal Court,[1] or whatever other form of investigation or judicial retribution might face them, was to make themselves indispensable to their new American ally in its 'global war on terror' (GWOT).

Also in Algiers, General Smaïn Lamari's staff in the DRS's Directorate for Documentation and External Security were hard at work preparing a raft of documentary briefing material and press releases on the al-Qaeda threat to both Algeria and the Sahara–Sahel that would be strategically placed in predominantly Algerian and French-language newspapers over the course of these three months.

A sample of the headlines (translated) from the time of the US reconnaissance of the Malian Sahara in November 2002 to the capture of the first hostages in February 2003 gives a clear message:

(1) 28 November 2002 'The bin Laden nebula: the worrying emirs of the Sahel'[2]

(2) 28 November 2002 'The introduction of 370 GSPC terrorists'[3]

(3) 30 November 2002 'Belmokhtar[4] met Imad Abdelwahid'[5]

(4) 2 December 2002 'Terrorism: Al-Qaeda in Mali'[6]

(5) 24 December 2002 'Portrait of the terrorist leader, Belmokhtar'[7]

(6) 30 December 2002 '17 Toyotas hijacked from an oil company at Illizi: the Emir Belmokhtar terrorises the South'[8]

(7) 7 January 2003 'Terrorist attack at In Guezzam: Belmokhtar's GSPC at it again'[9]

(8) 7 January 2003 'Abou Mohammed[10] turned out to be with the GSPC Batna underground: Al-Qaeda's agent shot dead'[11]

(9) 30 January 2003 'Mafia and terrorism are interlinked: the trail of the cannabis cartel'[12]

(10) 5 February 2003 'Tracking Al-Qaeda continues: members of Belmokhtar's network caught in Mali'[13]

(11) 10 February 2003 'Visit of an American mission to Algiers: FBI, CIA and NSA solicit the DRS'[14]

(12) 18 February 2003 'Belmokhtar supplied by Niger tribes: a powder keg in the South'[15]

These articles, and many others like them, painted an alarming, indeed terrifying picture of the Algerian and Sahelian Sahara. But they were almost all without any factual foundation. They were largely propaganda – disinformation, designed and crafted in such a way as to link 9/11, al-Qaeda, bin Laden, the GSPC, Hassan Hattab, Mokhtar ben Mokhtar and later El Para, Saharan rebels (the Tuareg), smugglers and traffickers. These linkages and associations not only gave some substance to what I have called Washington's developing 'banana theory', but also provided the backcloth to the stage on which the 32 hostages and El Para were soon to play their central roles in creating the 'big fact', the headline-holder, that was to justify the launch of a new, Saharan front in the GWOT.

Contextual Analysis of Algeria's 'Disinformation'

I outline and comment on the substance of each of these articles in the course of the next few pages. If the reader detects the occasional note of derision, it is because it is difficult to treat such cynical and largely fictional portrayals of the region seriously.

Article (1)[16] kicks off in blockbuster style, stating that the Saharan–Sahelian zone risks becoming a launch pad for armed fundamentalists striking at Western interests. Washington, we are told, is intending to tighten up controls across the entire zone, which is now the home of a number of extremists associated with or belonging to groups close to al-Qaeda. This frightening scenario comes from the US State Department's 'authoritative' Voice of America (VOA), which, citing a US Defense Department official, states that the Sahelian countries of Chad, Niger, Mali and Mauritania are particularly open to 'terrorist penetration' because of their borders with states like Algeria, Libya and Sudan. To back up this assertion, VOA cites intelligence sources to reveal the name of one such mysterious group, known only by the initials MBM, from the name of its leader, Mokhtar ben Mokhtar, who, we are told, is directly linked to Osama bin Laden's terrorist network, and who plunders the desert between northern Mali, southern Algeria and part of Mauritania (the area searched by the two US helicopters in November). Better known as 'Belaouer' (the one-eyed one) because of a wound received in his eye while fighting in Afghanistan, MBM has been in the sights of the Algerian army for more than a year as an arms trafficker for various Islamist groups – notably the GSPC of Hassan Hattab who, so the article informs us, is also known to be close to Osama bin Laden.

The article then focuses on northern Mali, particularly the region around Kidal and northwards to the Algerian border, and the region known as El-Khalil some 140km north of Tessalit. This region, MBM's field of operations, is described as being virtually a 'free zone', beyond the effective control of the Malian state, and open to arms traffickers, stolen-vehicle smugglers, illegal immigrants making their way to Europe, and so on. We are told that, according to the same unnamed intelligence sources, this region is Tuareg territory, and the focal point of the Tuareg rebellion in Mali (which, I should add, ended in 1995), thus making it an ideal hideout for terrorists. Even more alarmingly, we are told that the region – notably its main town, Kidal – has become a centre of radical Islamic fundamentalists, namely the 'Dawa' sect. (The journalist means the Tablighi Jamaat movement – see Chapter 12). The presence of radical Islamists in the region is linked to a similar phenomenon reportedly found around Agades, the centre of the Tuareg rebellion in Niger (which also ended in 1995), where many foreign radical preachers have also tried to establish themselves.

The article then gives forewarning of the Bush administration's Pan-Sahel Initiative (PSI), though without mentioning it by name. It merely states that the Pentagon is fearful of this region becoming a new sanctuary and rear base for al-Qaeda fugitives, and has accordingly decided to cooperate with the countries concerned by deploying the men and materials needed to beef up control over their frontiers. But Algeria – which has experienced so many years of attacks at the hands of the GIA and other armed dissident groups, especially Hassan Hattab's GSPC – is seen as the key to the region's overall surveillance and security.

In case readers do not appreciate the gravity of all this, the article reminds them that a document was found in the baggage of Mohamed Atta, the leader of the commando unit which flew the first plane into New York's World Trade Center, which describes plans for cooperation between Hassan Hattab's GSPC in Algeria and al-Qaeda.[17] Credible sources – the Pentagon, the State Department and US intelligence services – thus link the horror of 9/11 directly with the most remote and least known corners of the Sahara – Tuareg country – and with feared names and organisations such as Mokhtar ben Mokhtar, Hassan Hattab, the GSPC, and others who will presently be added to this dangerous nexus.

On the same day as *L'Express* published that alarming news, Algeria's *Le Matin* (article 2), citing military sources, confirmed that 370 GSPC terrorists were now established in Algeria. Of these, 180 were under the command of Saâdaoui Abdelhamid (known as Abou Yahia, alias Abou Haytham) in the central mountains around Bourmedès, Tizi Ouzou and Bouira. Another 150 or so were being led by Ammari Saïfi, known as Abderazak le Para (a new name to most of the paper's readers) in the eastern mountains around Sétif, Batna, Tébessa, Annaba and Souk Ahras, while some 40 or so terrorists belonging to the group of Mokhtar ben Mokhtar's (written as Belmokhtar Mokhtar), operated between Djelfa and the extreme south, including sorties into Niger, Mali and Mauritania. The southern group's mission was to provide arms for those in the north.[18]

Two days later, the link between 9/11, Osama bin Laden, al-Qaeda, Mokhtar ben Mokhtar, Hassan Hattab, the GSPC and El Para was firmed up a little more clearly. The story in Algeria's *L'Expression* (article 3) is that Mokhtar ben Mokhtar accompanied Osama bin Laden's emissary and al-Qaeda's representative in the Maghreb to a meeting with the terrorist Khelifa ben Kouider, alias Abou el-Hamam, in the Djelfa region in August 2001. The story is attributed to 'good sources' – a euphemism for the DRS's counter-terrorism unit. It is a story which has achieved increasing prominence as time has gone on, largely because the alleged emissary, Imad Abdelwahid Ahmed, alias Abou Mohamed, often known simply as 'the Yemeni', was reportedly killed in an army assault near Batna two months earlier (September 2002). We therefore have no other proof of either his existence or his alleged death except for the word of Algeria's army, which has scarcely managed to come up with one word of truth throughout this entire drama. Be that as it may, the story, now imprinted into contemporary Algerian history and US intelligence files, is that bin Laden's emissary was wanting to help sort out the question of the GSPC's leadership in the extreme south (i.e. the Sahara) between Hassan Hattab, Mokhtar ben Mokhtar, El Para (whose name is creeping ever more prominently into the public psyche) and Khelifa ben Kouider. The impression is thus given that bin Laden himself is overseeing the reorganisation of the GSPC in Algeria, especially in the Saharan region – and, to make the association, just a few weeks before 9/11.

Article (4), published two days later, is merely a 'proof by reiteration' article, reproduced in several newspapers and magazines, such as *Jeune Afrique L'Intelligent*, the Swiss French-language *L'Hebdo-International* and Niger's *Le Republicain*, which repeats the VOA broadcast already mentioned in Article (1), stating that the Americans suspect al-Qaeda of redeploying into West Africa under the aegis of Mokhtar ben Mokhtar. It reiterates his geographical field of operations in the Mali–Mauritania–Algerian border zones, while spicing up the story just a little more by saying that this region is occupied by *les barbus* (the 'bearded men' – a derogatory term for Islamic fundamentalists), and is a region that is difficult for the military to access. The article also reinforces Washington's 'banana theory' by raising the veil on the identity of *les barbus*, saying that they are Pakistanis, Afghans and Algerian Islamists belonging to the al-Qaeda network. (This was and is completely false. They are, in fact, members of the pacifist Tablighi Jamaat, introduced in Chapter 12).

The fifth of these articles presents a chilling portrait of the 'terrorist' chief, Mokhtar ben Mokhtar (Belmokhtar). Mokhtar is linked to a number of former GIA members – notably its leader Djamel Zitouni (d. 1996), who is reported to have charged Mokhtar in 1994 with assassinating foreign nationals working in the south of the country. This account is interesting for two reasons. Firstly, as explained in Chapter 9, Zitouni was a DRS infiltrator and under DRS command. Secondly, only one foreign national is known to have been killed in the south of the country during this period, if by 'south' one means the Saharan regions which are the focus of this book. The one isolated case was a German tourist who was allegedly killed by Mokhtar around 1995, when the German concerned resisted the theft of his vehicle – a circumstance which was rather different from the mass slaughter allegedly being advocated by Zitouni. Having portrayed him as a 'murderer of foreign nationals', the article reiterates Mokhtar's contacts with bin Laden's emissary and his key role of providing arms to the GSPC terrorist groups in the north of the country under the command of Hassan Hattab and El Para. These arms were coming from what is now described as 'the al-Qaeda rear base' that Mokhtar has set up in the border regions of Algeria, Mali and Mauritania, and which is being supplied with arms by the Islamic fundamentalist 'Dawa oua Tabligh' (Tablighi Jamaat) movement, which is now reported to have established itself in both northern Niger and Mali. (The reader should be aware that the Americans and Algerians have referred continuously to 'terrorists' bases' or 'rear bases' in northern Mali over the course of the last five or six years. It should be noted that not a single such base has ever been found in this region, in spite of the operations of US Special Forces and alleged satellite surveillance.[19])

Article (6), is particularly interesting in that it raises the question, almost as a premonition, of the threat posed to tourists in Algeria's extreme south by terrorists such as Mokhtar ben Mokhtar. The incident on which the article was based was the hijacking and theft of 17 four-wheel-drive vehicles belonging to an oil company in the Ouanet–Illizi region. According to the journalist's 'sources', the culprit was identified as Mokhtar ben Mokhtar. However, I was there shortly after the incident, and the opinion of most local people was that the bandits were more likely to have been one of many groups supposedly copying Mokhtar, than Mokhtar himself, who by this time was thought to have established himself in either Mauritania or Burkina Faso.

One week later, in article (7), the same newspaper used a similar incident to reiterate the linkages between Mokhtar ben Mokhtar, al-Qaeda, bin Laden, Afghans and the GSPC terrorists in the north of the country – notably Abderazzak El Para, whose name, previously unheard of, had in the course of a month become commonplace. The incident was a 'terrorist attack' on a road-gang working on the section of the main road at a point between 60km and 120km north of In Guezzam. Twenty heavily armed terrorists were reported to have distributed leaflets, said to be from Hassan Hattab, before stealing five vehicles and supplies and heading off in the direction of Niger. The leaflets and the direction of flight were proof to the authorities, who offered no other explanation, that the attackers belonged to Mokhtar ben Mokhtar's GSPC command. The army reportedly undertook a massive sweep, but, as so often, and in spite of its use of helicopters and hot pursuit into Niger, came up with nothing. The most interesting feature of the article is that it manages in a circuitous way to link these events to the infiltration into the region of al-Qaeda terrorists from Afghanistan. The purported evidence for this is threefold. The first is the usual unnamed but reliable security 'sources' – code for military propaganda. In this case the journalist states that 'it would not be wrong to believe the information in our possession which seems to indicate the presence of al-Qaeda fugitives [Afghans] who have succeeded in infiltrating national territory [Algeria] thanks to the assistance of Belmokhtar's terrorists'. Secondly, *L'Expression* refers to one of its earlier articles in which it mentioned the presence of a heavily armed group of Afghan Arabs in the Djanet region. The source of this information is not given, nor is the ethnic reference to 'Afghan Arabs' explained;[20] but in all probability the group concerned, even assuming that it existed, is likely to have been part of the extensive flow of illegal migrants moving from the Sahel to Libya who cut across the extreme south-east corner of Libya. They can be encountered on almost any day of the week if one cares to take a stroll along one of the world's most scenically beautiful pathways, the old caravan route that crosses the Tassili plateau from Djanet and Ghat. Some of the 'traffickers' of this business are Arabs and are armed. Thirdly, Afghan Arabs (whatever the ethnic meaning of this term) were reportedly thought to have been involved in an ambush of army troops the previous week near Batna, in the Aures region.[21] If the reader has trouble in making a connection between two incidents some 2,000km apart – bearing in mind that the distance from Algeria's southern frontier at In Guezzam to Algiers is further than the distance between London and Algiers – the journalist comes to our help: the ambush in the Aures took place in the same part of the country where Imad Abdelwahid, bin Laden's alleged emissary, had been killed three months earlier. That is the region in which El Para operates, and El Para is supplied with arms by Mokhtar ben Mokhtar – as the paper has explained in several earlier editions. QED!

Article (8), published in Algeria's *El Watan*, is another heavy piece of 'proof by reiteration', designed to establish verification of the association between al-Qaeda, bin Laden, and 9/11 with the GSPC, Hassan Hattab, El Para and Mokhtar ben Mokhtar.

It does this by adding another layer of detail to what has already been said in the articles mentioned above. For instance, for those who wonder if 'the Yemeni' (Imad Abdelwahid Ahmed Alwan, alias Abou Mohamed), bin Laden's emissary, really was killed near Batna on 12 September, *El Watan* (known for its close ties to the security establishment) confirms that his body was identified by *les services spécialisés*. If that were not convincing enough – and to show that *El Watan* is on top of every detail – we are told that, at the very moment of the 9/11 attacks in the US, Abou Mohamed was among the GSPC *maquis* of south-eastern Algeria, in the Aures region. Chilling. And even more so to learn that he spent the whole winter there, checking out whether the GSPC was up to the task that bin Laden allegedly had in mind for it – namely, to establish an al-Qaeda base in the Sahel to compensate for the loss of its bases in Afghanistan and Somalia. And so, with winter over, and the GSPC deemed up to it, Abou Mohamed set off for northern Mali, passing himself off along the way as Sidi Ahmed Habib Allah, a native of northern Niger, but also travelling under many other aliases and spending two or three weeks in each of Mauritania, Mali, Niger and Chad, checking out the scene. Then, according to *El Watan*'s 'guaranteed sources', Abou Mohamed returned to the Batna region for the summer of 2002, to meet and collaborate with the GSPC leaders of the region, notably El Para and Mokhtar ben Mokhtar.

By this time, even the least intelligent reader can only wonder why Algeria has a terrorist problem when its 'guaranteed sources' – the country's military intelligence services – have such detailed knowledge of the identities, numbers, movements and meetings of its terrorists. The compiler of the article has anticipated that obvious banana skin. We are told, in no uncertain terms, that Algeria's security forces knew absolutely nothing of all this at the time. The discovery of Abou Mohamed's presence in the region was entirely thanks to the Americans, who spotted him and immediately informed their Algerian counterparts. That should overcome our incredulity. But we are not given details of how the Americans achieved such an intelligence coup, which is truly amazing in the wake of their massive intelligence bungling in

Afghanistan (and later Iraq), and especially since they are known to have had little or no human intelligence of their own on the ground in Algeria. Indeed, such an uncharacteristically successful intelligence coup makes one wonder if there ever was an Abou Mohamed, and suspect that he was perhaps just another 'phantom' of Algeria's intelligence services. Like the other 'phantoms', he was reportedly killed off, on this occasion in an army ambush: killed and identified by the specialist services – in secret. In case, like me, the reader is becoming a little cynical, the compiler tells us that GSPC members who have taken advantage of the amnesty and turned themselves in have confirmed all this. They were able to tell their debriefing interrogators that Abou Mohamed had told them that he recognised all the participants in the 9/11 attacks as being members of al-Qaeda, and that he had taken part in the general organisation of the attacks. Thus, not only is 9/11 linked ever more closely with Algeria's domestic terrorists, but, as *El Watan* concludes, the death of Abou Mohamed in Algeria within the ranks of the GSPC is 'irrefutable proof' of ties of Hassan Hattab's GSPC to Osama bin Laden and 9/11.

Article (9), published by *L'Expression* on 30 January, is particularly interesting in the light of what we now know was to befall the European tourists a few weeks later. It paints the Sahara as a pretty rough and dangerous place, describing how the linkages between the 'terrorist' and 'mafia' groups – especially the drug networks and arms traffickers – have spawned a whole new type of 'mafia–terrorist' structure, whose member groups are heavily armed and operate more or less autonomously in the deep South (*le Grand Sud*).[22] The US Department of Defense is quoted extensively as saying that it believes these groups, notably the cannabis-and-heroin drugs 'mafia' that is now tied up with arms trafficking, are operating out of the 'ungovernable' 'free zone' that has been carved out of the frontier zones of northern Mali and southern Algeria: the region where Mokhtar Belmokhtar is one of the main operators. El Para, as we might now expect, also gets a prominent mention. However, what is particularly interesting about this article is that Algeria's security forces are said to have got their hands on many of the known wheeler-dealers in the east and south-east of the country, and that their confessions have enabled them to get inside the Tebessa arms-trafficking network (El Para's alleged region of operations) and its tentacles, which stretch into Libya and as far south as Illizi (the centre for the hostage operation a few weeks later). Thanks to these confessions, the security services claim to have gathered a lot of information about both active and dormant groups in this network – especially the fact that many of their members are foreigners operating on false papers. This has been deduced from the information given to the security services by their confessors, who, we are told, mentioned that the terrorists and traffickers mainly spoke foreign languages. Strangely, the nationality of these unidentified foreigners is not revealed. Particularly pertinent, however, is the fact that the security forces are reported to have turned their attention to Tamanrasset, Algeria's southernmost city and capital of the Ahaggar region, which shelters thousands of undocumented migrants of close to 40 African nationalities, who are known to be especially vulnerable to recruitment by the 'terrorist–mafia' groups. This last point is characterised almost as a novelty. What the reader is not told, and is unlikely to know, is that Tamanrasset, including its large population of foreign undocumented migrants, is heavily infiltrated by the security police. Indeed, there can be few other towns in the world that are kept under closer scrutiny. This, of course, is known to the local people, especially the Tuareg, who refer to the '*stasi*-fication' (after East Germany's *stasi* police) of Tamanrasset and its environs.

The article also offers an explanation of why Algerian and western intelligence services are working more closely together, and by implication in the southern margins of the country. The reason, we are told, is that Europe is being hermetically sealed: terrorist networks on the 'old continent' are coming under severe pressure, thus encouraging Algeria's terrorists to look more to African arms and drug trafficking networks to ensure their supply and to diversify their financial resources.

This article is not a brief news item – it is a detailed analysis almost 2,000 words long. And it is particularly significant to us for two very important reasons. The first is that it provides so much knowledge and detail of the 'terrorist–mafia' situation in the Algerian Sahara that anyone following this story must be in a state of utter bewilderment as to why, only a few weeks later, the same Algerian media, along with official military and ministerial spokespersons, were professing an almost imbecilic level of ignorance as to what was going on in their own Saharan territory. Indeed, the article almost boastfully describes how the security forces for several weeks have been putting in place a whole set of new tactics to match this restructuring of the 'terrorist–mafia' groups. We are told that several military 'search and intelligence' operations have been taking place concurrently in several places, and with such success that 'terrorist–mafia' support networks have been broken up right across the country: at Souk-Ahras, Batna, El-Oued, Biskra and Tebessa in the north-east (El Para's alleged domain), and also further south at Ghardaia, and right down to the extreme south of the country, at Djanet and Tamanrasset.

And that is the second very important point. Having told us that the security forces had got inside the Tebessa network, had extended their tentacles into the Illizi region, and broken up support networks right across the country from the Aures in the north-east down to Djanet and Tamanrasset in the extreme south, why was no attention paid to the nomads who, at this very same time, had reported to the military authorities in Illizi the presence of the *mujahideen* busily preparing the hostage site in Tamelrik? By now the answer is obvious: those preparing the Tamelrik hideout could only have been agents of the security forces, namely the DRS. And when we understand that 5,000 troops were reportedly deployed for months on end to search that very area, we can begin to get some idea of how enormous a lie was being prepared for the world.

Articles (10) and (12) reiterate much that has already been said in the preceding articles. The same names, places, networks and affiliations – not to forget the integral (but incredible) link back to 9/11 – are set before us again in what has become the standard Bush–Cheney style of proof by reiteration. However, there is one new and particularly interesting twist that the last of these articles tosses into the mix. In what can only be presumed to be an attempt to add some authority to the story, the Tuareg, who are to suffer considerably from the events that unfold from this point on, are dragged into the plot. We are told that two 'leaders' of two different Tuareg tribes – the E'Tawarek and El'Mcharka, who live close to the Niger–Algerian frontier zone, and who are in conflict – bought a substantial amount of arms and munitions at a place called Tazaret, and then sold them to a GSPC group operating under Mokhtar ben Mokhtar's rule in Algeria's extreme south. The story sounds plausible, especially to anyone unfamiliar with the ethnography of this remote part of the Sahara – wherein lies the sting. There is no place called Tazaret in that area, nor are there any Tuareg tribes of that name. On the assumption that Algeria's intelligence services did not make up the story entirely, it may possibly relate to a time in 1992 when the Niger government clandestinely supplied substantial arms to Arab groups (the Mcharka?) around Tassara, with the aim of attacking Tuareg groups (E'Tawarek?) in the area who at that time were in revolt against the Niger government. The Arabs, however, found it more profitable to use this sudden patronage to involve themselves in a little smuggling and gun-running!

What Did the Americans Know?

The most illuminating of all these articles is almost certainly article (11). It was written by Mounir B, of the *Quotidien d'Oran* – a paper known to be particularly close to the DRS. The article – published on 10 February 2003, a week before the first hostage-takings – reported that a delegation comprising several US intelligence agencies, notably the FBI, CIA and NSA, had undertaken a secret visit to Algeria to meet with the anti-terrorist services of the DRS and the Algerian army.

The article states that this was by no means the first such visit, and that although such meetings have been kept secret, contacts between the two countries' secret intelligence services have been intensifying since 9/11.[23] The most obvious question is: Why, if the delegation was so secret, was it leaked to the *Quotidien d'Oran*? Also, was it purely coincidence that such a seemingly significant meeting took place a week before the first hostages were captured? We do not know. Nor do we know what they discussed. Did they discuss what happened at Arak on 18 October? We must presume so, for the simple reason that the Americans, as we have now seen, had been busy telling the world that the Sahara–Sahel was at the centre of al-Qaeda's planning.[24] And what might the Algerians have told them? Were the Americans already 'in the loop'? Did the DRS tell their US counterparts that nomads had seen the Tamelrik preparations and reported them to the Illizi authorities? Also, did the Americans perhaps congratulate the Algerians on the exceptional inroads they claimed to have had made in unravelling the 'terrorist–mafia' networks in the Sahara? Perhaps they discussed the nature and management of the dis-information that would be given to the media regarding the hostage-taking. If so, did they discuss how they would manage their responses to the governments of the European countries involved? Was France onboard at this stage? Was the role of El Para discussed at this meeting, and, if so, did they discuss how the Algerian army would manage the logistics of his move to Mali and the related management of media disinformation?

We do not have definitive answer to these questions. However, let me play devil's advocate for a moment and assume that the Americans had absolutely no intelligence relations with Algeria or the Sahelian states, or any form of human intelligence on the ground in these Saharan regions. If that had been the case, there would still have been more than enough clues, such as the online news reports of the Swiss tourists' hijacking at Arak, my 'academic' memo (which was soon being quoted by Washington sources) on the smuggling and other businesses of Mokhtar ben Mokhtar, as well as all the articles (and many more like them) outlined above, staring the US intelligence services in the face for them to know that something was afoot in these Saharan regions. It is inconceivable – especially at this critical juncture in the GWOT, just a few months before the invasion of Iraq – that US intelligence would have missed on those clues.

But we know this assumption to be false. We know that the US and Algerian intelligence services collaborated closely after

Marion (Spike) Bowman had dispelled the anxieties of the Senate Select Committee on Intelligence on 31 July. We know that the CIA and/or US Special Forces had been reconnoitring the Malian side of the border in November. We know that officials from the US Office of Counterterrorism were simultaneously addressing the governments of Chad, Niger, Mali and Mauritania about the proposed PSI.[25] We know that several US intelligence agencies, notably the FBI, CIA and NSA, undertook at least one secret meeting with the DRS's anti-terrorist services in Algeria in February. And we know that the US State Department, notably through its VOA broadcasting service, along with other US media–intelligence services, was banging the drum about al-Qaeda networks in the Sahara–Sahel, and reiterating almost everything that was being written in these and other such articles. And that was probably only the tip of the iceberg.

We also know, in spite of all the disinformation and propaganda outlined above, that there had been no terrorist incidents, in the proper sense of the term, in this region prior to the Arak incident and the abduction of the 32 European tourists that was to commence in February. There was thus the preposterous situation of the world's two most prominent regimes in the war on terror – the USA and Algeria – both actively trying to portray a hitherto relatively tranquil region as one of the world's most dangerous 'terror zones'.[26]

Thus, if the Bush administration is to escape the charge of complicity in such a serious international crime as hostage-taking, it will have to plead a level of intelligence failure that defies credibility. Such a defence carries with it a number of tricky issues for the Americans. Firstly, it would follow that the collaboration between US and Algerian intelligence agencies was not as close as both parties had publicly stated. It would also follow, quite illogically, that the Americans actually believed much of their own intelligence disinformation associated with such things as Mohamed Atta's mislaid luggage; the existence and links of bin Laden's emissary in the Maghreb; the last wishes of al-Qaeda's military leader, Mohamed Atef (alias Abou Hafs el-Misri) to turn the mountains of the Sahara into another Tora Bora, before being reputedly killed by the US bombing of Kabul,[27] and so on. It also raises questions as to whether they knew or recognised El Para – highly profiled in the media between October and February – as 'one of their own'.

In fact, the more closely we analyse the events between 18 October 2002 (the Arak hijack) and February 2003, and the extraordinary series of press articles outlined above, we reach the almost inescapable conclusion that the intelligence services – US and Algerian – were establishing the media disinformation groundwork for the hostage-taking. If anyone had read these twelve articles in the order in which they were published – and it seems that very few people did until retrospectively – the taking of 32 European hostages in the Algerian Sahara would not have surprised them.

The Alliance Base: Paris

Another piece of incriminatory evidence only came to light in July 2005, two-and-a-half years later. This related to the question of what France, the former colonial power, and its intelligence services knew of the situation that was developing in the Algerian and Sahelian Sahara at this time. France's measured silence over the hostage affair was particularly noticeable, as it was the one European country that might be expected to have had an inkling of what was going on. The mystery of France's silence was solved in July 2005 when Dana Priest, the *Washington Post*'s Pulitzer Prize-winning specialist staff writer on national security, published a detailed report on Franco-US intelligence relations.[28] Priest revealed that the US and France had set up a top secret intelligence centre in Paris, code-named Alliance Base, in 2002. This was at the same time as the US was planning its Pan-Sahel Initiative (PSI), and shortly before the hostage-taking. The Base was largely funded by the CIA's Counterterrorist Center, but was headed by a French general assigned from France's secret intelligence service, the Direction Generale de la Sécurité Exterieure (DGSE),[29] France's equivalent of the UK's MI6. Priest revealed that the Base was multinational, having case officers from Britain, France, Germany, Canada, Australia and the US, and that it actually planned operations, rather than simply sharing information.

France's main contribution to the Base was that it brought what Priest described as 'its harsh laws, surveillance of radical Muslim groups and their networks in Arab states, and its intelligence links to its former colonies'.[30] More importantly as far as we are concerned, the French contribution also included its very close relationship with Algeria's military intelligence services, notably the DRS, headed by Generals Mohamed Mediene and Smaïn Lamari, which, as we have seen, was the focus of close collaboration in supporting the 'eradicators' in Algeria's Dirty War of the 1990s.

The *Washington Post*'s exposé of the Base lends much weight to the belief that the relationship between the US and Algerian intelligence services at that time was not a simple one-to-one relationship, but part of a triangle which included France's DGSE. Given Priest's reported timing of the establishment of the Base, it is almost impossible to believe that French intelligence services were not aware of the 'El Para affair', and the subsequent phases of the GWOT across the Sahara–Sahel.[31]

Justification for the GWOT and the Link with Iraq

From Washington's perspective, the hostage-taking was immensely beneficial, enabling it to kill a number of birds with one stone – not just regionally and in Africa as a whole, but also globally. It provided the US administration with 'proof' not only that an al-Qaeda network stretched from the Horn of Africa across the Sahel to Mauritania, but that al-Qaeda – or rather its subsidiaries in the form of Algeria's 'terrorist–mafia' groups, notably the GSPC – now straddled the Sahara from Niger and Mali, and perhaps elsewhere in West Africa, to northern Algeria and the Maghreb as a whole. The hostage-taking was proof of Washington's 'banana theory'. The terrorists dislodged from Afghanistan and elsewhere in Central Asia and the Middle East were now 'swarming', to use the US military's overheated language, across the Sahel and the Sahara, and into the Mahgreb. As General Carlton Fulford was quick to point out, terrorists training in the Sahel could be in Europe in a matter of hours.[32]

This 'proof' that al-Qaeda had established itself in the Sahara enabled the US to launch a new 'African' – or, more accurately, a Sahara–Sahelian – front in the GWOT. Expanding the GWOT into a pivotal region of Africa, the Sahelian border between Muslim–Arab Africa and 'black' sub-Saharan Africa, enabled Washington to create the ideological conditions for the US's invasion of Africa. It immediately provided US-EUCOM's commander, General (Jim) Jones, with all the legitimacy he required to pursue his mission of acquiring basing rights, and establishing what he referred to as a 'family of bases' across the continent.[33] General Jones was now able to talk with confidence of 'threats to the southern rim of the Mediterranean' from 'large uncontrolled, ungoverned areas across Africa that are clearly the routes of narco-trafficking, terrorist training and hotbeds of instability', and which 'are going to be potential havens for that kind of activity'.[34]

The launch of this new Saharan–Sahelian front in the GWOT has done more than anything else to legitimise the militarisation of the continent, and thereby the securing of US strategic national resources. The Pan-Sahel Initiative had been launched in the autumn of 2002. A year later, with the hostages released and the ideological base firmly established, the PSI was formally announced to the world, with the first US troops being deployed into the four Sahelian countries of Mauritania, Mali, Niger and Chad in January 2004. In an almost seamless transition, which I discuss in the *The Dying Sahara*, the PSI was expanded and upgraded in May 2005 into a $100 million, five-year programme officially known by Washington as the Trans-Saharan Counter-Terrorism Initiative (TSCTI), to include officially five more countries in the fold – Nigeria, Senegal, Morocco, Tunisia and Algeria – although it might be argued that Algeria had been more or less running the show from the outset.

On the global front, the hostage taking could not have been timelier for the Americans, coming as it did just before the US invasion of Iraq. The invasion of Iraq had been on the agenda of the militarists and neo-conservatives[35] of the Project for the New American century (PNAC) long before 9/11. As early as January 1998, they sent a letter to President Clinton urging him to use military force to remove Saddam Hussein. Several of them took over many of the more sensitive branches of the US government in the wake of George W. Bush's takeover of the White House – especially at the Pentagon, whose top three civilians, the secretary of state for defence, Donald Rumsfeld, the deputy secretary for defence, Paul Wolfowitz, and the under-secretary of defence for policy, Douglas Feith, were at the forefront in formulating the neocon agenda. The events of 9/11 provided an immense opportunity for them to put this agenda into practice. The key military-intelligence chain of command in this operation – particularly the management of 'intelligence disinformation'[36] and the responsibility for certain key Special Operations, including those running through USSOCOM (United States Special Operations Command) and its counter-terrorism branch, the JSOC (Joint Special Operations Command) – ran directly through the Rumsfeld–Wolfowitz–Feith hierarchy. Through their effective control over new command structures and offices within the Pentagon, such as certain SOCOM activities and Douglas Feith's controversial Office of Special Plans, they were able to manage and manipulate much of the intelligence and conduct of the GWOT.[37]

The initial justification for the US invasion of Iraq was based on the assertion that Saddam Hussein was either manufacturing or harbouring weapons of mass destruction (WMD). However, well before the invasion got underway, this disinformation was being exposed for the lie that it was. WMD were therefore replaced, rather at the last minute, by another line of intelligence disinformation which purported to show a 'terror link' between Saddam Hussein, Osama bin Laden and al-Qaeda. This claim was equally untrue, as was later confirmed by the US Senate's Select Committee on Intelligence.[38] Nevertheless, Wolfowitz and Feith had been hard at work fabricating and cherry-picking intelligence in an attempt to establish such links, and so justify the invasion. Even though the Sahara–Sahel was some distance from Iraq, hard evidence of al-Qaeda terrorist activity in the Sahara–Sahel, especially when shown to be part of a terrorist expansion from Afghanistan and the Middle East through this desert chain of predominantly Muslim countries to the very shores of Europe, helped the Bush administration muddy the waters sufficiently to associate Iraq with this enlarged geographical sphere of al-Qaeda activity. Moreover, by bringing the al-Qaeda threat to the gates of Europe so dramatically, the US was able to keep a sceptical 'old Europe' under threat and onboard in its GWOT, especially in the crucial months of the build-up to the invasion of Iraq.[39] Equally importantly, this expansion of al-Qaeda's terror network across the Sahel and beyond provided Washington with a whole new geographical arena with which to demonstrate the global threat of terrorism, and thus further to legitimise the globalisation of its war on terror – especially into Africa.

12

THE NATURE OF US INTELLIGENCE

One overriding question runs through the preceding pages, namely: what was the nature of the intelligence that underpinned the US administration's launch of its 'second' or 'Saharan' front in its GWOT?

The key operation in the launch of this 'second front' was President Bush's Pan-Sahel Initiative (PSI) – what locals called the US 'invasion' – in January 2004. It was predicated almost entirely on the actions of El Para. But, before El Para and Algeria's secret military service came on the scene, what was the intelligence that led the Americans to believe that the Sahara–Sahel might be even remotely dangerous, let alone a 'Swamp of Terror'? The answer, put simply, and incredible as it may sound, is 'virtually nothing'.

An Absence of Terrorism in the Sahel

As the much-respected International Crisis Group (ICG) was to conclude in its seminal 2005 report into 'Islamic Terrorism in the Sahel', 'there was little or no Islamic extremism and no terrorism in the Sahel at that time'.[1] Neither, as I have repeatedly emphasised, was there any firm evidence that terrorists from Afghanistan, Pakistan or the Middle East were making their way across the banana-shaped route from Central Asia or the Middle East to the Maghreb via the Sahel. And yet, that was the message that Washington and USEUCOM commanders were and still are broadcasting to the world. The Pentagon's fundamental explanation for its actions in the Sahara–Sahel, as it has kept telling us, is that 'as terrorist cells were uprooted from Afghanistan and elsewhere by US Central Command ... they shifted to ... the wide-open, relatively desolate areas of Africa ... an easy back door into Europe through Algeria, Morocco and Tunisia'.[2] Put another way: 'If you squeeze the terrorists in Afghanistan, Pakistan, Iraq and other places, they will find new places to operate, and one of those places is the Sahel/Maghreb.'[3]

'Back-of-the-envelope' Intelligence

So, if there was no terrorism in the region at that time and no evidence of passing terrorists traversing the Sahel on the way from Afghanistan to the Maghreb, what was the intelligence basis of Washington's assertions? As I mentioned in Chapter 10, I believe that Washington's intelligence at that time was based on nothing more than some of my own unpublished notes; the CIA's and possibly other US intelligence agencies' misreading and misunderstanding of the Islamic Tablighi Jamaat movement; the Algerian press; and wholly inadequate human intelligence ('HUMINT', in US military parlance) on the ground. Whichever way we dress up these snippets of information – for that is what they are – they were certainly not enough to justify the American claims. I will explain each in turn.

I have already referred to the unpublished notes that I sent to colleagues in the US, which mentioned the activities of Mokhtar ben Mokhtar, and which found their way into the hands of US intelligence agencies around mid-2002.[4] Let me explain their context and content. In 2001 I established a Saharan Studies Research Programme in the UK. Like many such enterprises, it was short of funds. I therefore undertook what was essentially a fundraising tour of a handful of US universities. The fundraising was unsuccessful, but at some of the universities I gave a brief seminar paper or a pitch to potential funding committees on the nature of the research programme. I described the upsurge of banditry across the Algerian–Nigerien–Malian border areas since the late 1990s, the activities of Mokhtar ben Mokhtar, the expansion of cigarette smuggling, the threat this posed to the region's security, and the possible links to the GSPC.

I subsequently learned that my talk, more in the form of a memo, had found its way to US intelligence agencies and almost certainly contributed to the US's heightened interest in the northern desert regions of Niger and Mali. Countless times since then I have heard phrases from it being misquoted in intelligence reports and media articles, usually with reference to the 'old Saharan caravan routes', and always completely out of context.

Although US military links to Mali go back to 1992, when US contingents arrived in Mali after the end of the first Gulf War,[5] the US's first active interest in Mali's northern desert areas appears to have begun only after my memo found its way to Washington. It was then, in November 2002, five months after my talk, that Robert Perry and Stephanie Kinney from the US Office of Counterterrorism met with officials in Mali, Niger, Chad and Mauritania to discuss combating terrorism, controlling illicit trade and enhancing regional security in their 'ungoverned desert areas',[6] while CIA agents simultaneously undertook helicopter reconnaissance of the desert regions north of Timbuktu, supposedly to check out terrorist training activities in that area.[7]

Confusing Pakistanis: the Tablighi Jamaat Movement

It was also around this time, as Washington was beginning to formulate what I have called its 'banana theory' of terrorism across the Sahel, that US intelligence agencies in Mali confused the possible links between Mokhtar ben Mokhtar and Hassan Hattab's GSPC, as suggested in my university memo, with their own misunderstanding of the Islamic (Salafist) Tablighi Jamaat movement.

The Tablighi Jamaat was founded in the 1930s in the Indian province of Deccan. After partition in 1947, it came to be labelled as Pakistani, though its organisational headquarters remained in India. The movement was established in Gambia in the 1990s, from where it spread to Mauritania and then south Mali. In Ramadan 1999, four Tablighi missionaries arrived in Kidal, in northern Mali.[8] Their number in the region remained small, and they were the butt of jokes and some hostility among the local population, although they won some influence among one of the more prominent clans. Although referred to by the local population as 'Bukstan' (Pakistani), most of them seem to have been of Bangladeshi origin. This reference to 'Pakistani' seems to have convinced US intelligence agencies that they were Taliban elements uprooted by US forces from Afghanistan and Pakistan, and were in search of new places to operate. The movement quickly lost popularity in the wake of 9/11, with the Malian authorities expelling most, if not all, of its Pakistani members.

Inadequate HUMINT

The two other US sources of intelligence on the region were the local media – especially Algeria's – and its own hopelessly inadequate human intelligence (HUMINT). Algeria's military intelligence service was and still is the ultimate source of most of the information underpinning most media reports on the GWOT in the Sahara–Sahel. Given its long and notorious record of counterinsurgency and associated disinformation, which the US intelligence services would certainly have been aware of, virtually all Algerian media reports, as illustrated in the previous chapter, should be treated with great caution.

The US's HUMINT in the region at that time was virtually nonexistent. That is not surprising, as US intelligence services are known to be notoriously thinly spread across the Arabo-Islamic world, especially when it comes to reliable human intelligence. Getting inside these countries and their regimes is not easy. With priority already given to Iraq, the Middle East and the Central Asian republics, it is not surprising that EUCOM intelligence officers had little intrinsic knowledge of the Sahara–Sahel region. In 2003, for example, a senior EUCOM intelligence officer contacted an academic colleague in an attempt to gain a basic understanding of what he called 'the tribal make-up' of the region. 'We haven't got a clue what's happening on the ground', the Colonel told my colleague.[9]

What little HUMINT US intelligence agencies were able to gather on the region seems to have been derived mostly from relatively young, ambitious military officers in the countries with which the US has reasonably good connections, such as Mali, and whom they were training. These are often the worst possible intelligence sources: not only do they see their careers as tied to the escalating strategic US dependency on Africa, and on Washington's associated and increasing militarisation of the continent,[10] but the vast majority of them come from ethnic groups that are alien to the region and whose knowledge of the indigenous Sahel populations, such as the Tuareg and Tubu, is usually prejudiced by their experience of the region's several recent rebellions and other, often longstanding inter-ethnic conflicts.

The resultant pattern of intelligence and of its flow from these sources means that the DRS and other Algerian channels, along with the HUMINT from the other countries in the region, have been telling the US intelligence agencies largely what they want to hear.[11]

These few 'snippets of information' were, I believe, close to being the sum total of intelligence available to the US administration before the DRS and El Para intervened. If that is what led the US, the world's only 'superpower', to launch its GWOT into the Sahara, then we are facing frightening possibilities. In fact, I believe that we are dealing with a far more serious and dangerous situation than that. As with the invasion of Iraq, the US was not really concerned with acquiring good intelligence. In Iraq's case, the decision to invade had been made irrespective of the nature of the intelligence. In like manner, the Bush administration was fully aware of the new strategic importance to the US of Africa's oil resources, and was determined to secure them. Securing Africa's oil meant militarising the continent – which, in the wake of 9/11, was justified by the GWOT. The fact that there was little or no terrorism in sub-Sahelian Africa, and West Africa in particular, was resolved by the 'banana theory' of terrorism, which provided Washington's philosophers with the ideological justification that they needed. They built the theory and then sought whatever facts might fit. And if the 'facts' didn't fit or exist, then, as we now know, they were invented.

The construction of such a theory made the need for good intelligence unnecessary. The US military-intelligence agencies knew that they were fabricating an elaborate deception – in short, a conspiracy theory – to which truth, normally ascertained through good intelligence, was irrelevant.

Parallels with Iraq

There is a certain parallel between the ways in which the Bush administration acquired its intelligence on Iraq and on the Sahara–Sahel region. In both regions the US has been operating on the basis of a more or less permanent 'Chalabi syndrome', as it became known. The US invasion of Iraq relied almost entirely on intelligence sourced to Ahmed Chalabi, a colourful and charismatic banker (among many other things) who had been convicted of fraud (in his absence) by a Jordanian court, but who was strongly supported and believed by the Pentagon, Congress and parts of the CIA. The State Department was a little more cautious – which was just as well, as most of Chalabi's information and judgments turned out to be disastrously wrong. In the Sahara–Sahel, the US has been similarly reliant on the filtration of equally disingenuous information through Algeria's intelligence services.

At another level, however, I believe that there may have been more sinister parallels between Iraq and the Sahara–Sahel that have yet to be revealed. In June 2003, the US Senate's Select Committee on Intelligence, under the chairmanship of Republican Senator Pat Roberts, commenced its investigation into the nature of the intelligence used to justify the Iraq invasion. The 'Senate Report on Iraqi WMD Intelligence', formally the 'Report of the Select Committee on Intelligence on the US Intelligence Community's Prewar Intelligence Assessments on Iraq', released its first report (Phase I) on 9 July 2004. It was a blistering indictment of the Bush administration. Phase II comprised five volumes. Two were released on 8 September 2006,[12] concluding that there was no prewar evidence that Saddam had been building weapons of mass destruction, and no evidence that he had had links to al-Qaeda. However, Senator Roberts procrastinated on the completion and release of the remaining three volumes, ensuring that they would not be published before the November 2006 mid-term elections. It was widely believed in Washington at the time that he would do everything within his means to stall the remaining reports, as it was thought they would open up, as one former intelligence officer suggested, 'an even bigger can of worms'.[13]

Following the Democratic Party's victory in the mid-term elections, Senator Rogers left the committee and was replaced as chairman by Democratic Senator John D. Rockefeller IV. A third volume of the report was released on 25 May 2007. The remaining two volumes, believed by the Republicans to be too damaging to American interests to be released, were finally released in June 2008. They confirmed, in the words of Senator Rockefeller, that 'In making the case for war, the administration repeatedly presented intelligence as fact when it was unsubstantiated, contradicted or even nonexistent.'[14]

It is unlikely, given the seriousness of what it will unearth, that the US Senate will initiate a similar investigation into the waging of the GWOT in Africa. If it did, the committee would find what I have documented here, and reach similar conclusions as it did with Iraq – namely that the GWOT in Africa, most notably its Sahara–Sahel front, has been based almost entirely on exaggerated and fabricated evidence.

Complicit in Conspiracy

There is no doubt that the Algerian and US military intelligence services have been complicit in exaggerating and fabricating the evidence used to launch the Saharan front in the GWOT. This suggests that the nature of the intelligence traffic between the US and Algeria may not have been as one-way as I might have hitherto suggested. While it is true that the US has been heavily dependent on Algeria's intelligence services for information on what is happening on the ground – the US almost certainly being duped on more than one occasion – the relation between the two countries' intelligence services would appear, at least on certain issues, to have become extremely close. For example, we know from European security sources[15] that the US was monitoring the radio (and probably also cell phone) traffic between the hostage-takers, and almost certainly between their leader (El Para) and their minders, from the outset of the hostage drama in 2003. This means that the US was almost certainly aware of the Algerian military's involvement in the abduction, as well as of El Para's true identity.

Whether the US was actually complicit in the planning of the hostage-taking, and whether it knew anything about the botched attempt at Arak, is less clear. However, US knowledge of the role and identity of El Para probably explains why it failed to attempt his capture when (and if) he was in Tibesti, why it raised no questions about the lack of due legal process on his return to Algiers, and why it has not once publicly queried the 'intelligence' being put out by Algerian and other Saharan/Sahelian government sources. Thus, while the US may have been duped with regard to some of the details of what was happening on the ground, it has certainly been party to the 'big lie'. Indeed, Dana Priest's exposé of the 'Alliance Base' makes it very difficult to believe otherwise.[16]

Most extreme-right-wing organisations tend to use the knee-jerk catchphrase of 'conspiracy theory' in attempting to deride or dispel criticism levelled against them. In this case, it is the Bush administration, not its critics, that stands accused of conspiracy. With the assistance of the DRS and El Para – Osama bin Laden's 'man in the Sahel' – the Bush administration has constructed an elaborate and grotesque conspiracy theory which, as I shall outline in the next chapter, has now taken on a life of its own and may well become a self-fulfilling prophecy.

13

'BLOWBACK' AND RESISTANCE

I began writing this book in 2005, at around the time that the Bush administration announced the expansion of its widely publicised Pan Sahel Initiative (PSI) into the even more widely publicised Trans-Saharan Counter-Terrorism Initiative (TSCTI). I thought it would take about four months to write. Instead, it has taken four years. One reason for that is because the story of America's duplicity in Africa continued to develop as I wrote. I was having to pin down a moving target. I was able to see the immense damage that the deception of its GWOT was causing to the livelihoods and well-being of the peoples of much of this part of the Sahara–Sahel (and beyond), and that it was only a matter of time before it would encounter blowback, to use the American term for what, in this case, I prefer to call resistance (not insurgency).

In Algeria, Tuareg anger against the Algerian government grew with an increasing awareness of Algeria's involvement in the hostage-taking, and as tourism, the main source of livelihood for many Tuareg, died almost instantaneously before their eyes. Many of them, even middle-aged men, were obliged to move into the smuggling and trafficking businesses, the borderline of criminality, just to eke out a living. Tuareg in the Sahel, in both Niger and Mali, were soon to suffer the same decimation of their livelihoods.

Many of them were also frightened. I remember being in a Tuareg camp in Niger in 2004 and listening on my short-wave radio to Voice of America (VOA) declaring that America's military commanders 'reserved the right to call in air strikes'. What right? And against whom? VOA was talking about the Sahel, where we were camped, in the context of alleged terrorism that my Tuareg friends knew did not exist. Who were the Americans targeting? Terrorists who did not exist, or innocent civilians who, based on the quality of US intelligence described in the previous chapter, would be written off, like those in southern Somalia and elsewhere, as collateral damage?

Even though these people lived in the middle of the Sahara, they were well informed on world affairs. They listened to the news on their radios and they watched television in the towns. And if they didn't get to town and watch it themselves, they quickly heard about it from others who did. News travels far and fast in the Sahara. They were well aware of America's invasion of Iraq, that there were no WMD, that Bush and Cheney were telling lies about the links between Saddam and al-Qaeda, and that the world's only superpower now presided over a debacle of its own making. America could no longer be trusted or believed. America told lies. And now their own camps and villages were being threatened with American air strikes. Why? It made no sense to them.

For many of these people, as in many other parts of the world, America – or, for those who articulated the difference, 'American imperialism' – had now become 'the enemy'. But this sentiment, at least from my experience, was rarely directed against individual Americans, who, on the few occasions they travelled to the region, were always treated with customary hospitality, and sometimes even sympathy for having to suffer being 'ruled by the stupidest man on earth'. Rather, America was more of an abstract and arm's-length enemy. This was partly because America was too far away, and because Americans – apart from the occasional traveller – were rarely, if ever, seen. They existed in satellites and planes overhead, on TV, and in the form of Special Forces flown into places like Tamanrasset and Gao, only to move on and disappear as fast as they had arrived, and in military bases that were rumoured but never found. But the main reason was that the anger that grew and spread further around the region after 2003 was directed primarily at their governments.

This was not simply because the regimes of the region were doing America's bidding. It was more complex and nastier than that: their alliance with the US in the GWOT has encouraged and enabled all of them, without exception – Morocco, Algeria, Tunisia, Libya, Egypt, Mauritania, Mali, Niger and Chad – to strengthen their repressive apparatus and to manipulate and use the GWOT for their own benefits and purposes. This has been done in two distinct but related ways. Firstly, the GWOT has provided them with the pretext to crack down on almost all forms of opposition, especially minority groups, and almost any expression of civil society democratisation. Secondly, it has provided them with what I call 'terrorism rents'. These comprise the military and other aid and largesse that these regimes receive from the US for allying themselves to the US in fighting the 'war on terror'.

However, with no terrorism (except state terrorism) in many parts of this region, notably the Sahara–Sahel, before the launch of the GWOT, it has had to be contrived. This has been done in varying degrees in every state within the region, most commonly by labelling or linking legitimate opposition and other such 'enemies of the regime' with 'terrorism' or 'Islamic extremism', or by deliberately provoking elements of the population into civil unrest and, as in the cases of Niger and Mali, into taking up arms.

Following the launch of the Saharan front in the GWOT and the overt US support for Algeria's *mukhabarat* state, local people, especially the Tuareg, soon noticed that the Algerian authorities became more openly confident in their abuse of power. One prominent local citizen expressed the views of many when he said, 'Now that [the Algerian authorities] have the Americans behind them, they have become even bigger bullies'. Corruption, especially through the embezzlement of local authority funds, became more brazen; repression of the population, especially crack-downs on those elements of civil society that were expressing concern for human rights and democratic organisation, and the harassment of individuals who were seen as potential opposition spokesmen,[1] became more widespread. Meanwhile the police, especially the DRS, became more pervasive,[2] more visible and open in their actions, and less observant of due legal process. For example, in January 2005, the security police (DRS) kidnapped an

Algerian citizen in public view, in daylight, in the crowded main street of Tamanrasset. He was grabbed by three men, bundled into the boot of a vehicle, handcuffed, covered with a tarpaulin and sat on, before being driven to a secret house on the edge of town where he was interrogated for two days before being released. While such police activity would be regarded as 'normal' throughout much of Algeria, it had not previously been so overt in the extreme south, where such actions were likely to be witnessed by foreign tourists. Within months of the launch of the GWOT into Algeria's Sahara, members of the Mouvement des Citoyens du Sud pour la Justice[3] had been gaoled; the Associations de Quartiers, a democratically-based organisation of representatives from each of Tamanrasset's suburbs, had been closed by court order; false charges had been brought against the president of the Union Nationale des Associations des Agences de Tourisme Alternatif (UNATA), while the regional government had attempted to proscribe the Association des Agences de Tourisme Wilaya de Tamanrasset (ATAWT).[4]

The Tuareg Take Up Arms

Tuareg first took up arms against such provocation in 2004, following the Niger government's arrest and detention of a prominent Tuareg leader on trumped-up murder charges. Following outbreaks of 'banditry' during the summer, the Niger government sent 150 of its recently US-trained troops into the Aïr Mountains in September, in a move that many thought was designed to ignite a new Tuareg rebellion. However, the troops were ambushed by the Tuareg, with at least one soldier being killed, four wounded, and four taken hostage. Then, in 2005, widespread unrest and rioting by Tuareg in Tamanrasset – which left at least 40 buildings in the town's commercial and administrative districts burned out, and which coincided with America's 'Operation Flintlock' to launch its TSCTI – was discovered (through legal interventions in court) to have been led by Algeria's own security police acting as agents provocateurs.

Both of these events encouraged further Libyan involvement and intervention in the region, which in turn led to Algeria's orchestration, with the backing of US Special Forces, of another Tuareg rebellion in Mali in 2006. With security experts warning that America's attempt to justify its GWOT in the Sahara–Sahel by fabricating and exaggerating terrorism in the region might lead to real terrorism or insurgency – thereby generating a self-fulfilling prophecy – it was only a matter of time before the unrest escalated into a regional conflagration. That conflagration began in early 2007 with almost simultaneous Tuareg rebellions in both Niger and Mali.

The Dying Sahara

By the time these multiple rebellions had turned much of the Sahara–Sahel from a US-imagined terrorist zone into a very real war zone, my manuscript, which had now become a six-year documentation of both the local and wider impact of this shameful episode in US foreign policy, had grown from 80,000 words to 160,000 – too much for one book! Rather than cut out valuable material and evidence, I rewrote it into two books: this one and *The Dying Sahara: US Imperialism and Terror in Africa*. This choice of title reflects the horrific loss of lives and livelihoods in the Sahara–Sahel over the last few years, for which the Bush administration, as for events in some other parts of Africa, must bear the ultimate responsibility.

The Dying Sahara records and analyses the US invasion that began with the arrival of its 'anti-terror' team of 500 troops at Nouakchott on 11 January 2004, continued with its build-up in 2005 into the TSCTI, and culminated, in October 2008, in the US military's ultimate objective: the establishment of an independent, fully autonomous and operational US military command for Africa – AFRICOM.

President Bush's authorisation of this new military command in December 2006 preceded by just seven weeks the outbreak of the conflagration that was to overwhelm much of the Tuareg Sahara. By a strange coincidence, the day before the first shots were fired by Tuareg rebels in Niger, President Bush explained how AFRICOM was intended to bring 'peace and security to the people of Africa and promote our common goals of development, health, education, democracy and economic growth in Africa'.[5] *The Dying Sahara* illustrates in fine detail how and why AFRICOM, while using the language of the new security-development discourse borrowed wholesale from Tony Blair's 2005 Commission for Africa[6] to present itself as something more benign than it really is, is achieving the precise opposite to what the US told the world.[7]

Far from bringing 'peace and security' to Africa, AFRICOM has been directly instrumental in creating conflict and insecurity. *The Dying Sahara* reveals how US-trained troops in the Sahel, and in Niger especially, have been responsible for appalling human rights abuses and atrocities in a government-directed 'ethnocide' against the Tuareg. The one obstacle to a peaceful settlement of the conflict is Niger's US-backed President, Mamadou Tandja. One wag of Washington's little finger would bring Tanja to the peace table. But no such wags have been forthcoming, for the simple reason that the regional insecurity caused by the rebellion has furthered US strategic interests, because that insecurity justifies AFRICOM and the US militarisation of Africa.

While AFRICOM's commander, General 'Kip' Ward, was selling the AFRICOM message of 'security and development' to a Royal United Services Institute audience in London in February 2008, his Special Forces troops were covertly accompanying Malian forces in a vicious reprisal against the civilian population of the northern desert town of Tin Zaouatene.

Although AFRICOM's commanders have been preaching security and development, their operations on the ground have so far created insecurity and undermined democratic expressions of civil society. In the case of the Sahara–Sahel region, the propaganda accompanying the launch of a second front in the GWOT has become a self-fulfilling prophecy. Six years of fabricated terrorism and provoked unrest have transformed large, hitherto relatively tranquil tracts of Africa into zones of more-or-less permanent instability, rebellion, war and terror. The tragedy of the Bush administration's militarisation policy for Africa is that few parts of the continent will be unaffected by its consequences and implications. Indeed, *The Dying Sahara* goes beyond the Sahara and explains the consequences of America's attempt to militarise the continent for people in other parts of Africa. It also explores the serious implications of this policy for social scientists at a time when the US government, as well as some of its western allies, is attempting to militarise academia and politicise research.[8]

At the time of writing, AFRICOM is not quite a fait accompli. Apart from the fact that no African country – except perhaps Liberia – is prepared to house AFRICOM's HQ, (which will therefore remain in Stuttgart!), the outcome of US Congressional appropriation committees' investigations makes it most likely that AFRICOM will not have the resources to accomplish its mandate. With no new military units being created for AFRICOM, and with no other US troops readily available because of the US military commitments in Iraq and Afghanistan, the indications are that AFRICOM's mission will be outsourced to 'contractors' or private military companies (PMCs), as they are now known. PMCs have become a multi-billion-dollar industry, and are wide open, as we have seen in Iraq, to corruption. The likely privatisation of AFRICOM's mission will open Africa up to the potentially horrific prospect of these mercenary forces – and not only American ones – turning Africa into their own 'plunder economy', where their own interests will be served and their fortunes made through the promotion and maintenance of conflict.[9]

Proof by Reiteration

In expanding and extending this research into *The Dying Sahara*, I have been able to do more than just expand the study of the impact of America's militarisation policy on other parts of Africa. I have also been able to acquire more evidence on the question of how the massive deception of the Bush administration's GWOT in Africa has been so easily and successfully maintained. It has enabled me to investigate an avenue through which this whole operation has almost certainly been at least part-financed, so raising disturbing questions as to whether UN agencies and the World Bank, regarded by many as the financial arm of US foreign policy, have also been complicit in this deception. It has also enabled me to examine the essential roles played by the media and academe in enabling the success of the Bush administration's 'information war', and especially the Bush–Cheney doctrine of 'proof by reiteration', or, as MIT Professor of Linguistics Noam Chomsky, put it, 'If you repeat it loudly enough it will become the truth'.[10]

Finally, in what no work of fiction could get away with, *The Dying Sahara* ends where it all began, with another DRS agent, an accomplice of El Para in the 2003 hostage-taking, once again taking Europeans hostage in the Sahara – but now in the name of al-Qaeda in the Islamic Maghreb!

NOTES

Introduction

1. François Gèze and Salima Mellah, '"Al-Qaida au Maghreb", ou la très étrange histoire du GSPC', *Algeria-Watch*, 22 September 2007, available online at www.algeria-watch.org/fr/aw/gspc_etrange_histoire.htm.
2. *Quotidien d'Oran*, 4 December 2003.
3. Philip Paull, 'International Terrorism: The Propaganda War' (thesis submitted in partial fulfilment of the requirements for the degree Masters of Arts in International Relations), San Francisco State University, California, June 1982, pp. 95, 99–100.

The Dossier

1. The contents of the dossier were also revealed to the Libyan authorities, who acted almost immediately in imposing restrictions on foreigners travelling in the country with their own vehicles, a move which effectively shunted the problem back into Algeria.

Missing

1. An *erg* is a sand sea.
2. This route ran just to the north of what is probably the least known part of the Tassili Mountains, including the Tamelrik massif, more or less equidistant from Illizi to the east and Amguid to the west.

Chapter 1

1. These data were compiled from statements by various Algerian government spokespersons.
2. 'Ahmed Zegri, guide et patron de l'Agence Mezrirène: "Ce sont les touristes pirates qui s'égarent"' ('Ahmed Zegri, guide and owner of [tourism agency] Agence Mezrirène: "These are freebooting tourists"'). Zegri is referring to the tourists travelling in their own vehicles, 'off-piste', and without guides. *El Watan*, 13 April 2003.

3. From the French word *contrabandier*. The actual business of smuggling is known as *trabendo* and its participants as *trabendistes*.

4. Smuggling of cigarettes and drugs is often referred to as narco-trafficking.

5. Tourism statistics in the Algerian Sahara are very unreliable. However, this figure is around the maximum annual amount, and roughly the same as the highest levels at the end of the 1980s, when tourism in the Algerian Sahara was at its peak.

6. 'The Marlboro boss/godfather'.

7. While the four may well have been part of a terrorist group, this was not proven, as the prosecution dropped the terrorism charges to help speed up the trial. Instead, the four were convicted of conspiracy to commit murder and to plant bombs, and of various weapons offences.

8. On 30 April, the Algerian press reported that the hostages were alive, in the hands of 'terrorists', had been located by the army, and were being held in several geographically separate groups, but all within the Illizi region. (*El Watan* and *Quotidien d'Oran*, 30 April 2003).

9. *Der Spiegel*, 12 April 2003.

10. Press reports, such as those in *L'Hebdo* on 8 and 22 May 2003, that he has been trafficking contraband cigarettes, fuel and vehicles between Mauritania, Niger, Mali and Algeria since the beginning of the 1980s, were misplaced, since he was not even a teenager at that time. Such reports were almost certainly associated with attempts by Algeria's security forces to construct their own histories of the Sahara. It is possible that journalists writing such stories have confused Mokhtar ben Mokhtar with another equally colourful character, Hadj Bettu, who became a local warlord in the Algeria–Mali–Niger frontier zones in the late 1980s, but who spent the 1990s serving a ten-year gaol sentence in Tamanrasset.

11. Information provided by security contractors working for foreign oil companies in the Algerian Sahara, and confirmed by members of Algeria's security forces.

12. J. Keenan, *Sahara Man: Travelling with Tuareg* (London: John Murray: 2001).

13. In spite of the government's sporadic but widely pronounced successes against smugglers, there is no firm evidence to indicate that the Algerian security forces were getting on top of the trans-Saharan trafficking businesses.

14. For example, the Swiss magazine *L'Hebdo* reported on 10 May that the kidnappers were demanding 1 million Swiss francs (US$775,000) for each hostage. The report was immediately denied by the Algerian media.

15. No formal confirmation of the release had actually been given by any of the governments of the European countries concerned.
16. This unit is part of the Direction des Renseignements et de la Sécurité (DRS), formerly the Sécurité Militaire (SM).
17. El Para's name had in fact arisen earlier, in an article in *El Watan* on 30 April, but at that time the attention was on Mokhtar ben Mokhtar.
18. The attack took place on 4 January 2003.
19. *Reuters*, Newsdesk, Algiers, 22 August 2003.

Chapter 2

1. In his State of the Union address of 29 January 2002, President Bush spoke of the expansion of the war on terror to new fronts. Since then, the term 'front', and especially the term 'second front', has become almost synonymous with the attempt to globalise the GWOT. Afghanistan is usually understood to be the first front. The term 'second front' has been applied at one time or another to most parts of the world, including Southeast Asia, Iraq, Latin America (in the context of the election of left-wing presidents in Brazil and Ecuador, and in relation to the FARC campaign in Colombia) and, after 2003, the Sahara. In the latter case the 'first' front is sometimes understood to be the Horn of Africa and East Africa. See, for example, David Pyne, 'The new second front in the war against terrorism', *American Partisan*, 19 December 2002; Michelle M. Clays, 'The interagency process and America's second front in the global war on terrorism' (Reference: Operation ENDURING FREEDOM [OEF] Philippines), Defense Technical Information Center, April 2003, Accession No: ADA424995.
2. Sahel means 'shore' in Arabic. The term is a geographical designation for the region covering the southern margins of the Sahara, encompassing southern Mauritania and much of Mali, Niger, Chad and Sudan.
3. This number was given by the hostages in their debriefings.
4. We also know from these telephone calls that El Para and a handful of his men left the group shortly after the freeing of the hostages, taking the only vehicle belonging to the tourists that has still not been found.
5. Statement made to a conference on terrorism in Bamako, October 2003.
6. Ahaggar and the Tassili-n-Ajjer are the two geologically intercon- nected massifs of southern Algeria which are the traditional homes

of the Kel (people of) Ahaggar and the Kel Ajjer Tuareg. Their combined size is roughly the same as that of France.

7. The *wali* is government's chief administrator in a *wilaya* (pl. *wilayat*, 'province'). He is appointed by the president.

8. The incident took place in early November, and was reported in the Algerian newspaper *El Watan*, which has close links to the Algerian military (*El Watan*, 11 November 2003).

9. Kel Aïr from Iferouane.

10. According to the Niger authorities, desperate to protect their tourism industry, Alembo was caught and gaoled in Niamey. The version given here was recounted by members of his village and confirmed on later occasions by several other local informants.

11. This apparent contradiction was a product of the fact that Alembo had several kinship ties to prominent members of the security apparatus in southern Algeria.

12. I was in the Chirfa region at the time of the attack, and crossed Alembo's tracks on several occasions.

13. According to Malian sources, this was done without official permission.

14. They were subsequently released, and thus able to report their experience.

15. No mention of the raid seems to have appeared in the Algerian press.

16. The group had at least three pick-ups, with heavy machine guns bolted onto them, as well as small arms. Subsequent reports in a German magazine would appear to be a gross over-dramatisation of what actually took place.

17. BBC, 29 January 2004. In 2004 the Paris–Dakar rally was cancelled for fear that Mokhtar ben Mokhtar was lying in wait for it.

18. The visit actually took place in October, but was not announced by the US Department of State until 7 November 2002.

19. Office of Counterterrorism, US Department of State, Washington, DC, 7 November 2002; Stephen Ellis, 'Briefing: The Pan-Sahel Initiative', *African Affairs* (2004), 103/412, pp. 459–64.

20. This statement is confusing and is typical of much US disinformation since 9/11. These figures must therefore be treated with caution. Subsequent communiqués by US officials in the region have given the impression that the number of US troops involved in the PSI might be a little less. However, while this sort of uncertainty is sometimes part of the disinformation associated with US military-security announcements, it is also an outcome of the Bush administration's privatisation of so much of US military activity. As in other parts of the world, the US government has been deliberately obtuse in

distinguishing between US forces and corporate contractors involved
in the PSI.

21. AP (Nouakchott), 12 January 2004.
22. AFP reports from 15–31 January 2004.
23. The arms haul comprised 17 mortars, machine guns and rocket
launchers; 220 light weapons, including 190 Kalashnikovs, automatic
guns and telescopic rifles; communications equipment including
eleven Thuraya satellite phones and a large amount of ammunition.
Algerian Press Service, 31 January 2004.
24. It should not be assumed that all arms trafficking in Algeria is from
south to north, nor destined exclusively for the GSPC. For example,
the Ivory Coast authorities appealed to the Mali government to put
a stop to the trafficking of arms through their territory from Algeria
to the rebel Forces Nouvelles in the north of the country. See *Le
Patriote*, 6 February 2004.
25. *Liberté*, 5 February 2004.
26. The European source also confirmed that Algerian and US intelligence
services had been working closely together since the beginning of
the hostage drama almost a year before.
27. The vehicle was later found abandoned near Gougaram, a little over
100km, as the crow flies, to the north-west.
28. These comprised two groups of French and one of Austrians.
29. Available online at www.worldtribune.com/worldtribune/
WTARC/2004/af_algeria_05_20.html.
30. Raffi Khatchadourian, 'Pursuing Terrorists in the Great Desert',
Village Voice, 24 January 2006.
31. Ibid.
32. Ibid.
33. There are many definitions of terrorism. By 'conventional', I mean
that terrorism is the threatened or actual use of violence against
civilian targets for political objectives. Jonathan Barker, paraphrasing
Boaz Ganor, elaborates:

> This applies to governments (and their agencies and proxies) as
> well as to non-governmental groups and individuals. It excludes
> non-violent political actions such as protests, strikes, demonstra-
> tions, tax revolts and civil disobedience. It also excludes violent
> actions against military and police forces.

Jonathan Barker, *The No-Nonsense Guide to Terrorism* (Oxford,
Between the Lines: 2003). See also Boaz Ganar, 'Defining Terrorism: Is
One Man's Terrorist Another Man's Freedom Fighter?' International
Institute for Counter-Terrorism, 23 September 1998, available online
at http://www.ict.org.il. 'Terrorism' does not include such fairly

normal Saharan pursuits as smuggling (now termed trafficking), acts of political rebellion (often referred to by the governments concerned as banditry and criminality) or the many forms of resistance of civil society towards the corrupt and authoritarian regimes which hold sway over most of this part of Africa.

34. US-EUCOM is the US European Command. It covers Europe, the former republics of the Soviet Union, and most of Africa. However, a number of countries in north-east Africa – namely Egypt, Sudan, Eritrea, Ethiopia, Djibouti, Somalia and Kenya, as well as the Seychelles – fall within the responsibility of US Central Command. Madagascar and the Comoros fall under the US Pacific Command. These commands are responsible for conducting active military operations in Africa, including training exercises, humanitarian relief, peacekeeping, evacuating civilians from unstable countries, and other operations. See Daniel Volman, 'US Military Involvement in Africa', *Review of African Political Economy (ROAPE)* 32 (103), March 2005, pp. 187–9.

35. Stewart M. Powell, 'Swamp of Terror in the Sahara', *Air Force Magazine* 87 (11), November 2004, available online at http://www.airforce-magazine.com/MagazineArchive/Pages/2004/November%202004/1104sahara.aspx.

36. Ibid. See also Jason Motlagh, 'The Trans Sahara Counter-Terrorism Initiative: US takes terror fight to Africa's "Wild West"'. *Global Research*, 30 December 2005, available online at http://www.globalresearch.ca/index.php?context=va&aid=1678. See also 'Leader of group tied to Madrid blast captured in Chad', available online at www.worldtribune.com/worldtribune/WTARC/2004/af_algeria_05_20.html.

37. We are indebted to US counter-intelligence services for noting that terrorists, like bees, swarm.

38. *Le Journal du Dimanche*, 4 July 2004.

39. http://www.jeuneafrique.com.

40. *Le Journal du Dimanche*, 4 July 2004. The report did not state whether the base was active or abandoned. Neither did this report, nor any of the international media which quoted it, question whether the base might not have been one of dozens of abandoned camps that litter this part of the Sahara after decades of almost continual military activity in the region.

    If the intention of the intelligence agencies was to establish an image of Tora Bora in the Sahara, they had probably not counted on the help of the BBC, which, in its three-part film exploring the roots of terror – 'The Power of Nightmares' – substituted film footage of the Sahara's mountains (those of the Ahaggar range) for those of Afghanistan! 'The Power of Nightmares', produced by Adam Curtis, was shown on BBC television on 20 and 27 October and 3 November 2004.

Chapter 3

1. See Chapter 9.
2. The population of Tamanrasset, for example, grew from around 40,000 at the end of the 1980s to around 100,000 by the end of the 1990s, and to perhaps as much as 150,000 or more by 2005. Nearly all of that growth was generated by Algerians moving into the region from the north.
3. Kel Ahaggar and Kel Ajjer (Kel means 'people of' in the language of the Tuareg).
4. Mustafa Barth, 'Sand-castles in the Sahara: US military basing in Algeria', *Review of African Political Economy (ROAPE)* 30 (98), 2003, pp. 679–85.
5. Jeremy Keenan, 1971, *The Social Consequences of Algerian Development Policies for the Tuareg of Ahaggar–Sahara*, Ph.D thesis (University of Exeter, 1971).
6. Jeremy Keenan, *The Tuareg: People of Ahaggar* (London: Allen Lane, 1977).
7. See Chapter 10.
8. See Chapter 6.
9. For example, during the course of the hostage drama, from March to August 2003 (and subsequently) few journalists, either local or international, bothered to check the map location of Tamelrik, the mountains in which the hostages were reportedly being held. Consequently, numerous newspaper reports, mostly relying on each other's errors, placed Tamelrik 150km north-east of Illizi, whereas it is in fact 150km to the south-west.
10. Deepak Lal, *In Praise of Empires: Globalization and Order* (New York: Palgrave Macmillan, 2004), p. 211.
11. The roles of the media and academe are examined in more depth in the sequel to this book. See Jeremy Keenan, *The Dying Sahara: US Imperialism and Terror in Africa* (London: Pluto, forthcoming).

Chapter 4

1. The other is the Arak gorge, which takes the main national road north from Tamanrasset to In Salah.
2. The name derives from the number of prehistoric tombs along its way.

3. A Land Rover, a Nissan and a Toyota.
4. This was (D) BT-MY 7.
5. Erich Christ, posted on www.sahara-info.ch/, 18 June 2003. See also 'theory three' at www.triotours.com/saharamissing/theories.html.
6. On their way out of the region – heading now towards Amguid – they ran across two more Austrians, Christoph Langes and Roland Mayr, who were also taken hostage.
7. '... is completely forbidden because of persistent dangers. It is necessary to have a special authorisation from the appropriate *wilaya* which requires additional security measures to those specified for Category B (routes) ... It is forbidden to leave roads and tracks (pistes)...'. (Algeria's official laws governing the use of its roads and pistes.)
8. Sadek had been appointed as head of the DRS in Tamanrasset in 2002.
9. Smaïn Lamari is no relation to Chief of Staff General Mohammed Lamari.
10. The debriefing took place at Amguid. The hostages were flown the short distance from Gharis, from where they had been liberated, to Amguid by army helicopter.
11. Harald Ickler, with Susanne Längsfeld, *Entführt in der Wüste* ('Kidnapped in the Desert') (Bergisch-Gladbach: Bastei Lübbe, 2003).
12. I was filming an extensive documentary film in the area six months later, and was told by the Algerian authorities that no filming had been undertaken in the area recently.
    The information obtained from hostage debriefings and later interviews must always be treated with circumspection. In this case, much of the hostages' information, perhaps not surprisingly, was equivocal. In addition to the almost inevitable 'Stockholm syndrome', which was clearly apparent among some of the hostages, the two groups were fraught with personal uncertainties and antagonisms and, for the most part, had a surprising lack of objective interest in and knowledge of their surroundings. Moreover, their inevitable psychological difficulties were almost certainly compounded by a number of other factors, such as the relatively low-level public reception, bordering in some instances on open criticism, on their return home; the knowledge, in the case of the first group, that a second group was still in captivity; and – for all of them – the tragic death of one of the second group on their journey to Mali. On top of these traumas, the authorities in all three countries (Germany, Austria and Switzerland) exerted varying degrees of pressure, and in some cases issued threats, for political reasons, not to publicise their experiences.

13. www.algeria-interface.com. See also issues of *El Watan* between 13 and 18 May 2003.
14. See, for example, www.algeria-interface.com.
15. Ingo Bleckmann was interviewed by me at great length on numerous occasions between 2003 (after his release) and 2007. See also the statement of hostage Axel Mantey in *El Watan*, 17 May 2003.
16. Salima Mellah, 'L'affaire des "otages du Sahara", décryptage d'une manipulation', Algeria-Watch, 22 September 2007.
17. Radio Report of Betina Rühl, Treibsand, WDR5, 5 August 2007; Mellah, 'L'affaire', n. 17.
18. Harald Ickler describes in his book how he later began to wonder if the Algerian military had staged his release. Ickler and Längsfeld, *Entführt in der Wüste*, p. 222–3.
19. Author interview with Ingo Bleckmann.
20. An Iveco 'people-carrier'.
21. The broadcast of 16 May 2003 on RFI (Radio France Internationale) was written by Richard Labévière, a specialist on Algeria and Islamist terrorism. It was quoted widely in both the Algerian and European press over the following few days. See, for example, *El Watan*, 17 May 2003. Labévière was soon after expelled from Algeria. The original transmission appears to have been removed from the RFI website. However, it was archived and can be accessed through Algeria Watch, at www.algeria-watch.org/fr/article/mil/groupes_armes/negociations_secretes.htm.
22. Salima Mellah and Jean-Baptiste Rivoire, 'El Para, the Maghreb's Bin Laden', *Le Monde Diplomatique*, February 2005.
23. Much of this information was obtained from the many interviews undertaken with members of the second group of hostages by various national and regional German media, as well as a number of groups and organisations working on behalf of the hostages and their families, and subsequently made available to me.
24. These events are described and explained in Chapter 9.
25. See Chapter 9.
26. This is reported by Salima Mellah ('L'affaire', n. 17) from the hostages' various debriefings and accounts of their capture.
27. There were only a limited number of French-speakers in the two groups of hostages.
28. Rainer Bracht and Petra Bracht, *177 Tage Angst* (177 days of anxiety), Euskirchen: Highlightsverlag, 2004.
29. As mentioned in Chapter 1, Reuters confirmed that it was not possible to authenticate the document independently (*Reuters* Newsdesk, Algiers, 22 August 2003).

30. Susanne Sterzenbach, 'Verschwörung in der Sahara' ('Conspiracy in the Sahara'), Auslandsreporter: WDR, 4 July 2007.
31. This is made clear by Salima Mellah (see note 16). It should be noted that this date (14 October 2004) is also after the alleged return of El Para to Algeria, as described in Chapter 6.
32. Mathieu Guidère, *Al-Qaida à la conquête du Maghreb: Le terrorisme aux portes de l'Europe* (Paris: Editions du Rocher, 2007). Guidère is Director of Research at St-Cyr, an Arabist, and a specialist on jihadist movements.
33. Richard Labévière, 'Les ravisseurs espèrent un million par otage' ('The kidnappers are hoping for 1 million per hostage'), *L'Hebdo*, 8 May 2003, 32 (19). The francs referred to in the price are Swiss francs. Other media, such as the BBC, picked up on the story. See, for example, BBC World News, 12 May 2003 (http://news.bbc.co.uk/go/pr/fr/-/1/hi/world/africa/3020131.stm/).
34. See, for example, *El Watan* 17 May 2003 (www.elwatan.com/); *Le Matin*, 16 May 2003; *Trio Tours*, 16 May 2003 (www.triotours.com/)
35. *Mouvement Algérien des Officiers Libres* (MAOL), 19 May 2003 (www.anp.org/)
36. The hostages painted and then photographed the date of 16 May on the wall of their rock shelter, saying it was the day they left for Illizi.
37. They could surely only have been supplied or delivered by the military or with the military's compliance.
38. This information came from the various debriefings of the Tamelrik group and from Harald Ickler's book. See Ickler, *Entführt in der Wüste*, p. 224, n. 11; Mellah, 'L'affaire', n. 17.
39. Tiger is built by Eurocopter, a subsidiary of the EADS (European Aeronautics Defence and Space) company formed by DaimlerChrysler Aerospace of Germany, Aerospatiale Matra of France, and CASA of Spain. For specifications, see www.army-technology.com/projects/tiger.
40. For specifications, see www.army-technology.com/projects/rooivalk.
41. The logic of this, if it is true, is that, as there were four Swiss among the 32 hostages, the Swiss share of the total ransom payment should be an eighth. However, none of the Swiss were in the first group – all four were in the second group at Tamelrik, which comprised ten Germans, four Swiss and one Dutchman. With the Austrians all freed in the first group, the Swiss feared that the ransom might become associated with the freeing of the second group only, in which case they might find themselves paying a disproportionate share – namely four-fifteenths!
42. Reported by AFP on algeria-interface.com, 16 May 2003.

43. *El Watan*, 17 May 2003.
44. This was revealed through interviews with soldiers involved in the search. The interviews were undertaken after their period of service in the army had ended.
45. The hostages knew that they had been spotted by Algerian army helicopters as early as 16 March, after which they were flown over regularly, sometimes daily, at very low altitude (Mellah, 'L'affaire', n. 17).
46. From interviews, it seems that it was probably always the same plane.
47. According to sources close to some of the hostages' families, it is perhaps significant that the US stopped providing them with information at about the time of the 'discovery' of this message.
48. The exact number of days spent travelling to Mali is not clear. The hostages left Tamelrik on 16 May and were in Mali around the first week of July, possibly by 5 July. That is approximately 50 days, of which around five days were spent in El Para's stop-over camp in Issaouane before setting off on their long journey.
49. Such an attack could have been undertaken at several places along the way, and especially when they were holed up in the Tassili-n-Ahenet Mountains on the Algerian side of the Mali border, where the captors would have had a safe escape route into Mali.
50. It is unlikely that we will ever know for certain whether the Algerians intended before the Tamelrik fiasco to move the hostages to Mali. There are vague reports of Algerian intelligence agents being seen in northern Mali sometime before the Tamelrik departure, as well as uncorroborated reports of French intelligence agents ensuring that Libyans were not in the area. If these reports are true, it would suggest that the Malian leg of the drama was planned some time beforehand.
51. The *Quotidien d'Oran* of 3 February 2004, estimated the sum as 4.6 million euros (quoted in Mellah, 'L'affaire', n. 17).
52. When they were 35km south of Timiaouine, the kidnappers allegedly took the mayor of the Timiaouine hostage, apparently fearing an attack by the Algerian army.
53. Iyad ag Ghali was named in the Algerian press on 3 August 2003 as the mediator acting on behalf of the Mali government.
54. After these meetings, at which the Algerians are believed to have fixed what we might regard as the 'ground rules' for the negotiations, the hostages met the mediators before being taken around 600km north towards Taoudenni while the negotiations were played out.
55. Harald Ickler and Bettina Rühl, *Treibsand*, WDR5, 5 August 2007; Susanne Sterzenbach, 'Verschwörung in der Sahara' ('Conspiracy in the Sahara') (Auslandsreporter: WDR, 4 July 2007).

Chapter 5

1. One reason why we may now never know is because Aboubacar Alembo (also known as 'Alambo') was killed in an engagement between the MNJ rebels and the Niger military at Tazerzait in Aïr, on 22 June 2007. The MNJ rebellion is introduced in Chapter 13 and discussed in detail in Jeremy Keenan, *The Dying Sahara: US Imperialism and Terror in Africa* (London: Pluto, forthcoming).

2. Information provided by local people who identified him as being in the Djanet area at around that time.

3. This network is not of local, Tuareg, origin. Its five founding members were all Arabs and foreigners to the region. Two came from Libya, two were Chaamba from the northern Algerian Sahara, and one was from Touat. They subsequently married into local families in Niger and Ajjer.

    In April 2007 I interviewed Captain Fancaro, the head of Niger's Force National d'Intervention et de la Sécurité (FNIS), at his headquarters in Agades. He confirmed to me that he too was a cousin of Alembo!

4. Given the complete absence of reliable verification of the events described by official Algerian and US sources in this Sahelian phase, all such reports must inevitably be regarded as disinformation.

5. See Chapter 2, note 23.

6. It should not be assumed that all arms trafficking in Algeria is from the Sahel and destined for GSPC cells in the north. For example, the Ivory Coast authorities appealed to the Mali government to put a stop to the trafficking of arms through their territory from Algeria to the rebel Forces Nouvelles in the north of the country. See *Le Patriote*, 6 February 2004.

7. The files make no other mention of the incident.

8. The two men were Abdellaoui Abderrazak (a.k.a. Abou Hafs) and Mahmoudi Aref (a.k.a. Talha).

9. *Quotidien d'Oran*, 17 August 2003.

10. The word *ishomar* is the Berberised version of the French word *chômeur* (an unemployed person or redundant worker). The word describes the young men who left Niger and Mali during the drought of the 1970s, and more recently, in search of work in Libya. Many joined Gaddafi's Islamic Legion. With the collapse in the oil price and Gaddafi's humiliating military withdrawal from Chad in the late 1980s, many of the them returned home and became the main fighters in the Tuareg rebellions in the 1990s. Many still sport their original arms – mostly AK47s.

11. Information provided by local Tuareg interviewed by me after the incident.

12. See bibliography.
13. Raffi Khatchadourian, 'Pursuing Terrorists in the Great Desert', *Village Voice*, 24 January 2006.
14. Ibid.
15. Ibid.
16. Ibid.
17. Ibid.
18. *Africa Analysis*, does not appear to be recognised among professional security firms as a specialist security firm, but rather as a subscription-based bulletin belonging to Oneworld, an organisation which claims to bring together more than 1,500 organisations from across the globe to promote sustainable development, social justice and human rights.
19. Khatchadourian, 'Pursuing Terrorists'.
20. I provided Khatchadourian with much detailed source material, including around four hours of telephone interviews, to which he makes absolutely no reference at all. For my analysis of Khatchadourian's article, see Jeremy Keenan, *The Dying Sahara*.
21. Notwithstanding his eloquent prose, it transpires that Khatchadourian never even visited Niger (personal communication with the author). See *The Dying Sahara*. It is journalism at its most imaginative, unethical and irresponsible.
22. Mustafa Barth, 'Sand-Castles in the Sahara: US military basing in Algeria', *(Review of African Political Economy* 30 (98), 2003, pp. 679–85; Jeremy Keenan, 'Americans & "Bad People" in the Sahara-Sahel', *Review of African Political Economy* 31 (99), 2004, pp. 130–9.
23. The file never reached the Bundeskriminalamt. Instead, it was 'diverted' through other channels before being passed to me in 2006. The names of the intermediaries cannot be divulged for their own safety. However, I have been able to interview them and have confirmation that the file in my possession is the same one that was destined for the Bundeskriminalamt.
24. This was in the Tamesna region. The officer said that there had been 'some deaths', but gave no details either of the number killed or of whether they were GSPC or FAN.
25. www.worldtribune.com/worldtribune/WTARC/2004/af_algeria_05_20.html.
26. US troops have been seen at the In Guezzam border post, while uncorroborated reports from nomads suggest that US troops have also been spotted at other Algerian posts in the Niger border area, such as In Azoua.
27. Note 13, above.

28. Note 21, above.
29. Saifi Ammari has many aliases, such as El (Al) Para, Abderezak, Abou (Abu) Haidara, Ammane Abu Haidra, Abderezak Zaimeche, Abdul Razzaq, Abdul Rasak, Abdalrazak, al Ammari Al Arussi, El Ourassi, and further combinations and alternative spellings of these. The names Arussi and Ourassi come from the name Aures, the mountain region in eastern Algeria in which he was born and in which he was allegedly the GSPC *emir*.
30. Tabarakatean is not found on non-military maps. That is because it is a new well, dug recently by narco-traffickers and other traffickers, as well as itinerant Tuareg (*ishumar*) travelling this route to Libya, at an old crossroads where all four compass-points meet, crossing the northern Ténéré.
31. El Para's men had acquired new petrol-fuelled Toyota four-wheel-drive pick-up trucks before leaving Mali. However, the vehicles they stole from the tourists at Temet were diesel-fuelled. The Chadian military reported the GSPC's Toyotas as having Algerian registration marks, while the accessory fog lamps, noted in photographs, also suggest a 'coastal' origin.
32. Tamgak is a large mountain in Aïr, just to the east of Iferouan.
33. This incident is described in Chapter 2.
34. Kaouar is the group of oases running down the eastern side of the Ténéré, from Orida in the north to Bilma in the south. The other oases, from north to south, are Djaba, Djabo, Chirfa, Séguédine, Aney and Dirkou.
35. Smugglers in Djanet passed on the information of Alembo's whereabouts to his family, who in turn gave it to the posse leader.
36. The source was a minister in the Niger government, whose name cannot be revealed for reasons of confidentiality.
37. Alembo apparently stated that he had no quarrel with the state, only with the leader of the posse, who, at the time of this alleged meeting with the minister, was in gaol on another matter.
38. £1 = approximately 1,000 CFA francs.
39. Tabarakaten might possibly have been the point at which the groups parted company.
40. If only 20 or 25 men had gone on to Chad, as the Temet tourists suggested, then 43 could not have been killed in Chad, as the Americans say.
41. As far as I am aware, there is only one reasonably safe route into the region from the west, which is well known to, and guarded by, the Chadian army.
42. To the Wour region.

43. Baz Lecocq and Paul Schrijver, 'The War on Terror in a Haze of Dust: Potholes and Pitfalls on the Saharan Front', *Journal of Contemporary African Studies* 25 (1), January 2007, pp. 141–66.

44. As mentioned earlier in this chapter, Alembo had close kin ties to the director of security for the Tamanrasset *wilaya* and close ties to key officials at Djanet. He was killed in a military engagement between Niger's MNJ rebels and the FAN on 22 June 2007.

45. *Quotidien d'Oran*, 10 March 2004.

46. Reuters, 11 March 2004.

47. *L'Expression, El Watan* and AFP, 15 March 2004.

48. *Jeune Afrique L'Intelligent*, 24 April–1 May 2004.

49. AFP, 19 March 2004.

50. *El Watan*, 20 March 2004.

51. 'Pentagon Africa Terror', Voice of America, 24 March 2004.

52. *Paris Match*, 5–11 August 2004.

53. At this time the MDJT was split into at least two factions. El Para was being held by one faction and his men by another. Forestier had to travel some distance between the camps of the two factions to conduct his interview with El Para.

54. If there was no battle with the Chadian army, and if El Para's men had split into two groups after Temet, as seems likely, it is possible that this group of captives represented all of his group that actually travelled into Chad.

55. Information provided to me by senior members of MDJT.

56. Author interviews with Tubu nomads from the region. According to the Americans the battle lasted for three days (see Khatchadourian, 'Pursuing Terrorists', n. 14). It is almost inconceivable that there would be no traces of such a prolonged battle, such as spent shells, on the ground, and less likely still that nomads could not have found them.

Chapter 6

1. The names Arussi and Ourassi come from the name Aures, the mountain region in eastern Algeria in which he was allegedly born, and where he was allegedly the GSPC *emir*.

2. At the beginning of 2007, the GSPC changed its name to Al-Qaeda in the Islamic Maghreb (AQIM).

3. Raffi Khatchadourian, 'Pursuing Terrorists in the Great Desert', *Village Voice*, 24 January 2006.

4. Transparency International defines itself as a global civil society organisation leading the fight against corruption (www.transparency.org).

5. ExxonMobil is the major partner (with a 40 per cent share) in a consortium also comprising Petronas Malaysia (35 per cent) and ChevronTexaco (25 per cent), and part-funded by the World Bank, which is regarded by many as the financial arm of US foreign policy. See Jeremy Keenan, 'Chad–Cameroon Oil Pipeline: World Bank and ExxonMobil in Last Chance Saloon', *Review of African Political Economy* 104/5 (2005), pp. 395–405.

6. Youssouf Togoïmi founded the MDJT in 1998. He died in mysterious circumstances in Tripoli in 2002.

7. The claim of one of the faction leaders, Choua Dazi, to be at the head of 1,000 men is almost certainly an exaggeration.

8. Reported by Radio France Internationale, 'Le Matin', 3 June 2004.

9. See note 3, above.

10. Algeria has a proven track record of using 'phantoms' in its war against Islamic militants. The best known is probably Mokhtar ben Mokhtar, who has many aliases, and who has been reported killed on at least six occasions. Algerians know that Mokhtar ben Mokhtar and El Para are two such 'phantoms', who are invariably credited with actions undertaken by the DRS; or, as is often the case, with incidents that didn't actually occur. Not surprisingly, as soon as El Para was reportedly taken into detention by the Algerians in October 2004, Mokhtar ben Mokhtar was immediately credited with alleged attacks on security services along the south-eastern border of the country. This pattern is so familiar that Mokhtar ben Mokhtar is actually referred to by many Saharan peoples as 'le phantom'.

11. *Agence France-Presse*, 12 September 2004.

12. These would either have been placed or at least approved, by the DRS.

13. *Paris Match*, Paris, 5–11 August 2004. *Paris Match*'s biographical details on El Para presumably came from Algerian military–media sources.

14. According to the Algerian press, the first date comes from the records of the Gendarmerie Nationale, the second from the army. *L'Expression*, 30 October 2004.

15. Chaouia (Shawiyya) are the indigenous Berber people of the Aures region.

16. See note 13, above. El Para's Gendarmerie Nationale file (mentioned in Chapter 5) reads: 'Né P / 1968 à Kef Errih / commune de Bouhechana / Daïra de Ben S'mih / Wilaya de Guelma, fils de Abdallah et Belenchir Draham, Ex-djoundi des Forces Spéciales (caserne de Beni Messous)'.

17. See note 13, above.

228 THE DARK SAHARA

18. Groupe(s) Islamique(s) Armée(s).
19. *L'Expression*, 30 October 2004.
20. Although the GSPC was formed in 1998, internal discussion over such a breakaway from the GIA had been in hand since 1996.
21. *Le Matin*, 9 August 2003.
22. *Le Monde Diplomatique*, February 2005.
23. www.jihad-algeria.com.
24. A few ambiguous references to El Para before this time may well have been to another 'El Para', namely Abbi Abdelaziz, alias Okacha El Para, who was reportedly killed alongside the GSPC leader Nabil Sahraoui on 18 June 2004 (or thereabouts).
25. See note 22, above. See also Chapter 4.
26. See Chapter 4.
27. Ibid.
28. There is a possible reference to El Para in a Spanish article in 1999, but it is imprecise and possibly a reference to another El Para. This appears to be the first media reference to his name, based on extensive, but not necessarily infallible, searches.
29. Even if that were to happen, there is probably much that is confined to the mental records of its leading generals.
30. See Chapter 9.
31. There have been three amnesties during Bouteflika's presidency. The first was the Civil Harmony Law, which gave a six-month amnesty to most Islamists from 13 July 1999. It was renewed in January 2000, but without clear legal status. In 2006 the Charter for Peace and National Reconciliation was passed by decree, giving the security forces effective immunity from prosecution.
32. The number of dead varies according to different reports.
33. See note 22, above.
34. This botched abduction is detailed in Chapter 10.
35. For example, a report in the Saudi-owned, Arabic-language London daily, *Asharq al-Awsat*, on 15 February 2003 states that El Para was being encircled by the Algerian army in the Tebessa Mountains with 100 of his followers. This encirclement, if it happened, is more likely to have taken place immediately after the attack at Teniet el-Abed. Also, 15 February was within a week of the first tourist disappearances, making it unlikely that El Para could have extricated himself from the army net, travelled deep into the Sahara, and organised the abductions in such a short space of time. The London report may have been placed by the DRS, hence the delay. The newspaper's report that El Para had summoned groups of GSPC leaders in the east to discuss their transfer of loyalty to him and his overthrowing

of Hassan Hattab as leader, also has the ring of information from a DRS plant.

36. For an illuminating analysis of these practices, see Luis Martinez, *The Algerian Civil War 1990–1998* (London: Hurst, 2000).

37. The problem with this possibility is that the information relating to El Para's *trabendo* activities comes from the Algerian media, and hence the security services. While it cannot, of course, be ruled out, it merely highlights the possibility that the method of El Para's infiltration into the GSPC was through his *trabendo* operations, into which he was possibly launched and almost certainly controlled by the DRS.

38. Attention was probably first called to El Para's possible association with US Special Forces by A. Chevalérias, 'Qui A Enlevé Les Otages Du Sahara?' (http://www.recherches-sur-le-terrorisme.com/Documentsterrorisme/sahara.html/).

39. This behaviour fits that noted by the hostages, namely that he rarely prayed and was often busy doing other things at prayer times, such as sitting in his vehicle or working the radio.

40. Mohamed Boudiaf's official position was as chairman of the High State Committee (HCE), Algeria's five-man collective presidency, which stepped in following the displacement of President Chadli Benjedid in January 1992. See Chapters 8 and 9.

41. Both Toufik and Smaïn are well known to US intelligence agencies, with Toufik having his own representative in Washington, DC (information provided personally by the FBI in Washington, DC, August 2006).

42. Gen. Sahab also had good experience of the US military, having been on several training missions to the US.

43. Executive Outcomes had more than two-dozen subsidiary companies that were particularly difficult to unravel and trace.

44. See Chapter 4.

45. *El-Khabar* ('Joint military operation leaves 50 "terrorists" dead'), 7 March 2001.

46. Lounis Aggoun and Jean-Baptiste Rivoire, *Françalgérie, crimes et mensonges d'Etats: Histoire secrète de la guerre d'indépendance à la "troisième guerre" d'Algérie* (Paris: La Découverte, 2004), pp. 365–7.

47. B. Mounir, 'Nabil Sahraoui et trois de ses ajoints abattus', *Le Quotidien d'Oran*, 21 June 2004.

48. 'Favorable au projet d'amnistie générale, Hassan Attab exclu du GSPC', *El Watan*, 13 February 2005.

49. 'L'émir' national de GSPC abattu par ses rivaux', *Le Jour d'Algérie*, 31 May 2005.

50. François Gèze and Salima Mellah, 'Clashes between factions against the backdrop of geopolitical conflicts', *Algeria-Watch*, 21 April 2007 (translated from French), available online at www.algeria-watch. org/en/analyses/geze_mellah.htm.
    Their comment is based on information published by, among others, Mohammed Sahraoui, *Chronique des années de sang. Algérie: comment les services secrets ont manipulé les groupes islamistes* (Paris: Denoël, 2003).

51. The name of the border post was 'El Sirri'. Two Tunisians were injured, and three of the 20 terrorists who carried out the operation were killed. *El-Khabar*, 3 June 2000.

52. *Africa News* ('Spillover Effect of Terrorism in Algerian–Tunisian Border'), 7 June 2000.

53. Rainer and Petra Bracht, *177 Tage Angst* (Euskirchen: Highlights Verlag, 2004), p. 204.

54. As the radios were old Warsaw Pact stock, it would have been surprising if the BKA had not been able to break the code.

55. This information was provided by certain international oil companies whose own aircraft movements were affected by this airspace closure.

56. See note 22, above.

57. According to the Gendarmerie Nationale files (mentioned in Chapter 5) , Abdelhak's real name is Laïche Dhaou. He was born on 5 August 1964 at Debila, El Oued, son of Chaabane and Aïcha Dhaou.

58. There are inconsistencies in the hostages' evidence over this length of time. It varies between one and three weeks, possibly because they were captured on different dates. Salima Mellah, for example, says that he spent three weeks with the first group (Salima Mellah, 'L'affaire des "otages du Sahara", décryptage d'une manipulation', Algeria-Watch, 22 September 2007). The evidence that I have from the hostages is that it may have been as little as a week.

59. Ibid.

60. Ibid.

61. Not only have many of the soldiers who had been on these patrols subsequently spoken to both me and my many informants in the region; they have also confirmed that they were pulled back whenever they got too close to the hostage locations.

62. Alvaro Canovas and Paul Comiti, respectively.

63. Patrick Forestier's photo-interview was published in *Paris Match*, 5 August 2004.

64. I myself raised questions at the time of Forestier's 'scoop' as to whether he may have been aided and abetted by the French secret

service, as his account certainly gave credibility to the US–Algerian version of events. However, I have subsequently heard from reliable intelligence sources that the French intelligence services were extremely angry with Forestier, which suggests that he was not in cahoots with them and that his scoop was genuine.

65. See Chapters 9–11.

66. This has never been absolutely clear, and it may even have been revoked.

67. One request was by phone; the other was made in a personal visit to the embassy.

68. My motives were twofold: to pass information of a serious 'international crime' to the appropriate authority, and to protect myself from being accused of withholding information on a terrorist action, especially one that had led to the death of an innocent German citizen. The same offer was made to the 'security section' at the US embassy in London, which took my name and contact details and told me that I would be called if needed. My information, quite understandably, was clearly not needed!

69. The question of whether Germany's intelligence services were gullible, inept or in collusion with the DRS is encapsulated in the information given to Ingo Bleckmann (a hostage at Gharis) by the Germans after his release. Bleckmann was told by the Germans that they had been given access by the Algerians to El Para's radio communications with the two groups of hostages. Two weeks before his release from Gharis, El Para had apparently ordered his captors to kill one of the hostages in Ingo's group, as arrangements were not going well. Ingo's captors reportedly replied that they could not do that, as the hostages were nice people. Does this mean that German intelligence services were in collusion with the DRS, or simply that they had not considered that the DRS had managed the hostage-taking and was contriving radio broadcasts to dupe the Germans? (Source: author interviews with Bleckmann).

70. My own view is that, while Germany's intelligence services certainly demonstrated their incompetence, it is difficult to accept that the German Foreign Ministry, and perhaps other elements of the German government, were not in some degree of collusion with the Algerians, and perhaps also the Americans.

71. This was reported in most Algerian newspapers and by AFP between 28 and 31 October, 2004. See, for example, AFP (Alger), 28 October 2004 and Le Quotidien d'Oran ('La Libye extrade Abderezak Al-Para vers l'Algerie'), 30 October 2004.

72. US State Department, daily press briefing, Washington, DC, 29 October 2004.

73. In the same trial three other Algerians were acquitted, and two – both minor players – sentenced to three years in gaol.

74. Hamid Ould Ahmed, 'Algeria jails top Islamic desert militant for life', Reuters (Algiers), 25 June 2005.

75. Ibid.

76. In February 2007 Algeria's media reported that El Para was to be brought to court for trial on further terrorist charges on 18 March 2007. That date came and went, as most El Para watchers anticipated, in stony silence.

77. Holger Eichele, 'Jede Geisel hat ihren Preis', *Muenchner Merkur*, 1 December 2005 (my translation).

78. Algeria's minister of the interior, Yazid Zerhouni, was quoted in several media reports after the attack as saying that Islamic rebel leaders (*emirs*) do not trust young suicide bombers who might decide at the last minute not to die. The solution (for the *emirs*) is to make sure the bomb can be detonated externally. This statement is particularly strange as Algeria, unlike the Palestinian territories and Iraq, and in spite of its long history of terrorist atrocities, has little or no experience of suicide bombings. The basis of Zerhouni's statement is therefore not at all clear.

79. His name was known to the hostages and confirmed on the National Gendarmerie file mentioned in Chapter 5.

80. See Chapter 5.

Chapter 7

1. George W. Bush, 'State of the Union Address', 31 January 2006, available at www.whitehouse.gov/stateoftheunion/2006.

2. In 2006 the US produced 6,871,000 barrels daily, compared with 10,859,000 for Saudi Arabia and 9,769,000 for the Russian Federation (source: *BP Statistical Review of World Energy*, June 2007).

3. Knowing that it was only a matter of time before such reliance became inevitable, the Roosevelt administration sought to establish an American protectorate over Saudi Arabia.

4. The Truman Doctrine pledged unstinting US assistance to any nation threatened with Communist subjugation. The Eisenhower Doctrine authorised the president to use US combat forces to defend friendly Middle East countries against Soviet-backed aggressors and to provide additional arms and military assistance to pro-American regimes. See Michael Klare, *Blood and Oil* (London, Penguin: 2004).

5. While the Gulf states may have been the major beneficiary of the Nixon Doctrine, it was focused primarily on extricating US troops from Vietnam and trying to avoid any other such entanglements.

6. Richard Nixon, *U.S. Foreign Policy in the 1970s*, report to Congress, 18 February 1970 (Washington, DC: US Government Printing Office, 1970), pp 53–9. Cited in Klare, *Blood and Oil*, pp. 42–3.

7. Robert E. Ebel, 'The Geopolitics of Energy into the 21st Century', remarks to the open forum, US Department of State, Washington, DC, vol. 1, pp. 24, 30. Cited in Klare 2004, *Blood and Oil*, pp. 14–15. As Klare remarks, 'Nothing in these proposals really sought to reverse the nation's growing reliance on imported oil; nor did they eliminate America's dependence on the Persian Gulf.' Ibid., p. 15.

8. *National Energy Policy*, report of the National Energy Policy Group, May 2001 (available at http://www.whitehouse.gov).

9. Per capita oil consumption peaked in 1978 at 31 barrels a year. By 2000 it had fallen by 20 per cent to 26 barrels (source: US Department of Energy). In 2003, oil comprised 39 per cent of energy consumption in the US by fuel type. Natural gas was second, at 23 per cent, followed by coal at 22 per cent, nuclear at 8 per cent, hydroelectric at 3 per cent, and renewables at 4 per cent. Latest figures from the US Energy Department's Energy Information Administration (EIA) forecast that by 2025 the contribution of oil will have increased to 42 per cent. Gas is forecast to remain at 23 per cent, with coal, nuclear, hydroelectric and renewables all declining by approximately 1 percentage point. This forecast, three years later than the Cheney Report, indicates that oil will become an even more important contributor to the massive levels of US energy consumption than was forecast by the Cheney Report.

10. Natural gas consumption is predicted to increase by more than 50 per cent over the same period. The EIA Report for 2005 forecast that US petroleum demand would grow by 37 per cent by 2025. *Annual Energy Outlook (AEO2005)*, Energy Information Administration, US Energy Department (www.eia.doe.gov/oiaf/aeo/). These forecasts look like they will be met: according to the International Energy Agency, US oil consumption for 2004 rose by 2.9 per cent – the fastest rate of growth in 23 years.

11. In 2000 oil accounted for 89 per cent of net US energy imports (source, US Department of Energy).

12. As a result of increased production offshore, predominantly from the deep waters of the Gulf of Mexico, output will increase slightly over the next few years to peak at 6.2mb/d in 2009. Thereafter, domestic crude oil production will resume its decline, which is estimated to fall to 4.7mb/d by 2025, as the country's mature production basins are tapped out.

13. LNG is natural gas super-cooled to –259 degrees Fahrenheit, which shrinks and changes to a liquid.

14. This figure is in line with the 2005 US Energy Department forecast, which expects the US to import 68 per cent of its petroleum needs in 2025.

15. For instance, as a result of the secrecy surrounding Vice-President Cheney's dealings and affairs, it has taken six years to obtain confirmation of what everyone suspected – namely, that representatives from the oil industry were given privileged access to the Cheney team, to the exclusion of environmentalists and other concerned lobbies, and that the report was little more than a blueprint for the oil industry, riding roughshod over civil liberties and environmental safeguards. See, for example, Michael Abramowitz and Steven Mufson, 'Papers Detail Industry's Role in Cheney's Energy Report', *Washington Post*, 18 July 2007: p. A01.

16. The roots of the American neo-conservative movement go back several decades. However, the impetus that neocons have given the Bush administration stems largely from the Washington-based think tank (Chairman: William Kristol) called Project for the New American Century, which describes itself as 'a non-profit educational organization dedicated to a few fundamental propositions: that American leadership is good both for America and for the world; and that such leadership requires military strength, diplomatic energy and commitment to moral principle'. Details of PNAC can be found at: http://www.newamericancentury.org.

17. 17 May 2001.

18. Remark by President George W. Bush to Capital City Partnership, RiverCentre Convention Centre, St Paul, Minn., 17 May 2001, available at www.whitehouse.gov.

19. *National Energy Policy*, report of the National Energy Policy Group, May 2001. (available at http://www.whitehouse.gov), Ch. 8, p. 6. See also Daniel Volman, 'The Bush Administration & African Oil: The Security Implications of US Energy Policy', *Review of African Political Economy* 30 (98), December 2003: pp. 573–84.

20. Data for 2006 shows that the five leading Persian Gulf states contain 59 per cent of proven global reserves and are responsible for 28 per cent of global output. The figures for the Middle East as a whole are 61.4 per cent and 31.3 per cent, respectively. In 2000 the percentage of global reserves and output for the Gulf states and the Middle East as a whole were slightly higher. That is because proven global reserves increased from 1.03 trillion barrels in 1999 to 1.21 trillion barrels at the end of 2006, with the greatest increases being in other regions, such as Africa (*BP Statistical Review of World Energy*, June 2007).

21. The most detailed and informative analysis of Saudi oil is provided in Matthew R. Simmons, *Twilight in the Desert: The Coming Saudi Oil Shock and the World Economy* (London: Wiley, 2005).

22. US Dept of Energy, EIA, IEO 2003, table D1, p. 235.
23. US Dept of Energy, EIA, IEO 2001, tables D1, D6, pp. 235, 240.
24. Jeff Gerth, 'Forecast of Rising Oil Demand Challenges Tired Saudi Fields', *New York Times*, 24 February 2004.
25. Ibid.
26. US House of Representatives, Committee on International Relations, 'Statement of the Honorable Spencer Abraham, secretary of Energy, Before the Committee on International Relations, US House of Representatives, June 20, 2002', p. 4 of electronic version, available at http://www.house.gov/international_relations.
27. US Department of Defense News Transcript, 'DoD News Briefing – Deputy Assistant Secretary of Defense for African Affairs Michael A. Westphal', 2 April 2002.
28. Kofi Akosah-Sarpong, 'Washington eyes Africa's oil', *West Africa* 4,354, 2–8 December 2002, p.10. Quoted in Daniel Volman, 'The Bush Administration & African Oil'.
29. The top four African producers in 2006 were Nigeria, Algeria, Libya and Angola, producing respectively 2,460, 2,005, 1,835 and 1,409 thousand barrels daily (*BP Statistical Review of World Energy*, June 2007).
30. *National Energy Policy*, report of the National Energy Policy Group, May 2001, Ch. 8, p. 11. This explains why Nigeria has been trying to negotiate a higher OPEC quota.
31. 'Light' and 'sweet' refer respectively to the low density and low sulphur content of the crude. Details of these physical properties can be found in the extended version of this chapter (for access details, see note attached to the title of this chapter).
32. Source for all data on African countries cited below is *BP Statistical Review of World Energy*, June 2007.
33. The leading foreign oil companies are ExxonMobil and ChevronTexaco from the US, together with the Franco-Belgian company TotalFinaElf.
34. Amerada Hess is the main US oil company operating in the country, alongside Shell, TotalFinaElf and ENI/Agip from Europe.
35. Although TotalFinaElf and ENI/Agip dominate production, US companies ExxonMobil and ChevronTexaco are partners in the development of several fields.
36. The pipeline is operating illegally as a result of ExxonMobil's failure to follow strict safety regulations and the consequent absence of Area Specific Oil-Spill Response Plans (ASOSRPs). See Jeremy Keenan, 'Chad–Cameroon oil pipeline: World Bank and ExxonMobil in Last Chance Saloon', *Review of African Political Economy* 32 (104/5), June–September 2005, pp. 395–405.

37. Four American companies – namely Amerada Hess, ExxonMobil, Marathon Oil and Ocean Energy – dominate oil production and exploration in the Gulf of Guinea.

38. Barry Meier and Jad Mouawad, 'No Oil Yet, but African Isle Finds Dealings Slippery', *New York Times*, 2 July 2007.

39. Between 2000 and 2006, proven reserves grew from 35.5 to 51.9 billion barrels; production increased from 3,687 to 4,937 thousand barrels daily (*BP Statistical Review of World Energy*, June 2007).

40. US Central Intelligence Agency, National Security Council, *Global Trends 2015*, December 2000, p. 50 of electronic version, available at http://www.cia.gov/nic/; John Bellamy Foster, 'A Warning to Africa: The New US Imperial Grand Strategy', *Monthly Review*, June 2006.

41. Exxon and Mobil withdrew from Libya at that time. Amerada Hess, Conoco, Grace Petroleum, Marathon Oil Corporation and Occidental Petroleum Company remained in Libya until sanctions were imposed in 1986.

42. Libyan oil had been discovered in 1959. Initially output had been so great that its biggest problem was finding markets.

43. Production in state-owned fields was falling at the rate of around 7–8 per cent per annum. For example, Occidental's assets, which were producing 170,000bpd in 1986, were down to about 50–60,000bpd by 2005.

44. Libya began pipeline gas exports to Italy at the end of September 2004, with the opening of the US$6 billion Green Stream Line, owned jointly by Libya and Italy's ENI. Of 10 billion cubic metres of gas, 80 per cent will be exported to Italy and 20 per cent retained for domestic use.

45. Libya claims that only 25 per cent of the country has been explored, and that there are up to 100 billion barrels waiting to be found. However, most oil experts believe that Libya's best areas have been explored and that this claim is unrealistic.

46. The initial problem for Libyan exports is that US refineries are reluctant to experiment with an oil they have not run for two decades. However, at least three of the original Ocean group companies have their own refineries, and exports to the US are expected to pick up steadily.

47. Algeria has proven oil reserves of 12.3 billion barrels and proven natural gas reserves of 159 trillion cubic feet (4.545 trillion cubic metres). Algerian gas exports are expected to exceed 3tcf by 2010, and to meet some 30 per cent of future European demand. Algeria commenced LNG production in 1964, and by 2000 had become the world's second-largest LNG exporter (after Indonesia), with significant exports to America's New England coast. (Algeria's

LNG plant at Skikda was destroyed in an explosion, attributed to poor maintenance, in January 2004. A new plant is currently being built.).

48. US Department of Commerce statistics show that petroleum products continue to account for the largest portion of total US imports from sub-Saharan Africa under the African Growth and Opportunity Act [AGOA], making up an 87 per cent share of US–Africa trade.

49. Council on Foreign Relations, *More Than Humanitarianism: A Strategic US Approach Toward Africa*, 2006, p. xiii.

50. The Heritage Foundation, *Africa's Oil and Gas Sector: Implications for US Policy*, 13 July 2007, available at http://www.heritage.org/Research/Africa/bg2052.cfm, citing US Department of Energy, Energy Information Administration, 'US Imports by Country of Origin', updated 19 April 2007, at http://tonto.eia.doe.gov/dnav/pet/pet_move_impcus_a2_nus_ep00_im0_mbblpd_a.hm.

51. National Intelligence Council, 'External Relations and Africa', discussion paper, 16 March 2004, available at www.dni.gov/nic/PDF_GIF_2020_Support/2004_03_16_papers/external_relations.pdf.

52. John C. K. Daly, 'Questioning AFRICOM's intentions', *ISN Security Watch*, 2 July 2007. BP (*BP Statistical Review of World Energy*, June 2007) puts the increase in African oil production between 2004 and 2007 as being from 8.4 million bpd to just over 10 million bpd.

53. Daniel Volman, 'The Bush Administration & African Oil', p. 573.

54. US Department of Defense News Transcript, 'DoD News Briefing – Deputy Assistant Secretary of Defense for African Affairs, Michael A. Westphal', 2 April 2002, p. 1 of electronic version, available at http://www.defenselink.mil.

55. 'African Oil: A priority of US National Security and African Development', symposium proceedings, *Institute for Advanced Strategic and Political Studies*, Washington, DC, 25 January 2002.

56. National Intelligence Council, 'External Relations and Africa', discussion paper, 16 March 2004.

57. Fred Kempe, 'Africa Emerges as a Strategic Battlefield', *Wall Street Journal*, 25 April 2006.

58. AFRICOM is explained in detail in Jeremy Keenan, *The Dying Sahara* (forthcoming). See also Jeremy Keenan, 'US militarization in Africa', *Anthropology Today* 24 (5), October 2008, pp. 16–20. AFRICOM will unify Africa (with the exception of Egypt, which will remain under Central Command) under a single US military command. Previously Africa fell under three commands: Pacific Command (PACOM), which covered Madagascar; Central Command (CENTCOM), which covered most of the Horn of Africa, Sudan

238 THE DARK SAHARA

and Kenya; and European Command (EUCOM), which covered the rest of the continent.

59. Quoted by John Bellamy Foster, 'A Warning to Africa'.
60. Fred Kempe, 'Africa Emerges as a Strategic Battlefield', *Wall Street Journal*, 25 April 2006.
61. Council on Foreign Relations, *More Than Humanitarianism: A Strategic US Approach Toward Africa*, 2006, p. 40.
62. John Bellamy Foster, 'A Warning to Africa'.
63. Council on Foreign Relations, *More Than Humanitarianism*.
64. Keenan, *The Dying Sahara*.
65. Klare, *Blood and Oil*, p. 15. When Klare made this observation, he also provided the sobering warning that 'as this growing reliance on military force parallels America's growing dependence on imported energy, the risks of miscalculation are bound to increase', (p. 24).
66. Daniel Volman, 'The Bush Administration & African Oil'.
67. Noam Chomsky, *Hegemony or Survival: America's Quest for Global Dominance* (New York: Metropolitan Books, Henry Holt & Co., 2003).
68. The two main terrorist acts in the Maghreb, outside Algeria, were five near-simultaneous suicide bombings in Casablanca, Morocco, on 16 May 2003, which killed 33 civilians and 12 of the bombers, and a bomb attack on a synagogue on the resort island of Djerba, Tunisia on 11 April 2002, killing 21 civilians, mostly tourists.
69. The first was the Horn of Africa.
70. America's 'invasion' of Africa, as local people called it, and the continent's increasing militarisation and its consequences, are explored and explained in Keenan, *The Dying Sahara* (forthcoming).

Chapter 8

1. In the first instance of economic unrest since independence, spontaneous protests erupted in April 1985 against appalling housing conditions ... These developed into a large demonstration and march on the FLN headquarters in central Algiers, Oran, Skikda and Constantine in November 1986 and tensions deepened further when the military used excessive force to suppress a student protest against changes to the *baccalauréat* examination in Constantine ... Growing frustration with the government's economic policies and resentment of the military's use of force ensured that the spate of sporadic student protests and labour unrest persisted into 1987 and 1988.

   Martin Stone, *The Agony of Algeria* (London: Hurst & Company, 1997), p. 63.

2. The principal reason for this was the removal of OPEC oil price restraints in 1985.
3. Stone, *Agony of Algeria*, p. 97.
4. Ibid.
5. Layachi and Entelis, 'Democratic and Popular Republic of Algeria', in D. E. Long and B. Reich (eds), *The Government and Politics of the Middle East and North Africa* (Boulder, CO: Westview Press, 2002), p. 441.
6. Many believe the number killed was much higher.
7. Many people also claim this figure to be a gross underestimate.
8. Stone, *Agony of Algeria*, pp. 65–6.
9. Ibid., p. 68.
10. Ibid. p. 70.
11. For example, one southern seat had 2,000 voters, compared to 160,000 in the FIS stronghold of Bab El-Oued.
12. Hugh Roberts, *The Battlefield: Algeria 1988–2002: Studies in a Broken Polity* (London: Verso, 2003), p. 120.
13. The FFS (Front des Forces Socialistes) is Algeria's oldest opposition party. It is secular and has a strong Berber base.
14. Cited in *Algérie-actualité*, 9–15 January 1992.
15. Cited in Frédéric Volpi, *Islam and Democracy: The Failure of Dialogue in Algeria* (London: Pluto, 2003), p. 53.
16. Quoted in *Le Monde*, 16 January 1992 – cited by Volpi, *Islam and Democracy*.

Chapter 9

1. Habib Souaïdia, *La Sale Guerre: le témoignage d'un ancien officier des forces spéciales de l'armée algérienne* (Paris: La Découverte, 2001).
2. Nesroulah Yous, with Salima Mellah, *Qui a tué à Bentalha? Algérie: chronique d'un massacre annoncé* (Paris: La Découverte, 2000).
3. Hugh Roberts, 'France and the lost honour of Algeria's army', in Hugh Roberts, *The Battlefield: Algeria 1988–2002* (London: Verso, 2003), pp. 305–16.
4. Ibid., p. 309.
5. Ibid.
6. Ibid., p. 310.
7. Souaïdia served in the Mitidja region, the site of most of the massacres, and then at Lakhdaria, 40 miles or so south-east of Algiers, from early 1993 until mid-1995, before being mysteriously detained for theft, court-martialled, and sentenced to four years in a military prison. On his release in 1999, he managed to get to France, where he wrote his book.

8. Mohammed Samraoui, *Chronique des années de sang* (Paris: Editions Denoël, 2003).

9. Nafeez Mosaddeq Ahmed, *The War on Truth: 9/11, Disinformation and the Anatomy of Terrorism* (Moreton-in-Marsh, Gloucestershire: Arris Books, 2005), p. 97.

10. Interviewed by Yasser Za'atreh in *Palestine Times*, London, no. 72, June 1997 (quoted by Nafeez Ahmed, *War on Truth*, p. 70).

11. Amirouche, Hamou, 'Algeria's Islamist Revolution: The People versus Democracy?' *Middle East Policy* 4 (4), January 1998 (quoted in Nafeez Ahmed, *War on Truth*, p. 67).

12. *Paris Match*, 9 October 1997. (Quoted in Nafeez Ahmed, *War on Truth*, p. 67).

13. *Independent*, 30 October 1997. (Quoted in Nafeez Ahmed, *War on Truth*, p. 67).

14. Ibid. (Quoted in Nafeez Ahmed, *War on Truth*, p. 68).

15. *Sunday Times*, 16 July 2000 (quoted in Nafeez Ahmed, *War on Truth*, p. 67).

16. Pierre Sane (secretary-general of Amnesty International), 'Algerians: Failed by the Government and by the International Community', *Amnesty International*, New York, 18 November 1997.

17. J. Sweeney and L. Doyle, 'Algerian Regime responsible for Massacres: Algerian Regime was Behind Paris Bombs', *Manchester Guardian Weekly*, 16 November 1997.

18. John Sweeney, 'We Accuse 80,000 times', *Observer*, 16 November 1997.

19. Jeremy Keenan, *Sahara Man: Travelling with the Tuareg* (London: John Murray, 2001), p. 2.

20. See Luis Martinez's incisive analysis of *Algeria's Civil War 1990–1989* (London: Hurst & Co., 2000), p. 57.

21. Mohammed Samraoui, 'DRS, GIA and Impunity', *Algeria Watch*, July 2003.

22. Ibid.

23. Ibid.

24. See Fernando Imposimato, preface to Habib Souaïdia, *La Sale Guerre.*

25. Appointed chief of the general staff on 10 July 1993.

26. Martinez, *Algeria's Civil War*, p. 92.

27. The ratio of debt service to imports fell from 93 per cent in 1993 to 47 per cent in 1994 and 37 per cent in 1995.

28. See Martinez, *Algeria's Civil War*, p. 119; J.-F. Bayart, S. Ellis, and B. Hibou, *La criminalization de l'Etat en Afrique* (Brussels: Complexe, 1997), p.58.

29. Eleven thousand new trading companies opened between 1994 and 1996. Applications in 1996 reached 60 per day.

30. Often referred to as Smaïl.
31. François Gèze and Salima Mella, 'Al-Qaeda in the Maghreb and the April 11 2007 attacks in Algiers', *Algeria-Watch*, 21 April 2007.
32. Jeanne Kervyn and François Gèze, 'L'organisation des forces de répression', *Comité Justice pour l'Algérie*, dossier no. 16, September 2004.
33. Le Mouvement Algérien des Officiers Libres. Algeria-Watch MAOL file, available online at www.algeria-watch.org/infomap/infom08/i8maol.htm/
34. See Lounis Aggoun and Jean-Baptiste Rivoire, *Françalgérie, crimes et mensonges d'Etats*, La Découverte, Paris, 2004; Salima Mellah and Jean-Baptiste Rivoire, 'Who Staged the tourist kidnappings?' *Le Monde Diplomatique*, February 2005.
35. Habib Souaïdia, *Le procès de 'La Sale Guerre'*, (Paris: Éditions La Découverte, 2002), p. 242.
36. Aggoun and Rivoire, *Françalgérie*.
37. Jeanne Kervyn and François Gèze, 'L'organisation des forces de répression', *Comité Justice pour l'Algérie*, dossier no. 16, September 2004, quoted by Naima Bouteldja, 'Who really bombed Paris?' *Guardian*, 8 September 2005.
38. Arnaud Dubus, 'Les sept moines de Tibehirine enlevées sur ordre d'Alger,' *Libération*, 23 December 2002. For an earlier reference to the DRS involvement, see John Sweeney, 'Seven monks were beheaded. Now the whistleblower has paid with his life', *Observer*, 14 June 1998.
39. Sweeney, 'Seven monks were beheaded'.

Chapter 10

1. Nafeez Mosaddeq Ahmed, *The War on Truth: 9/11, Disinformation and the Anatomy of Terrorism* (Moreton-in-Marsh, Gloucestershire: Arris Books, 2005), p. 3.
2. Ibid., p. 5.
3. Philip Paull, 'International Terrorism: The Propaganda War' (San Francisco State University, California, June 1982 – thesis submitted in partial fulfilment of the requirements for the degree Masters of Arts in International Relations), pp. 9–10, quoted in Ahmed, *War on Truth*.
4. Ibid., pp. 59–91.
5. Ibid., pp. 95, 99–100.
6. Noam Chomsky, 'The New War against Terror', *Counterpunch*, 24 October 2001, available online at www.counterpunch.org/chomskyterror.html.

7. Founded in Panama in 1946, the School of the Americas was relocated to Fort Benning, Georgia, in 1984, before being renamed the Western Hemisphere Institute for Security Cooperation (WHISC or WHINSEC) in 2001.

8. See, for example, William Blum, *Rogue State* (London: Zed Books, 2006), Chapter 3.

9. According to the Mouvement Algerien des Officiers Libres, a named CIA agent worked closely with Algerian military intelligence throughout this period. The CIA's response to this is that it was concerned for the security of Algeria's oil and Mediterranean waters, and therefore needed to maintain, or perhaps deepen, its links with Algeria's secret services.

10. Martin Stone, *The Agony of Algeria* (London: Hurst, 1997), pp. 245–7.

11. Military relations, however, were not cut entirely. For instance, in 1997 the US delivered six Gulf Stream carriers to Algeria; America's Vice Admiral Joseph Lopez, second-in-command of Nato's southern European flank, visited Algiers in 1998, while a visit to Algiers in February 1999 by US Admirals Steve Abbot (deputy commander US forces in Europe) and Daniel Murphy (US Sixth Fleet) preceded joint naval manoeuvres in 2000 between the small Algerian navy and warships and aircraft from the US Sixth Fleet.

12. The two presidents did hold informal private talks.

13. Mounir B., 'Bush écrit à Bouteflika', *Le Quotidien d'Oran*, 5 November 2005.

14. Details of this visit have not been made public. The Algerian newspaper *Le Quotidien d'Oran* published an article on 10 February 2003 saying that the visit was made by Robert Mullen, director of the FBI. However, the director of the FBI was Mueller, not Mullen, and Robert Mueller did not take over the directorship until July 2001. However, since the article was written two years after the visit, from sources clearly provided by Algeria's military intelligence services, the failure to point out that the visit was made before Mueller took over as director of the FBI is probably an editorial error.

15. *Algeria Amnesty Newsletter*, July–August 2002, available online at www.amnesty-volunteer.org/uk/algeria/02Jul.php.

16. Chapter 9 showed that most of the apparent reprisals in France, such as the RER bombings, were organised by elements within the Algerian and French secret intelligence services.

17. *National Energy Policy*, report of the National Energy Policy group, May 2001, available online at www.whitehouse.gov. See Chapter 7, above, for details.

18. Thomas Gorguissian, 'Bouteflika goes aid-hunting', *Al-Ahram Weekly Online* 543, 19–25 July 2001, available online at http://weekly.ahram.org.eg/2001/543/re6.htm.

19. *World Tribune*, 16 July 2001.

20. 'Eradication' refers to the Algerian army's policy towards the Islamists. It is explained in more detail in Chapter 9.

21. This argument was made most forcibly by José Garçon, writing in *Libération* (quoted in *Algeria Amnesty Newsletter*, September–October 2001), available online at www.amnesty-volunteer.org/uk/algeria/01Sep.php.

22. *El Hayat*, Quoted in *Algeria Amnesty Newsletter*, September–October 2001. See also *Human Rights Watch*, online at http://hrw.org/wr2k2/mena1.html.

23. *Algeria Amnesty Newsletter*, September–October 2001.

24. While in Washington, Bouteflika also had discussions with a number of military and aeronautic suppliers, including Northrop Grumman, Lockheed and Raytheon. *Algerian Interface* and *El Watan*, 5 November 2001. Also reported in *Algeria Amnesty Newsletter*, November–December 2001, available online at www.amnesty-volunteer.org/uk/algeria/01Nov.php.

25. *Algerian Amnesty Newsletter* and *El Watan* (see n. 24).

26. Human Rights Watch, available at http://hrw.org/wr2k2/mena1.html.

27. Notably EUCOM's Supreme Allied Commander, General Ralston (General Jones's predecessor).

28. From a modest US$121,000 in 2001 to US$200,000 in 2002 – and to $550,000 in 2003.

29. Although direct military aid was not forthcoming at this stage, economic cooperation was developing significantly. The US government-run Export–Import Bank, which provides loans and guarantees to assist US investment abroad, stated that its exposure in Algeria rose in the fiscal year ending 30 September 2002 to nearly US$2 billion – a level matched in the Middle East and North Africa only by the bank's exposure in Saudi Arabia. Total private US investment in Algeria was about US$4 billion, nearly all in the energy sector. *Human Rights Watch*, available online at http://hrw.org/wr2k2/mena1.html.

30. An American official was reported in December 2002 as saying that the US would proceed slowly on the military aid package, partly because of criticism by human rights groups (*New York Times*, 10 December 2002). Washington also stated publicly that no approval had been given to the sale of lethal weapons systems to Algeria.

31. For example, the US abuse of and opposition to human rights has been manifested in its consistent opposition to the adoption of the UN Declaration of Indigenous Rights and of the UN Arms Trade Treaty – two of the most urgently needed measures in Africa. On 28 November 2006, the US succeeded, through its manipulation of proxy powers in Africa, in blocking the UN General Assembly's adoption of the UN Declaration of Indigenous Rights. Nine days later, on 7 December, the US was in a global minority of one in voting against the UN's proposed Arms Trade Treaty. Most of the world's governments, as Amnesty International commented, recognise the urgent need for this treaty 'to stop the present flow of weaponry to serious abusers of Human Rights'.

32. An analysis of statements by US officials on arms sales to Algeria around the end of 2002, although seemingly positive on the subject of military collaboration, reflects America's caution on the sale of lethal weapons systems. One US spokesman, when pressed, said, 'down the road we might consider it. We will consider requests if we believe they contribute to the counter terrorism effort' (*New York Times*, 10 December 2002). It was also noticeable that William Burns, assistant secretary of state for Near East affairs, made no reference to lethal weapons systems when he said 'We are putting the finishing touches to an agreement to sell Algeria equipment to fight terrorism' (*Guardian*, 10 December 2002).

33. In spite of this more optimistic perspective, it is highly debatable whether the Algerian regime has ever wanted to end the violence entirely. As one authority on the Algerian political situation noted,

> There is little or no evidence of a serious will within the regime to end the violence, as distinct from reducing it to tolerable proportions. It should be noted that the violence in itself serves to justify the annual renewal of the state of emergency, and that the regime may be considered to have an interest in maintaining the restrictions on opposition political activities which the state of emergency authorises.

Hugh Roberts, *The Battlefield: Algeria 1988–2002: Studies in a Broken Polity* (London: Verso, 2003), p. 270.

34. New York Times, 10 December 2002.

35. *Guardian*, 10 December 2002.

36. See, for example, Princeton N. Lyman, Fellow for Africa Policy Studies, Council on Foreign Relations, 'The Terrorist Threat in Africa' (testimony before the House Committee on International Relations Subcommittee on Africa – hearing on 'Fighting Terrorism

in Africa', 1 April 2004), available online at http://www.cfr.org/
publication/6912/terrorist_threat_in_africa.html.

37. International Crisis Group, *Islamic Terrorism in the Sahel: Fact or Fiction?* ICG, Africa Report 92, 31 March 31 2005.

38. See Chapter 2.

39. Maj.-Gen. J. Kohler, quoted in *Stars and Stripes*, 15 January 2004.

40. Col. Victor Nelson, quoted in Jim Fisher-Thompson, 'US–African partnership helps counter terrorists in Sahel region: New Maghreb co-operation central to Pan Sahel Initiative', Washington File, US Department of State information service, 23 March 23 2004. See also Donna Miles, 'US Must Confront Terrorism in Africa, General Says', US American Forces Press Service, US Department of Defense, Washington, 16 June 2004; S. Powell, 'Swamp of Terror in the Sahara', *Air Force Magazine* 87 (11), (2004): pp. 50–4.

41. *National Energy Policy*, report of the National Energy Policy Group, May 2001, available online at www.whitehouse.gov.

42. See Daniel Volman, 'The Bush Administration and African Oil: The Security Implications of US Energy Policy', *Review of African Political Economy* 30 (98), December 2003, pp. 573–84.

43. 'African Oil: A Priority of US National Security and African Development', symposium proceedings, Institute for Advanced Strategic and Political Studies, Washington, DC, 25 January 2002.

44. US Department of Defense News Transcript, 'DoD News Briefing – Deputy Assistant Secretary of Defense for African Affairs, Michael A. Westphal', 2 April 2002, electronic version, p. 1, available online at www.defenselink.mil.

45. Kofi Akosah-Sarpong, 'Washington eyes Africa's oil', *West Africa* 4,354, 2–8 December 2002, p.10, quoted in Volman, 'Bush Administration and African Oil'.

46. The August 1998 blast at the US embassy in Nairobi killed 219 people and wounded 5,000. The attack on the US Embassy in neighbouring Tanzania killed 12 people and injured more than 80.

47. See Chapter 12, below.

48. The movement originated in India in 1927 and subsequently moved its headquarters to Pakistan.

49. An indication of US unfamiliarity with the region comes from reported incidents of translation errors in intelligence reports, such as 'nigérien' (native of Niger), for example, being confused with 'nigerian' (Nigerian).

50. Statement of Marion E. ('Spike') Bowman to Senate Select Committee on Intelligence, 31 July 2002, available online at www.fas.org/irp/congress/2002_hr/073102bowman.html.

246 THE DARK SAHARA

51. This name is not recognised as that of any of the known armed Islamic groups, and was probably made up for the occasion.
52. It is not known whether these communications were by radio or satellite phone. The source of this information comes from conversations between local people and some of the gendarmes involved. By chance, I was in the region at the time and was able to interview some of the former, as well as one of the guides to the gendarmerie.
53. The order is believed to have come from General Abdennour Aït-Mesbah (Sadek) who had been appointed as head of the DRS in Tamanrasset shortly before this incident. Indeed, it is possible that he was posted to the region to oversee it.
54. For instance, none of the official local or regional organisations responsible for tourist management and safety, such as UNATA or ATAWT, were officially notified of the incident. Local people in Tamanrasset were only able confirm the incident by reading a Swiss website! The report of the incident was published in detail on the Swiss Saharan travellers website: sahara-info.ch, and a few other Internet news sites.
55. This information comes from author interviews with the Kel Ajjer nomads concerned.
56. Office of Counterterrorism, US Department of State, Washington, DC, 7 November 2002. Secretary of State Colin Powell had visited Mali on his first tour of Africa in May 2001. In June 2002, with rumours of US involvement in the Sahel in the air, Chad's interior and security minister, Abderamane Moussa, asked the US secretary of state for money and arms to combat terrorists (a euphemism for political opponents), who he claimed were based in the neighbouring states of Libya, Sudan and Nigeria.
57. 'African Oil: A priority of US National Security and African Development', symposium proceedings, *Institute for Advanced Strategic and Political Studies*, Washington, DC, 25 January 2002.
58. Although the PSI was announced in 2002, it was not funded and put into operation until November 2003. A small number of US Special Forces were already in the region, notably in Mali, but the PSI forces were not officially brought into the region until January 2004.

Chapter 11

1. Not surprisingly, neither Algeria nor the US is a signatory to the ICC Treaty.
2. Christine Holzbauer (-Madison), 'Les inquiétants émirs du Sahel', *L'Express*, 28 November 2002. The journalist is regional

correspondent for the right-of-centre *L'Express*, centrist *La Tribune* and the Catholic *La Croix*. Her sources rely heavily on the US military and State Department. Her contact address in Dakar, Senegal is given as c/o the US embassy. Prior to the *L'Express* article, she published a similar article in *La Croix* (19 November 2002) under the title 'Al Qaeda est pistée en Afrique de l'Ouest', saying that the US believed that al-Qaeda was attempting to establish itself in the heart of the Sahara, along the borders of Algeria, Mauritania and Mali. On 28 June 2004 she published a further article in *L'Express*, 'La Chasse aux salafistes du désert', based almost entirely on US military sources (EUCOM) in Stuttgart, and on information from the commanding officer of the PSI in the Sahel.

3. *Le Matin*, 28 November 2002.
4. Mokhtar ben Mokhtar.
5. B. Azzedine, 'Dernières Révélations: Belmokhtar a recontré Imad Abdelwahid', 30 November 2002, available online at www.lexpressiondz.com. Imad Abdelwahid is bin Laden's emissary to the Maghreb.
6. C. H. Sylla, 'Terrorism: Al-Qaïda au Mali', *Le Républicain*, Niger, 2 December 2002.
7. 'Portrait du chef terroriste Belmokhtar: Un viage sur un émir', 24 December 2002 available online at www.lexpressiondz.com.
8. Ibid. '17 Toyota d'une compagnie pétrolière détournées à Illizi: l'émir Belmokhtar terrorise le Sud', 30 December 2002.
9. B. Azzedine, 'Attaque terroriste à Aïn Guezzam: Le GSPC de Belmokhtar récidive', L'expressiondz.com, 7 January 2003.
10. Alias Imad Abdelwahid.
11. Salima Tlemçani, 'Abou Mohamed se trouvait dans le maquis du GSPC à Batna: l'agent d'Al Qaîda abattu', *El Watan*, 7 January 2003.
12. *Algeria-guide*, 30 January 2003, available online at www.lexpressiondz.com.
13. 5 February 2003, available online at www.lexpressiondz.com.
14. *Le Quotidien d'Oran*, 10 February 2003.
15. 18 February 2003, available online at www.lexpressiondz.com.
16. This article (see n. 2, above), from the French weekly *L'Express*, appears to have been based mainly on West African US military and diplomatic sources. The information contained could only have come from DRS sources, indicating the close working relationship between the US and Algerian intelligence services at this time.
17. Mohamed Atta's suitcase must have been a veritable Pandora's box, given the extraordinary amount of intelligence that it is alleged to have contained.

18. Part of the fictive narrative is that the GSPC groups in the north are provided with arms from those in the Sahel, thus justifying the trans-Saharan link. Given that the north has been heavily involved in such fighting (see Chapter 9) for some ten years, and is awash with arms, it would seem most unlikely that they were needed anymore, least of all from the south. This is an enigma that has been ignored by virtually all so-called 'security experts'.

19. The Americans have become increasingly embarrassed at having this fact pointed out to them. Over the last year or so, they have explained their inability to find any of these bases by saying that they are 'mobile'. (Iraq's chemical WMD factories, never discovered, were also said to have been 'mobile').

20. The notion of an 'Afghan Arab' – especially in this context – is a politically derogatory term without any scientific ethnic content. The ethnic composition of Afghanistan is complex. Around 90 per cent of the population are Pashtuns (the majority), Tajiks, Hazaras and Uzbeks. Small minority groups of Turkmans, Baluchs, Nuristanis, Kirghis and Pashaes make up the remainder. The majority are Sunni Muslims, although the Hazzaras are Shia Muslims and the Nuristanis have their own religion. Ummayad Arabs entered the region of what is now Afghanistan in the seventh century and some stayed on, mixing with the local population and speaking Persian, not Arabic. A survey in the fifteenth century confirmed that the Arab language had completely disappeared. A second wave of Arabs moved into the region to escape Russian expansion in the late eighteenth century and the Bolshevik Revolution. Some 30,000 Arabs moved from the Bukhara region to Afghanistan, and mixed quickly with the local population, speaking Persian and/or Uzbek. A third wave of Arabs were those who came to help the Afghans in the Soviet–Afghan War. Some of these stayed on, but most returned to their home countries, where they were often dubbed 'Afghans'.

21. This is presumably a reference to the ambush of Algerian army troops at Teniet El-Abed on 4 January, for which El Para was said to have been responsible (see Chapter 6).

22. The drug and other trans-Saharan trafficking networks are largely run or protected by powerful elements in the politico-military elites of the countries of the region, notably West Africa, the Sahel and Algeria, in which the DRS is generally regarded as having more than a passing interest.

23. Prior to Robert Mueller's visit in early 2001, American intelligence services were wary of their Algerian counterparts because of their supposed former KGB ties and 'pro-Palestinian' stance. Mueller's visit seems to have helped dispel such views, with collaboration being

strengthened further by the submission of Marion Bowman's report to the US Senate in July 2002.

24. It is inconceivable that US intelligence in Stuttgart would not have picked up the reports of the hijack on the Swiss-German news and travel websites.

25. Office of Counterterrorism, US Department of State, Washington, DC, 7 November 2002.

26. The Pentagon, especially, has produced numerous maps, marking in the banana-shaped zone of terror across the Sahara–Sahel region.

27. See Chapter 3, n. 37, above.

28. Dana Priest, 'Help from France Key in Covert Operations', *Washington Post*, 3 July 2005.

29. The DGSE, subordinate to the Ministry of the Defence, is responsible for military intelligence as well as for strategic information and electronic intelligence. It is also responsible for counterespionage outside the national territory.

30. For example, there is now evidence that French troops stationed in France's former Sahelian colonies have served as a proxy army for US interests. In Chad, for example, French troops played a far greater role than was initially reported in thwarting the attack on the Chad capital of N'Djamena in April 2006, by rebels trying to overthrow the despotic 'president for life', President Déby. The US has been supportive of the Déby regime through its PSI, and in supporting ExxonMobil's lead role in developing the country's oil resources. While the French say that their military intervention was intended purely to protect French citizens and interests, reports from N'Djamena indicate that the US encouraged France to assist Déby's forces.

31. This raises questions about the complicity of the Base's other partners – especially Britain and Germany, who have also both been remarkably reticent on this subject. The death of a German subject, Michaela Spitzer, while in El Para's hands raises legal questions which, under the circumstances, the German state has clearly preferred not to address. In this context it should be noted that the German authorities placed considerable pressure on the former hostages to remain silent.

32. Retired General Carlton W. Fulford. Quoted by C. Cobb Jr, 'General sees expanding strategic role for U.S. European Command in Africa', *American Enterprise Institute*, 16 April 2004, available online at http://allafrica.com/stories/200404150758.html.

33. For clarification on US military basing in Algeria and America's new concept of basing rights at that time, see Mustafa Barth, 'Sand-Castles in the Sahara: US Military Basing in Algeria', *Review of*

African Political Economy 30 (98), 2003, pp. 679–85; Jeremy Keenan, 'Americans and "Bad People" in the Sahara–Sahel', *Review of African Political Economy* 31, No. 99, 2004, pp. 130–9.

34. *World Tribune*, 6 May 2003; *New York Times*, 4 July 2003.
35. For a general description and background, see Khurram Husain, 'Neocons: The Men behind the Curtain', *Bulletin of the Atomic Scientists*, 59 (6), November/December 2003, pp. 62–71.
36. In 2006, 80 per cent of the US intelligence budget was being managed through the Pentagon. See Jay Solomon, 'CIA Hearings May Bring Oversight Debate', *Wall Street Journal*, 13 May 2006, available online at http://online.wsj.com/.
37. One of their aims was to keep 'out of the loop' other branches of government who might be expected to check their activities, including desks within both the State and Defense Departments.
38. The US Senate's Select Committee on Intelligence confirmed in 2006 that there had been no evidence of WMD or terrorist links between Saddam Hussein and al-Qaeda.
39. The coincidence in the dates of the start of the invasion of Iraq, on 20 March 2003, and the disappearance of the first hostages three to four weeks earlier seems almost conspiratorial. However, if the two were linked in the way that I have suggested, one might have expected the launch of the Saharan front in the war on terror to have slightly preceded the invasion of Iraq. The fact that there had been an earlier hostage-taking attempt (see Chapter 10) – in October 2002, exactly five months before the Iraq invasion – is therefore possibly much more significant than it otherwise appears.

Chapter 12

1. International Crisis Group, *Islamic Terrorism in the Sahel: Fact or Fiction?* ICG, Africa Report 92 (31 March 2005).
2. Major General J. Kohler, quoted in *Stars and Stripes* (European edition), 12 January 2004.
3. Colonel Victor Nelson, quoted by Jim Fisher-Thompson in 'US–African Partnership Helps Counter Terrorists in Sahel Region: New Maghreb Co-operation Central to Pan Sahel Initiative', Washington File, distributed by the Office of International Information Programs, US Department of State, available online at http://usinfo.state.gov (23 March 2004). See also General Charles Wald, quoted by Donna Miles, 'US Must Confront Terrorism in Africa, General Says', US American Forces Press Service, US Department of Defense, Washington, 16 June 2004; S. Powell, 'Swamp of Terror in the Sahara', *Air Force Magazine* 87 (November 2004), p. 50–4.

4. See Chapter 10.
5. *Le Monde Diplomatique*, 8 July 2004.
6. Office of Counterterrorism, US Department of State, Washington, DC, 7 November 2002. See S. Ellis, 'Briefing: The Pan-Sahel Initiative,' *African Affairs* 103 (412), 2004, pp. 459–64.
7. See Chapter 10 (last paragraph).
8. For details of the Tablighi Jamaat's presence and activities in northern Mali, see Baz Lecocq and Paul Schrijver, 'The War on Terror in a Haze of Dust: Potholes and Pitfalls on the Saharan Front,' *Journal of Contemporary African Studies* 25 (1), 2007, pp. 141–66.
9. This lack of elementary knowledge appears to have led to some bizarre intelligence failures. For example, it appears that there may have been a failure to distinguish between *nigérian* (Nigerian) and *nigérien* (native of Niger). This may account for the number of reports claiming Nigerians to be part of GSPC groups operating in the Sahara–Sahel – something which is not borne out by those who know the GSPC. The strongly racist nature of the GSPC makes it extremely unlikely for it to include Nigerians. However, part of US strategy is to link Saharan–Sahelian 'terrorism' to Nigeria as part of the ideological conditions to justify the securitisation of Nigerian and West African oil in general, in which case the difference between *nigérian* and *nigérien* may not be a mistranslation after all.
10. See, for example, Daniel Volman, 'The Militarization of Africa', *ACAS* [Association of Concerned Africa Scholars] *Bulletin* 65, Fall 2003; 'Privatizing and Militarizing Africa', *ACAS Bulletin* 66, Winter 2003/04.
11. A two-part BBC World Service programme in 2005 investigated the nature and impact of the US war on terror in the Sahara–Sahel. When the presenter suggested to a senior US military officer with responsibilities for the region that the US military had been duped by Algeria as a result of its lack of intelligence, he denied that that was the case, simply repeating, 'We have our sources ... We have our sources.' ('Secrets in the Sand', BBC World Service, August 2005). They are, however, mostly Algerian.
12. US Senate, 'Report of the Select Committee on Intelligence on Post-War Findings about Iraq's WMD Programs and Links to Terrorism and How They Compare with Pre-War Assessments', US Senate, Washington, DC, 8 September 2006.
13. John Byrne, 'Prewar intelligence probe grinds towards end as parties accuse each other of delay', Raw Story, 11 April 2006 available online at www.rawstory.com/news/2006/Prewar_intelligence_probe_grinds_to_end_0411.html. That 'can of worms' was believed to relate to Douglas Feith's role at the Pentagon's Office of Special

Plans. Douglas Feith resigned from his position as Under Secretary of Defense for Policy on 8 August 2005. US Army General Tommy Franks reportedly described Feith as the 'fucking stupidest guy on the face of the earth'. Bob Woodward, *Plan of Attack*, New York: Simon & Schuster, 2004. See also http://slate.msn.com/id/2099277.

14. US Senate Select Committee on Intelligence, 'Report on Whether Public Statements regarding Iraq by US Government officials were Substantiated by Intelligence Information', available online at http://intelligence.senate.gov/080605/phase2a.pdf/; and 'Report on Intelligence Activities Relating to Iraq Conducted by the Policy Counterterrorism Evaluation Group and the Office of Special Plans Within the Office of the Under Secretary of Defense for Policy', Washington, DC, 5 June 2008, available online at http://intelligence. senate.gov/080605/phase2b.pdf. See also a press release of the Intelligence Committee, 'Senate Intelligence Committee Unveils Final Phase II Reports on Prewar Iraq Intelligence', 5 June 2008, available online at http://intelligence.senate.gov/press/record. cfm?id=298775.

15. Personal communications.

16. Dana Priest, 'Help from France key in Covert Operations', *Washington Post*, 3 July 2005.

Chapter 13

1. This includes such things as physically impeding local businessmen bidding for local public work contracts; the arbitrary confiscation of driving licences; the forging of documents by government officials to be used as court evidence in trumped-up charges against representatives of civil society, and so on. This latter practice was uncovered by defence lawyers in the trial of a prominent Tuareg, subsequently acquitted, in the Tamanrasset court in the autumn of 2004.

2. Local people termed this behaviour, notably the bribing of local people for information and to spy on their friends and neighbours, as *sovietique*.

3. Established in 1999 and associated to the Ligue Algérienne de Défense des Droits de l'Homme, established in 1989.

4. UNATA was founded in 1991, and ATAWT in 1989.

5. The White House Office of the Press Secretary, 'President Bush Creates a Department of Defense Unified Combatant Command for Africa', press release, 6 February 2007.

6. www.commissionforafrica.org/english/report/introduction. html#report.

7. Jeremy Keenan, 'US Militarization in Africa: What Anthropologists Should Know about AFRICOM', *Anthropology Today* 24 (5), October 2008, pp. 16–20; and 'Demystifying Africa's security', *Review of African Political Economy* 35 (118), 2008, pp. 634–44.

8. Catherine Lutz, 'Selling our Independence? The Perils of Pentagon Funding for Anthropology', *Anthropology Today* 24 (5), October 2008, pp. 1–3; P. Baty, 'Life-Risking "Spy" Plan Pulled', *Times Higher Education Supplement*, 20 October 2006; A. Frean and M. Evans, 'Universities "Asked to Act as Spies for Intelligence Services"', *The Times*, 19 October 2006, available online at www.timesonline.co.uk/tol/life_and_style/education/student/news/article605728.ece; Jeremy Keenan, 'My Country Right or Wrong', *Anthropology Today* 23 (1), 2007: 26–8.

9. See n. 7, above.

10. Noam Chomsky, *Hegemony or Survival: America's Quest for Global Dominance*, New York: Henry Holt, 2003.

LIST OF JEREMY KEENAN'S WORKS ON THE SAHARA, THE WAR ON TERROR AND THE TUAREG SINCE 2000

(listed by type, in reverse chronological order)

Books

The Sahara: Past, Present and Future (ed.), London: Routledge, 2007.

The Lesser Gods of the Sahara: Social Change and Contested Terrain amongst the Tuareg of Algeria, London: Routledge, 2005.

The Tuareg: People of Ahaggar (new edn), London: Sickle Moon Books, 2002 (London, Allen Lane Penguin, 1977).

Sahara Man: Travelling with the Tuareg, London: John Murray, 2001.

Chapters

'Resource Exploitation, Repression and Resistance in the Sahara–Sahel: the Rise of the Rentier State in Algeria, Chad and Niger', in Kenneth Omeje (ed.), *Extractive Economies and Conflicts in the Global South: Multi-Regional Perspectives on Rentier Politics*, London & Burlington, VT: Ashgate, 2008.

'Tourism, Development and Conservation: a Saharan Perspective', in D. J. Mattingly, S. McLaren, E. Savage, Y al-Fasatwi, and K. Gadgood, *Natural Resources and Cultural Heritage of the Libyan Desert: Proceedings of a Conference Held in Libya, 14-21 December 2002*, London: Society for Libyan Studies, 2006.

'Sedentarisation and Changing Patterns of Social Organisation amongst the Tuareg of Algeria', in D. Chatty (ed.), *Nomadic Societies in the Middle East and North Africa: Entering the 21st Century*, Leiden (Netherlands): Brill, 2006.

'Sustainable Nomadism: The Case of the Algerian Tuareg', in D. Chatty (ed.), *Nomadic Societies*.

'The Tuareg People: Drought, Politics and Corporate Encroachments', in *The Indigenous World 2006*, Copenhagen: International Work Group for Indigenous Affairs (IWGIA), 2006.

'The Development or Re-Development of Tourism in Algeria', in Margaret Majumdar and Mohammed Saad (eds), *Transition and Development in Algeria: Economic, Social and Cultural Challenges*, Bristol: Intellect, 2005.

'The Tuareg People: Paying the Price for the US Militarisation of Africa', in *The Indigenous World 2005*, Copenhagen: International Work Group for Indigenous Affairs (IWGIA), 2005.

'The Tuareg People: The Continuing Insecurity of Tuareg Regions', in *The Indigenous World 2004*, Copenhagen: International Work Group for Indigenous Affairs (IWGIA), 2004.

'The Tuareg People: The Threat of Insecurity in Tuareg Regions', in *The Indigenous World 2002–2003*, Copenhagen: International Work Group for Indigenous Affairs (IWGIA), 2003.

'The Situation of the Tuareg Peoples in North and West Africa', in *The Indigenous World 2001–2002*.

'How and Why the Tuareg Poisoned the French: Some Reflections on *Efelehleh* and the Motives of the Tuareg in Massacring the Flatters Expeditions of 1881', in Barnaby Rogerson (ed.), *North Africa Travel*, London: Sickle Moon Books, 2001.

Journal Articles and Briefings

'Demystifying Africa's security', *Review of African Political Economy* 35 (118), 2008: pp. 634–44.

'US Militarization in Africa: What Anthropologists Should Know about AFRICOM', *Anthropology Today* 24 (5), October 2008: pp. 16–20.

'Uranium Goes Critical in Niger: Tuareg Rebellions Threaten Sahelian Conflagration', *Review of African Political Economy* 35 (117), 2008: pp. 449–66.

'US Silence as Sahara Military Base Gathers Dust', *Review of African Political Economy* 34 (113), 2007: pp. 588–90.

'Who Thought Rock-Art Was about Archaeology? The Role of Prehistory in Algeria's Terror', *Journal of Contemporary Africa Studies* 25 (1), 2007: pp. 119–40.

'The Banana Theory of Terrorism: Alternative Truths and the Collapse of the "Second" (Saharan) Front in the War on Terror', *Journal of Contemporary Africa Studies* 25 (1), 2007: pp. 31–58.

'The Making of Terrorists: Anthropology and the Alternative Truth of America's "War On Terror" In The Sahara', *Focaal – European Journal of Anthropology* (48), 2006: pp. 144–51.

'Conspiracy Theories and "Terrorists": how the "War on Terror" is Placing New Responsibilities on Anthropology', *Anthropology Today* 22 (6), December 2006: pp. 4–9.

'Turning the Sahel on its Head: The "truth" behind the Headlines', *Review of African Political Economy* 33 (110), 2006: pp. 761–9.

'Military Bases, Construction Contracts and Hydrocarbons in North Africa', *Review of African Political Economy* 33 (109), 2006: pp. 601–8.

'North Africa: Power, Politics and Promise' (with R. Bush), *Review of African Political Economy* 33 (108), 2006: pp. 175–84.

'Security and Insecurity in North Africa', *Review of African Political Economy* 33 (108), 2006: pp. 269–96.

'Tuareg Take Up Arms', *Review of African Political Economy* 33 (108), 2006: pp. 367–8.

'Waging War on Terror: The Implications of America's "New Imperialism" for Saharan Peoples', *Journal of North African Studies* 10 (3–4), 2005: pp. 610–38.

'Looting the Sahara: The Material, Intellectual and Social Implications of the Destruction of Cultural Heritage', *Journal of North African Studies* 10 (3–4), 2005: pp. 467–85.

'The UNDP, the World Bank and Biodiversity in the Algerian Sahara' (with D. Giurovich), *Journal of North African Studies* 10 (3–4), 2005: pp. 585–96.

'Funerary Monuments and Horse Paintings: A Preliminary Report on the Archaeology of a Site in the Tagant Region of Southeast Mauritania – Near Dhar Tichitt', (with W. Challis, A. Campbell, and D. Coulson), *Journal of North African Studies* 10 (3–4), 2005: pp. 455–66.

'The Sahara: Past, Present and Future' (editorial) *Journal of North African Studies* 10 (3–4), 2005: pp. 247–52.

'Famine in Niger is Not All that It Appears', *Review of African Political Economy* 32 (104–105), 2005: pp. 405–7.

'Political Destabilisation and "Blowback" in the Sahel', *Review of African Political Economy* 31 (102), 2004: pp. 691–8.

'Terror in the Sahara: The Implications of US Imperialism for North and West Africa', *Review of African Political Economy* 31 (101), 2004: pp. 475–96.

'Americans and "Bad People" in the Sahara–Sahel', *Review of African Political Economy* 31 (99), 2004: pp. 130–9.

'Indigenous Rights and a Future Politic amongst Algeria's Tuareg after Forty Years of Independence', *Journal of North African Studies* 8 (3–4), 2003: pp. 1–26.

'From Tit (1902) to Tahilahi (2002): A Reconsideration of the Impact of and Resistance to French Pacification and Colonial Rule by the Tuareg of Algeria (the Northern Tuareg)', *Journal of North African Studies* 8 (3–4), 2003: pp. 27–66.

'Ethnicity, Regionalism and Political Stability in Algeria's Grand Sud', *Journal of North African Studies* 8 (3–4), 2003: pp. 67–96.

'Dressing for the Occasion: Changes in the Symbolic Meanings of the Tuareg Veil', *Journal of North African Studies* 8 (3–4), 2003: pp. 97–120.

'The End of the Matriline? The Changing Roles of Women and Descent Amongst the Algerian Tuareg', *Journal of North African Studies* 8 (3–4), 2003: pp. 121–62.

'The Last Nomads: Nomadism amongst the Tuareg of Ahaggar (Algerian Sahara)', *Journal of North African Studies* 8 (3–4), 2003: pp. 163–92.

'The Lesser Gods of the Sahara', *Journal of North African Studies* 8 (3–4), 2003: pp. 193–225.

'Contested Terrain: Tourism, Environment and Security in Algeria's Extreme South', *Journal of North African Studies* 8 (3–4), 2003: pp. 226–65.

'The Sahara's Indigenous People, the Tuareg, Fear Environmental Catastrophe', *Indigenous Affairs* (1), 2002: pp. 50–7.

'The Lesser Gods of the Sahara', *Journal of Public Archaeology* 2 (3), 2002: pp. 131–50.

'The Theft of Saharan Rock-Art', *Antiquity* 74, July 2000: pp. 287–8.

'The Father's Friend: Returning to the Tuareg as an Elder', *Anthropology Today* 16, August 2000: pp. 7–11.

Conference Presentations

'Africa Unsecured: The Consequences and Implications of Using the Global War on Terror to Militarise Africa', conference on 'The War on Terror: Perspectives from the Global South', Centre for the Study of 'Radicalisation' and Contemporary Political Violence, Aberystwyth University, 11–12 December 2008.

'The ethics of Anthropological Engagement in a Neoliberal World', WDO 80th anniversary, memorial seminar, Leiden University, 27–28 November 2008.

'Uranium Goes Critical in the Sahel: Tuareg Rebellion Targets Mining and Oil Operations', conference on 'The State, Mining and Development in Africa', Leeds University Centre for African Studies and *Review of African Political Economy*, Leeds University, 13–14 September 2007.

'Anthropology in the Firing-Line: Alternative Truths in the US War on Terror', European Association of Social Anthropologists, Bristol University, 18–21 September 2006.

'Rights, Resources and Rebellions: "Rebranding" the Tuareg for the 21st Century', conference on 'The Berbers and other Minorities in North Africa: A Cultural Reappraisal', Portland State University, Portland, Oregon, 13–14 May 2005.

'Who Thought Rock-Art was about Archaeology!? The Political Economy of Saharan Rock-Art', special session on 'The War on Terror in the Sahara' at the joint annual meetings of the African Studies Association and the Middle East Studies Association of North America, Washington, DC, 17–22 November 2005.

'The Political Economy of the Discovery and Looting of Central Saharan Rock Art: The Case of the Henri Lhote Expedition to the Tassili-n-Ajjer in 1957–58', Canadian Council of Area Studies Learned Societies, Montreal, Canada, 27 April–1 May 2005.

'The Impact of America's War on Terror on the Peoples of the Sahara', Canadian Council of Area Studies Learned Societies, Montreal, Canada, 27 April–1 May 2005.

'Who Thought Rock Art was about Archaeology!? The Political Economy of Saharan Rock-Art', paper presented at the 70th Annual Meeting of the Society for American Archaeology, Salt Lake City, Utah, 30 March–3 April 2005.

'The Language of Terror: US Engagement in Africa', paper delivered at 47th annual meeting of the African Studies Association, New Orleans, 11–14 November 2004.

'Waging War on Terror: The Implications of America's "New Imperialism" for Saharan peoples', conference on 'The Sahara: Past, Present and Future', Saharan Studies Programme, University of East Anglia, 22–24 June 2004.

'Looting the Sahara: The Material, Intellectual and Social Implications of the Destruction of Cultural Heritage', conference on 'The Sahara: Past, Present and Future', Saharan Studies Programme, University of East Anglia, 22–24 June 2004.

'Crises and Insecurity in the Sahara: Indigenous Perceptions of America's War on Terror', paper delivered at 'Middle East Studies Centre Fordham University, New York, and the Department of Social Anthropology, University of Vermont, November 2003.

'Bad Lands and Borderlands: The Insecurity of Central Saharan Frontiers', 46th annual meeting of the African Studies Association, Boston, US, 30 October–2 November 2003.

'Geopolitics of the Destruction and Conservation of Saharan Rock-Art: The Price of Patrimony', workshop on 'Practices in Rock-Art Research', Cambridge Rock-Art Group, Department of Archaeology, Cambridge, UK, 3 May 2003.

'Tourism, Development and Conservation: A Saharan Perspective', conference on Natural Resources and Cultural Heritage of the Libyan Desert, Tripoli, Libya, 14–21 December 2002.

'Social Change and Gender Issues among the Tuareg of Algeria', seminar series: 'The Meanings of Gender in the Development Context',

Queen Elizabeth House, International Development Centre, Oxford University, 14 January 2002.
'The Development or Re-Development of Tourism in Algeria', conference on 'Restructuring the Algerian Economy: Trends, Patterns and Implications', Bristol Business School, 30 June 2001.
'Algeria's Soft Underbelly. The Role of Trans-Saharan "banditry" and International Cigarette Companies in the Economic and Political Destabilisation of Algeria', presentation to the Algerian Society, SOAS, London University, March 2001.
'Crumbs that Fall from the Rich Man's Table: Algeria's socio-economic Strategy towards the Tuareg', conference of the British Society for Middle East Studies, Cambridge, UK, 2–5 July 2000.

Other Articles

'Reply to Stephen Ellis', *Anthropology Today* 23 (3), 2007: pp. 21–2.
'On Her Majesty's Secret Disservice', *Times Higher Education Supplement* (1,780), 9 February 2007: p. 18.
'A Sift Through Sands Reveals No Grain of Truth', *Times Higher Education Supplement* (1,773), 15 December: pp. 16–17.
'The Collapse of the Second Front', *Foreign Policy in Focus*, Washington DC, 26 September 2006.

Professional Services

Sahara Focus, political risk analysis, London: Menas Associates, quarterly (by subscription), from April 2005.

Films

'A Forgotten Civilisation (The Garamantes – Libya)', A&AB Productions, Malta, 2007.
'Waters Under the Earth (Libya)', A&AB Productions, Malta, 2007.
'Travelling with Tuareg', A&AB Productions, Malta, 2006.
'The Lesser Gods', A&AB Productions, Malta, 2006.

INDEX

Rogerson, Barnaby 255
Rolling Rover 12
Rome 140, 146, 151, 156
Rommel 16
Roosevelt, F.D. (former US
  President) 116, 232
Royal United Services Institute
  (RUSI) 209
Royce, Ed. (Senator) 127, 168
Rühl, Bettina 220, 222
Rumsfeld, Donald 81, 194
Russia (Russian Federation)
  22–3, 117, 232, 248
Rwanda 146

Saad, Mohammed 255
Saadaoui, Abdelhamid 97, 179
Sahab, Abdelmajid (General)
  102, 229
Sahara *passim*
Sahel xii, 2–3, 5–9, 23, 33,
  36–40, 45–6, 50, 52–3, 65, 71,
  74–96, 98, 102, 109, 111–12,
  115, 126, 128, 131, 167–71,
  174–9, 183–4, 189–204, 206,
  208–9, 214–15, 223–4,
  245–51, 254–7
Sahraoui, Nabil 97, 104–5,
  228–9
salafist (-ism) xvi, 1, 20, 24,
  63–4, 85, 94, 198, 247
Samraoui, Mohammed 230
San Francisco State University
  159, 212, 241
San Salvador xviii, 46, 91
sanctions 47, 125, 236
Sane, Pierre 145, 240
Sant' Egidio 140, 151, 156, 161
São Tomé and Principe 123–5
Saudi Arabia xviii, 117, 121–2,
  126, 228, 232, 234–5, 243
Saudi Aramco 122
Saudi Royal Family 117

Savage, E. 254
Schlesinger, James 118
School of the Americas (SOA)
  xiv, 160, 242
Schrijver, Paul 91, 226, 251
Sécurité Militaire (SM) (*see* DRS)
  xiv, 4, 144, 147, 214
security forces 1, 11, 18–19,
  23–4, 29–30, 41, 43, 46–7, 59,
  71, 74, 77–8, 87, 90, 92, 99,
  104, 136–7, 145–9, 152, 155,
  175, 184–7, 213, 228
Seguedine xviii, 91, 225
Senegal xviii, 193, 247
September 11, 2001 (9/11) 6, 8,
  20, 51, 118, 120–1, 127,
  132–3, 141, 150, 158–9,
  162–5, 167–8, 176–7, 179–80,
  183–5, 187–8, 194, 199–200,
  215, 240–1
Sétif 104, 180
Seychelles 217
Shah of Persia 117
Shell 235
Shia Muslims 248
Shin Bet 103
shott (Ar.) xvi, 172
Silet xix
Simmons, Matthew R. 234
Skikda 237–8
social services 134
Solomon, Jay 250
Solzhenitsyn, Aleksandr x
Somalia xviii, 2, 184, 205, 217
Sonatrach 23, 150
Souaïdia, Habib 142–4, 147,
  176, 239–41
Souk Ahras 180, 187
South Africa 67, 103, 160
Soviet Union 128, 134, 158–9,
  217
Soviet-Afghan war 248
Spitzer, Michaela 1, 31, 249